The *Vivaraṇapramēyasaṅgraha* of Viḍyāraṇya

"A Summary of the Topics of the Elucidation"

Sri Garib Das Oriental Series No. 175

The *Vivaraṇaprамēyasaṅgraha* of Viḍyāraṇya

"A Summary of the Topics of the Elucidation"

Translated by

G. Thibaut

Comprising Varnaka I.

Sri Satguru Publications
A Division of
Indian Books Centre
Delhi-India

Published by:
Sri Satguru Publications
Indological and Oriental Publishers
A Division of
Indian Books Centre
40/5, Shakti Nagar
Delhi - 110 007
(INDIA)

First Edition: Allahabad, 1915.
Second Edition: Delhi, 1994.

ISBN 81-7030-391-5

Laser Typeset by: ShiKi Associates, New Delhi - 110 058.

PRINTED IN INDIA

Note

The translation of *Vivaraṇaprameyasaṅgraha* was being done by our late lamented colleague, Dr. Thibaut. The last instalment was printed in Indian Thought, Vol. III, ending on page 120. His duties at Calcutta—as Registrar of the University and latterly as Professor of *Ancient Indian Culture*—left him no time to go on with the work. Before leaving for home in April last, he told me he was now in a position to resume his work for 'Indian Thought'; and I was looking forward to his important contributions. All that hope however has now gone for ever. I have therefore thought it fit to finish Varṇaka I, and thus enable our subscribers to have the translation bound up as Vol. I. I wish I could go on with this translation; but my hands are full of other work; and I must forego, however unwillingly, the privilege of completing this important treatise on Vedānṭa. I have the satisfaction however that the volume as it stands presents a complete explanation of "*Aḍhyāsa*," which forms the essence of the *Aḍvaiṭa Veḍānṭa*, from which the rest of its doctrines follow, more or less, as necessary deductions.

Ganganatha Jha

Muir College
Allahabad,
Feb. 26th, 1915.

Viḍyāraṇya's

Vivaraṇa-pramēya-saṅgraha

Preliminary Note

The work, a translation of which is here begun is entitled 'Vivaraṇa-pramēyasaṅgraha,' *i.e.*, "a Summary of the Topics of 'Elucidation'." The 'Elucidation,' the contents of which our work claims to exhibit in a comprehensive form, is the commentary, by Prakāshātman, on the so-called Pañchapādikā which itself is a commentary on the introductory section of Śaṅkarācārya's Commentary on the Vedānta Sūtras. The latter work, the Pañcapādikā and the Vivaraṇa together form the most authoritative exposition of that aspect of Vedānta theory which is associated with Śaṅkarācārya's name. A translation of Pañcapādikā has been begun by Mr. A. Venis in the Benares 'Pandit,' and a translation of the Vivaraṇa might, therefore, possibly be considered as what is just now most needed to help us to a full understanding of the Śaṅkara Mata.' But the Saṅgraha, although a later work, has the very great advantage of not being a *formal* commentary, and therefore capable of being read and understood by itself; while the Vivaraṇa imposes upon the reader the exceedingly irksome task of constantly referring not to one but to two previous works, the elucidation of which is its avowed object.

For the convenience of readers who may wish to refer to the Sanskrit text, the numbers of the pages in the edition of the Vivaraṇapramēya-saṅgraha published in the 'Vizianagram Sanskrit Series' are noted at the due places.

Vivaraṇaprameyasaṅgraha

by

Viḍyāraṇya (Mādhavācārya)

Introductory Verses

1. The abode of supreme bliss* which shines within the lotus of the heart—delighting all living beings here below by a mere fraction of itself, and, in a higher state of being, by completely absorbing them within itself,—into that holy ascetics devoutly enter!

2. What is undertaken in this work is a concise exposition of the topics treated of in the 'Elucidation' (*i.e.*, the Vivaraṇa composed by Prakāśātman) of the Gloss (ṭīkā, *i.e.*, the Pañcapādikā composed by Padmapādācārya) on the 'Commentary' (*i.e.* Śaṅkarācārya's great commentary on the Vedānta-Sūtras); to the end that the student may be saved the trouble and fatigue connected with the reading of such works as stand to each other in the relation of texts to be explained and formal explanations of such texts.

3. And (if the question be asked to what class of readers systematic works on the Vedānta address themselves,—we reply that) those who, urged by the injunction of the reading of the Veda as an absolute duty, have read the Vedānta-texts (*i.e.*, the Upaniṣads) and thereupon are troubled by doubts as to their purport, are the proper persons to study the Vedānta-Sūtras (in which the teaching of the Upaniṣads is systematized), the Commentary thereon and all further subsidiary works.

---

* Or 'the feet of Śaṅkarānanda' (the teacher of Mādhavācārya).

Sūtra 1 — Varṇaka (1)

I

[It is an absolute duty incumbent on every Brāhmaṇa to study the Veda. He there meets with texts declaring that the cognition of the Highest Self is the means to attain to Immortality (Final Release—which naturally is the highest aim of man). And other texts further declare that, in order to arrive at the cognition of the highest Self, it is needful to hear, reflect and meditate upon, that Self.]

*The injunction 'the Veda is to be read' is an absolute (*nitya*) injunction of such reading, in agreement with the declaration** 'the Veda with its six auxiliary disciplines is to be read and understood, as a religious duty, independently of any special motive.' For if the injunction of such study were one valid for him only who desires to attain certain objects, the following vicious circle would result—when there is an understanding of the matter of the Veda there arise certain desires (as being capable of being fulfilled through acting in accordance with Vedic injunctions); and, on the other hand, when there are certain desires in a man's mind, he engages in the study of the Veda with its auxiliary disciplines, and thus attains to an understanding of the sense of the Veda. We therefore hold fast to the view that, what prompts men to the study of the Veda together with its auxiliary disciplines is nothing else but the force of that absolutely binding injunction of study, and that they in this way come to comprehend the sense of the Veda. Now, owing to the influence of the maturation of long-accumulated religious merit there springs up, here and there, in the mind of some individual man, the desire to attain to the very highest good

---

* A Vedic injunction (*vidhi*) is either absolute, unconditional, permanent (*nitya*)—*i.e.*, enjoins a duty which is absolutely binding on an individual man or a class of men; or it is *kāmya*, —*i.e.*, it prescribes a certain course of action for him who is desirous of obtaining a certain wish (*kāma*) or end. The Jyotiṣṭoma-sacrifice is to be performed by him who desires, on death, to pass into the special heavenly region called Svarga. The study of the Veda, on the other hand, is unconditionally incumbent on every Brāhmaṇa.

** In Patañjali's *Mahābhāsya*, I.1.1, page 1, Bombay Sans. Series.

of man, and, looking in the Veda for means of realizing that good he comes across the following text—'For the love of the Self everything is dear';* and as this text means that everything else is dear only in so far as it subserves the Self, he loses his desire for all things other than the Self, and thus becomes qualified for 'the knowledge of the Self.'

Now a further text, beginning with the words 'when the Self has been seen heard, reflected on and known, then all this is known,' concludes with the words 'this much indeed is Immortality.'** From this the student learns that the 'seeing' of the Self is a means towards Immortality which itself is the highest object of man. But as 'seeing' is something that does not depend on the wish and exertion of man and hence cannot be enjoined or commanded, the student understands that the clause 'the Self is to be seen' (although an injunction in form, is not a genuine injunction, but) is a mere mention of that 'seeing' for the purpose of enjoining the 'hearing' of the texts as the principal means through which 'seeing' is to be attained, along with such useful aids as 'reflecting' and 'meditating'—the injunction being conveyed by the imperative sentence 'the Self is to be heard, to be reflected on, to be meditated on.'*** [*i.e.* what this sentence enjoins, for the accomplishing of the 'seeing of the self,' as the principal matter (aṅgin) is *hearing,* towards which reflection and meditation stand in the relation of useful subordinate matters (aṅga)]****

---

* *Bṛhadāraṇyaka-Upaniṣad.* (II.4.5).

** Ibid. (IV. 5.15).

*** *Bṛi-Upa.* (II. 4.5).

**** The introductory part of the Saṅgraha which deals with *vidhi* (injunction), may be passed over by the reader interested in Vedānta *philosophy,* but not anxious to enter into the details of Indian scholastics. The following remarks, however, will be useful to him who may wish to understand why this book, no less than other systematic Vedānta works, begins with discussions of *vidhi* (injunction). The Vedāntins consider the fundamental truths of their system to be set forth, or revealed, in one of the two great sections of the Veda. By the 'Veda' itself we have to understand a certain group of literary compositions—or, to use a more genuinely Hindu expression—a certain aggregate of sentences or texts (*vākyas*)—which are distinguished from all other literary works 'or aggregates of sentences' by two main circumstances—they are not of human nor indeed of divine origin, for they are absolutely self-existent and eternal; and they impart to the hearer truths which cannot be attained by any of the ordinary means of true cognition. The body of the Veda, no doubt, contains numerous texts or passages which are not *original,* inasmuch as they merely tell us what is, or may be, known by other means, *e.g.* Perception; passages of this character indeed make up the bulk of the Veda. But in the midst of these passages of secondary importance there appear a limited number of texts or enunciations of primary importance on which the

But, an objection is raised, although he who studies the Veda with its auxiliary disciplines thereby arrives at an understanding of its literal sense, he will not grasp its real purport without further thought; and hence the text quoted can hardly refer to that understanding of the Veda which results from mere hearing! Not so, we reply. There are passages in

---

unique character of the Veda depends. These texts teach man what otherwise he could not know at all. And of texts of this character two different classes has to be distinguished. The first class comprises so-called *vidhis* or injunctions, *i.e.* enunciations which, owing to their imperative form, move men to certain courses of action, the injunctions themselves declaring those courses of action to lead to certain desirable results; of this kind is *e.g.* the well-known text 'Let him who is desirous of the heavenly world perform the Jyotiṣṭoma-sacrifice.' The aggregate of such injunctive passages, together with secondary texts connected with them in some way or other, constitutes the so-called Karma-kāṇḍa, *i.e.*, that section of the Veda which is concerned with action, mainly of a ritual kind. The second, and in the opinion of the Vedāntin infinitely more important, class of Vedic texts does not urge man to action, but enunciates certain theoretical truths (more accurately *one* supreme truth, *viz.*, that the individual soul is identical with the universal principle of intelligence or thought—Brahman), the result of which is illumination of the hearer's mind—such illumination taking place without any choice or endeavour on the hearer's part; just as a sound eye perceives without effort, and cannot choose but perceive, an object placed before it in bright day-light. The aggregate of such non-injunctive, purely declaratory or instructive, texts—together with a considerable mass of secondary passages of a character merely explanatory, illustrative, etc.—constitutes the Jñāna-kāṇḍa, *i.e.*, that part of the Veda which is concerned with knowledge. Roughly speaking that part consists of the Upaniṣads.

But now it is a patent fact that even the Jñāna-kāṇḍa of the Veda contains numerous enunciations of an injunctive—imperative or hortatory—form, somehow bearing on the cognition of theoretic truth; and this fact has to be accounted for without an infringement of the general theory that the insight into truth which the Upaniṣads bring about flashes upon the hearer's mind with a sudden irresistible illumination, and that nobody can be *ordered* to know. The explanation given is that while knowledge in itself is spontaneous, involuntary, it yet accomplishes itself in the mind of him only who has gone through certain preliminary activities—hearing, studying, pondering and the like—which *do* depend on the will and energy of man, and therefore may be objects of injunction. Wherever therefore we meet in the Upaniṣads with texts which appear to say that man should endeavour to know Brahman, we have to understand that what is enjoined there is only those preliminary mental operations of which cognition itself is the spontaneous result. It thus remains true that the knowledge of Brahman is something that can be declared, but not enjoined. Nor, in the next place, may it be said that we do not require Vedic texts to tell us that in order to apprehend the truths enounced in the Upaniṣads we must study, and ponder the meaning of, sacred texts. For the possible modes of learning and studying are various, and the originality (the truly *Vedic* character) of the injunctions in question lies therein that they prescribe one certain definite mode of study of the sacred texts as alone capable of bringing about the desired result, *viz.*, cognition of the identity of the individual with the universal Self, and thereby Final Release.

the Purāṇas which clearly set forth that the *grasping of the purport* is included in the *hearing.**

"'Hearing,' *viz.*, from scriptural texts, and 'reflecting' with the help of proving arguments, and 'meditating'—these are the causes of the *seeing, i.e.*, the intuition of the Self.

(*Page* 2). Among these several causes, 'hearing,'—*i.e.*, the hearing of all the Vedānta texts from the beloved mouth of a venerated teacher,—consists in the ascertainment of the true purport of the texts, help being given by the drift of introductory clauses and the like.

By 'reflecting' is meant the repeated turning over in one's mind of arguments supporting the meaning of the texts; and by 'meditating' the steady concentration of the mind in the act of 'hearing' as well as 'reflecting.'

Both meditation and reflection are auxiliary means contributing towards the general result (*viz.*, the intuition of Brahman); through the former, non-knowledge (of Brahman) is put an end to; through the latter, contrary conceptions (such as the view of atoms or the like being the cause of the world) are utterly destroyed. 'Hearing' is superior in importance to both 'reflecting' and 'meditating:' for it stands in a more intimate relation towards the origination of knowledge; further off there stand 'reflection' which excludes other views, and 'meditation;' while calmness of mind, restraint of the senses, &c., fall under the head of 'details of procedure.'

In the mind of a man, then, who is fortified with all these subsidiary helps, there arises through the action of the word of the Veda, a mental modification (*vṛtti*) of a pure nature which has for its object the oneness of the soul and Brahman; and the manifestation, within that mental modification, of the universal intelligent principle—self-accomplished and divine—that it is which constitutes Brahman-cognition, that it is which destroys Nescience.

Through the instrumentality of the sacred word there arises a modification, perfect and firm, of the internal organ (*manas*)—which has the form of oneness of soul and Brahman; the 'seer' of that modification is the self-luminous internal Self; insofar as manifested therein (in that modification of the *manas*), in its own being, which is Brahman, that Self

* The Purāṇa passages are quoted in the text as proving that the main means of grasping the purport of the Veda is the 'hearing' of the sacred texts. They however extend over other matters also—on which we do not comment in this place, because they will be dealt with much more fully in the body of the work.

is called 'knowledge of Brahman.' Nescience is something merely illuminated (manifested) by the intelligent Self, and hence exists in consciousness only; comparable to the darkness which, in day-time, exists in the consciousness of the owl. This non-real Nescience and all its effects the serene Self naturally destroys by itself; so that the Self only remains in its full Brahma-nature. And that state of cognition which establishes the Self, thus remaining and being the sole object of its consciousness, is what we call 'divine cognition'."

II

[The texts declaring that the highest Self must be heard, reflected on, etc., are injunctive (*vidhi*) in character, and belong to the special class of injunctions (technically called 'defining' injunctions) the object of which is to restrict the agent to one of several *prima facie* possible course of action.]

[*Page 3*] But, our opponent argues, even with these explanations we cannot allow that the *hearing* of the Veda is something that can be enjoined. For if there is an injunction at all, it must be one of the three recognised kinds of injunction*—*i.e.*, it must either be an injunction which, like that of the Jyotiṣṭoma-sacrifice, establishes something not known through any other means of knowledge (*apūrva-vidhi*); or a 'defining' or 'restrictive' injunction (*niyama-vidhi*), like that which prescribes that the shelling of the rice-grains required for the sacrificial cake is to be effected by beating the grains in a mortar (not by removing the husks with the finger-nails, which, apart from the special defining injunction, would be the natural way of proceeding); or else an injunction

* The nature of the several *vidhis* cannot be discussed here at length; the difference between the three kinds may, however, shortly be stated as follows: An *apūrva-vidhi* enjoins what, apart from that *vidhi*, is absolutely non-established (unknown); it is the Vedic injunction only which moves us to offer the Jyotiṣṭoma-sacrifice in order to attain to the heavenly world. A *niyama-vidhi* defines the course of action, in cases where several alternatives are possible—each of which is partially non-established or unknown, insofar as without the *vidhi*, other courses of procedure would be equally likely to be resorted to, and thus exclude the procedure enjoined by the *vidhi*. The function of a *parisaṅkhyā-vidhi* is to restrict the agent to certain lines of action out of a number which are all equally *established* and are not mutually exclusive; as when the Veda lays down that the flesh of five kinds of five-nailed animals only is lawful food; while natural appetite moves man to eat the flesh of animals of any kind.

of exclusion (*parisaṅkhyā-vidhi*), such as the injunction 'five five-nailed animals may be eaten' (the purport of which injunction is to exclude from being used as food, all other five-nailed animals). Now the alleged injunction of 'hearing' cannot be of the first kind; for positive and negative experience alike prove that the hearing of, reflecting on, etc., the Vedānta texts is a means towards the cognition of Brahman; which is a result accessible to perception or observation (so that no Vedic text is required to enjoin the hearing of the Veda as a means of cognizing Brahman). For ordinary experience teaches, that in any case the study of a certain branch of knowledge is the means towards understanding the matter concerned; he, *e.g.*, who studies the standard works on medicine apprehends the matters with which that science deals. Nor can an injunction of 'hearing' the Veda be a so-called *niyama-vidhi*. For there is in this case nothing enabling us to assume a non-perceived (transcendental) result to be effected by action defined by the *niyama*-injunction. It is otherwise in the case of the beating of the rice grains; for there the general* supersensuous result of the sacrifice (the so-called *paramāpūrva*) obliges us to assume a supersensuous result of the beating of rice through which that general result is produced. Nor may you argue that, in an analogous way, the cognition of Brahman also is produced through some such unseen result; for negative experience does not favour this conclusion;—that is to say, we do not observe that where the Vedānta texts are learned, etc., the cognition of Brahman does not arise merely owing to the imperfection consisting in the fact that some unseen result due to some defined course of action is absent. And even if the cognition of Brahman were in some way due to 'unseen results,' the interpretation of the text concerning the learning of the Veda as an injunction would be in conflict with Śankara's Great Commentary where, under the 4th Sūtra, this view is forcibly impugned. The chief argument

* According to the Mīmāmsā-theory of the sacrifice, the sacrifice as a whole produces a certain supersensuous result, in the form of an energy, which, in due time, brings about that special fruit or result with a view to which the sacrifice was undertaken. When, *e.g.*, the actual *Soma* sacrifice has come to an end, there survives that unseen energy or force which later on puts the performer of the sacrifice in possession of the heavenly world. And this general supersensuous result again must be held to be the joint outcome of all those minor unseen results which spring from all the particular actions or steps of procedure which together constitute the total sacrifice. Thus the beating of the rice-grains prescribed by the Veda (as *the* only valid procedure of freeing the grains from their husks) must be supposed to have its own super-sensuous result; and it is for this reason that the *beating* is specially prescribed (to the exclusion of other methods of shelling the grain).

employed there is that if the Vedānta texts were at the same time to enjoin certain activities (*e.g.*, the learning of the Veda) and to set forth the nature of Brahman, there would be an objectionable 'split of the sentence' (*vākyabheda*).* Nor, again, can the injunction be of the nature of *parisankhyā-vidhi*. For in the case of the injunction of the eating of five kinds of animals possessing five nails, the eating of animals of any kind—whether having, or not having, five nails—is established by some other means (*viz.*, by natural desire which prompts men to use for food animals of any kind); and hence there is an opening for the 'injunction of exclusion' which enjoins that only certain animals should be eaten. The intuition of the Self, on the other hand, cannot possibly be attained by any other means than the Upaniṣads (and hence there would be no sense in excluding other means). The conclusion therefore is that the hearing of the Veda is not something that can be enjoined.

To this we make the following reply: As a matter of fact, defining injunctions (*niyama-vidhi*) are admitted with regard to the study of the Veda insofar as instrumental towards the comprehension of active religious duty (*dharma*), although such comprehension has results that can be perceived by the senses. Now if this is so in the case of the knowledge of outward religious duty, which is not of the nature of direct perception and constitutes only a minor good of man, how much more reason is there for *niyama*-injunctions in the case of that 'hearing' which is the means for accomplishing man's highest good,—*viz.*, the direct intuition of Brahman. And if in the case of the reading of the Veda, that which makes us assume an unseen result due to a *niyama* is the general unseen result of the sacrifice, which can only be produced through such minor unseen results,—we may with equal right assume that the cognition of Brahman demands us to assume *niyama*-injunctions with regard to the 'hearing' of the Veda. For the intuition of Brahman is just what is produced through all unseen results whatever (and hence it would not be wrong to say that it is produced by the unseen result produced by the *niyama*). As Smṛti says— 'All work whatever finds its proper termination in knowledge.'** For this text, in order to preclude the erroneous notion of the word 'all' referring only to such well-known works as sacrifices, employs the additional word 'whatever' in order to include thereby such

* A 'split' or 'break' of the sentence (*vākyabheda*) occurs when one sentence is made to express two different matters. According to the canons of interpretation laid down by the Pūrva-Mīmāṃsā, recourse to the assumption of a *vākyabheda* should be avoided wherever possible.

** Bhagavadgīta IV. 33.

activities as 'hearing' also.* On any other interpretation (if 'all' and 'whatever' were supposed to mean the same) there would be redundancy of expression. And if it be said that in the case of active religious duty (such as sacrifices), we are obliged to admit an injunction of study, because misfortune is threatened to him who does not study in the proper way, *e.g.* in the passage (Manu-Smṛti II. 168).— 'the Brāhmaṇa who without having studied the Veda in the proper way, labours after other things, falls, even in his present life, to the condition of a Śūdra, together with his descendants,'—we reply that the case under discussion does not differ; for here also we have an authoritative text threatening disaster (to him who does not do the 'hearing' of the Vedānta-texts)—'the Sannyāsin who, having abandoned all works of permanent obligation, lives without *hearing* the Vedānta-texts, doubtless falls into sin.'**

But, our adversary objects, that 'hearing,' 'reflecting,' etc., are means towards the cognition of Brahman, can be established neither by positive nor negative instances, since Brahman free from all difference is to be known through the Vedānta texts *only;* how then can the text, in question, be proved to be a defining injunction? (the conditions of the *case* excluding the possibility of *defining*, for which there is room only when there are more *means* than one).

This objection also, we reply, is without force. In the case of (the stock-example of defining injunctions, *viz.,*) 'he beats the rice-grains,' there is nothing to establish the use of the finger nails or the like as means of unhusking the rice-grains, which are to bring about the 'unseen result;' since such rice-grains are known from Scripture only; and yet we admit of the express defining injunction telling us to *beat* them. In the same way, there may be a defining injunction of the *Hearing* of Scripture, although there is no other alternative means of comprehending Scripture. "But," our adversary resumes, "in the case of the rice-grains there is occasion for the special defining injunction of *beating*, since the other means of unhusking have a preliminary *locus standi* with regard to grains in general (of which the sacrificial grains are only a species)." Well, we reply, in the case under discussion also there is room for the injunction of *Hearing* the Veda, considering that there are many different means towards the

---

* And thus the Smṛti text declares that the intuition of Brahman is produced, not only by such 'unseen results' as spring from sacrificial action, but also by such other 'unseen results' as that due to the 'hearing,' etc., of the sacred texts. And this latter 'unseen result' is the ground for assuming the *niyama-vidhi* of 'hearing.'

** Sāmba Purāṇa I.

knowledge of things in general (of which knowledge the 'cognition of Brahman' is only a special case). "Let it then be said that the injunction of the beating of the rice-grains really is an injunction establishing something altogether new (an *apūrva-vidhi*), but is on account of its practical effect spoken of as a defining injunction!" Then, we reply, the same will hold good with regard to the injunction of *Hearing*! Nor will this imply a contradiction of what the Bhāṣya says (as the opponent had urged above); for what is denied there is only the injunction of the Self being *seen*, not that of its being *heard*. According to the principle 'that the root and the affix of a verb conjointly signify *principally* what the affix denotes,' in the sentence 'the Self is to *be seen*' (*draṣṭavyaḥ*), the word '*draṣṭavyaḥ*' would express principally the injunctive force which belongs to the affix '*tavya*,' while 'seeing'—which is denoted by the root-element of '*draṣṭavyaḥ*'—would occupy a secondary subordinate position; and hence the Self or Brahman —which in the sentence quoted occupies the position of a mere determination of 'seeing' (of which it is the object)—would all the more be reduced to a subordinate place. The result of this would be that Brahman could not be viewed as the principal object which the Vedānta texts aim at establishing. This difficulty is removed if—with the Bhāṣya—we view the *seeing of Brahman* as the principal thing,—*i.e.*, as the final result of what Scripture enjoins,—for the accomplishment of which the *Hearing* of the Self is enjoined as a mere means.

As to the objection raised above that, if the Vedānta texts were at the same time to set forth Brahman *and* to convey an injunction, this would imply an objectionable syntactical split—is this objection, we ask, urged by one of ourselves (*i.e.*, the Vedāntins) or by the Mîmāmsaka? The former has no right to urge this objection; for the Vedāntins also assume that the sentence 'they desire to know Brahman by means of the sacrifice' enjoins the sacrifice as a means of knowing Brahman, although this interpretation implies a syntactical split (the sentence thus interpreted meaning 'cognize Brahman' *and* 'effect this by means of the sacrifice'). Nor, in the second place, can the objection be rightly urged by the Mîmāmsaka. For in that section of the Veda which treats of the Pretāgnihotra we have at first the clause 'he is to walk holding the fuel below (the handle of the sacrificial ladle),' which enjoins the *holding below* of the fuel; and after this we have the clause, 'for he holds it above for the gods.' Now here the decision of the Mîmāmsakas* is that this latter clause

* Mîm. Sūtras III-4. This Sūtra is not commented upon by Śabara Svāmin (See Bibl. Ind. edition I, p. 316); reasons for which omission are given in the Tantra-Vārttika (Benares Sanskrit Series Edition, pp. 920-22).

must be taken as *enjoining the holding above* of the fuel in the case of oblations made to the gods, although the clause stands in a section not treating of those latter oblations (but concerned with an oblation to the pitṛis.* It might be urged that one section of the Mīmāmsakas, *viz.*, the followers of Prabhākara do not accept this view as to the interpretation of the passage quoted (and that, hence, to them it is open to raise the objection as to 'syntactical split' against the Vedāntins). But in that case we point out another head of discussion where the Prābhākaras also admit a 'syntactical split': In the section on the Darśapūrṇamāsa sacrifice we have the clause 'the observances should be kept up for three nights,' and this clause the Prābhākara also accepts as an injunction of observances for a woman in her courses.** Considering these cases of admitted 'syntactical split' what harm can there be in allowing that the 'hearing' of the Veda is enjoined in a section which mainly treats of the cognition of Brahman?

[*Page 5*] You perhaps will deny the analogy, on the ground that in the case of the text referring to the 'observances' there is no possibility of connecting these observances with the matter of the section in which they occur, and that hence we have no choice but to accept a syntactical split; while in the text as to the 'hearing of the Veda' the affix '*tavya*' (in '*śrotavyaḥ*,' so far translated by 'is to be heard') may very well be taken, in the context in which it stands, as denoting capability (the clause '*ātmā śrotavyaḥ*' then meaning 'the Self is capable of being heard'), so that a recourse to 'syntactical split' would not be justified. In that case, we reply, we point to the text*** — 'hence the Brāhmaṇa having fully attained learning should seek to stand firm in strength (*viz.*, of reflection); and having fully attained learning and strength he should become a Muni'—as enjoining 'hearing' and the rest—a text which does not stand under any specific heading and therefore is not open to the objections stated above. For although this text does not at first sight convey the idea of 'hearing the Veda' &c., yet on more careful consideration we find that it *does* enjoin 'hearing' and the connected mental operations. Nor can this our view of that text be charged with not being the traditional one; for the author of the Vedānta-Sūtras himself (in III.4.47), taking it for granted

* The point of the reasoning is that the Mīmāmsakas declare the second clause (*upari hi devebhyaḥ*, etc.) to be, not an *anuvāda*, but an injunction, although on this view a *vākyabheda* has to be admitted.

** And this apparently implies *vākyabheda*. We are not in a position to give details as to the interpretation of this text according to the Prābhākaras.

*** Brih. Up. III. 5.1.

that the words 'pāṇḍitya,' ('learning,') and 'bālya' ('strength') imply the injunction of 'hearing' and 'reflecting', explains the concluding clause '*atha muniḥ*' as enjoining 'silence' *i.e.*, meditation.

But even if this be so, our opponent resumes, my main contention remains valid; *viz.*, that the particular text 'the Self is to be heard' with which the student meets in the sacred texts read by him, cannot be an injunction of 'hearing!' Not so, we reply. An authoritative grammatical rule teaches that the suffix *tavya* expresses *injunction* also (not only *capability*). Moreover in the case of other Vedic texts also—such as 'seek to know that,'* which appears along with many other sentences occurring in the same context,—we have necessarily to admit injunctions of 'hearing,' in spite of such admission implying 'syntactical splits;' and hence there really is no reason why you should be dissatisfied with our explanation of the sentence 'the Self is to be heard.' Nor may you raise an objection on the ground that there would be a needless repetition if we had two injunctions of 'hearing' in one and the same *śākha*—of the Veda (the two texts 'the Self is to be heard' and 'having fully attained learning' both occurring in the Bṛihadāraṇyaka). For the two texts differ in so far as one is a pure injunction, while the other states some details with reference to the injunction. Or else, we may consider the case of the two injunctions of 'hearing' as analogous to that of the two Maitreyi-Brāhmaṇas (also met with in one and the same book, *viz.*, the Bṛihadāraṇyaka) one of which is a recapitulation of the other—so that there is no idle repetition. All which proves that the text 'the Self is to be heard' may be taken as an injunction (*viz.*, a defining injunction) of the 'hearing' of the Self.

III

[In order fully to carry out what is implied in the texts enjoining the 'hearing,' etc., of the Self, a systematic enquiry into the purport of all the Vedānta texts must be undertaken. And this was the task proposed to himself by Bādarāyaṇa the author of the Vedānta-Sūtras. The first *sūtra* properly interpreted means that in order to attain to final Release a man must make a thorough investigation of the meaning of the Vedānta texts; from this there will result cognition of the highest Self or Brahman, and from that again there will result Release.]

* Taitti. Up. III. 1, 1.

*As declared in the Purāṇa passages quoted above, we have to understand by the 'hearing' of the Vedānta texts in its full sense the determination of the purport of those texts, which results from a ripe consideration of them, with the help of the various means of interpretation such as 'the drift of introductory clauses,' etc. We may then otherwise say that he who has renounced all desire for other things, and thus become preliminarily qualified for the cognition of the Self, should undertake a full consideration of the Vedānta-texts to the end of attaining to that intuition of the Self which is a means of Immortality. But when a man has thus studied the Veda and, in a general way, apprehended its meaning, doubts will begin to present themselves to his mind:—Is the mere absence or desire for worldly objects a sufficient qualification for the cognition of the Self, or are there other qualifications also? What are the means to cognize those qualifications and the nature of him who possesses them? Is the method of the enquiry into the meaning of the Vedānta texts already settled by the method of the enquiry into practical religious duty or not? or, how is the meaning of those texts to be enquired into? What is the true nature of the Self? What means are there to cognise it? Are those means in conflict with something else, or not? Has the knowledge of the true nature of the Self to be combined with meritorious works, in order to act as a means of Immortality; or has it that power by itself? And in the

* The exposition of Vedānta doctrine proper may be said to begin at this place; although the reader interested in *Philosophy* will now find himself hampered by a further complication. The fact is that to the Vedāntin philosophic truth is inextricably bound up, in the first place with that section of the Veda which deals with 'knowledge,' *i.e.*, the Upaniṣads; and in the second place with the so-called Vedānta-Sūtras *i.e.*, a body of concise aphorisms, ascribed to the Ṛṣi Bādarāyaṇa, in which the teaching of the Upaniṣads is systematized. The consequence of this view is that in all Vedānta books genuine philosophical reasoning is constantly interrupted by appeals, firstly to the text of the Upaniṣads, and secondly to the Vedānta-Sūtras—a quotation frequently taking the place of an argument. What the author tries to establish in the present section is that the central tenet of the Vedānta—*i.e.*, that all that prevents the individual soul from realizing its true nature, *viz.*, its identity with Brahman, is a mere unreal figment of Nescience which may at once be destroyed by true knowledge—is, if not explicitly enounced, at any rate implied in the very first of the Sūtras already. The Sūtras are so concise, and frequently enigmatic, in expression that many of them admit of most diverse interpretations; and it of course is a well-known fact that essentially differing theories appeal to the Sūtras—no less than to the Upaniṣads—in confirmation of their tenets. The unbiased student will, in this place, hardly see his way to accepting our author's view of the implied meaning of the first aphorism. And he may comfort himself with the reflection that, in refusing to follow our author's lead, he is not an 'innovator;' for his attitude in no way differs from that of many Hindu authorities of high standing and competence.

latter case, what proof is there for its having that power? Of what nature is Immortality and what proof is there for it?—All these and other similar questions and doubts demand to be solved by various arguments and lines of reasoning.

[*Page 6*] Now it was the intention of the reverend teacher Bādarāyaṇa, animated as he was by supreme compassion for suffering man, to set forth all those arguments in a body of concise aphorisms. Accordingly, in order rationally to determine the full meaning of the injunction conveyed by the text 'the Self is to be heard'—with its threefold reference to the object of the injunction, its result, and the qualified person to whom it is addressed—he in his first Sūtra, 'now therefore the enquiry into Brahman,' declares the need of an enquiry into the meaning of that injunction,—such need being indeed the prompting cause of the setting forth of the entire body of doctrine introduced by that Sūtra. The word 'now' in this first Sūtra points to the person qualified for the enquiry about to be undertaken, *i.e.*, him who, in accordance with the text 'for the love of the Self, &c.,' can lay claim to such qualification, insofar as possessing the four preliminary spiritual conditions of success which may be comprised under the term 'absence of desire for worldly objects' (*virakti*). The word *therefore* intimates the reason of the enquiry about to be made—that reason being what is declared by the text, 'there is no hope of Immortality by wealth,'* *viz.*, that Immortality is not to be attained by works of any kind, either worldly or enjoined by the Veda. And the compound word 'enquiry-into-Brahman,' finally, intimates what is expressed by the Vedānta-text 'when the Self has been seen, heard' etc., *viz.*, that to the end of attaining to that intuition of Brahman which is the means of Immortality, 'hearing'—which implies a full consideration of the Vedānta texts—has to be undertaken.

But, our opponent asks, is this first Sūtra to be understood as *enjoining* something, or merely as making a statement about something already established (*i.e.*, already known through other means of knowledge)? The former alternative cannot be accepted since the Sūtra exhibits none of those verbal forms (imperative, gerundive, etc.), which express command or injunction. And, on the latter alternative, the Sūtra would not possess any *motive* force, and hence could not be taken as conveying the injunction of 'hearing.' This objection is unfounded, we reply. For, as a matter of fact, we have to supply in the Sūtra a word with injunctive force *viz.*, '(is) to-be-made' (so that the complete Sūtra would

* Bri. Up. II. 4.1

run as follows: 'Now therefore the enquiry-into-Brahman is to be made.') And if to this you object that,—since cognition and desire depend on their objects (in the presence of which they spontaneously arise, and hence are not things which a man can be *ordered to do*)—the word *jijñāsā* (which so far has been translated 'enquiry' but which literally means 'desire-to-know') does not properly connect itself with the word supplied (*viz.*, 'has-to-be-done.'); we reply that, just for this reason the word 'desire-to-know' must be taken to denote, by implication, *consideration* or *enquiry (vichāra)* which is something that can be *done* (if the agent so wills, and to which therefore he can be urged.) The necessary connexion of *enquiry* with the *desire-to-know* can easily be established, the case being one of those where one thing or term is 'grasped tight as with pincers' between two others: *Rational consideration* or enquiry is 'grasped tight' between *desire* and *cognition*; for at first there is the *desire to know*; this inevitably leads to *enquiry*; and from this there originates *knowledge*. Nor must it be objected to this that, if we take the term 'desire-to-know-Brahman' to denote by implication 'enquiry into Brahman,' then the Sūtra would indeed establish that reference to the object which is termed 'enquiry,' but not that reference to the result of enquiry which is termed 'knowledge of Brahman.' For the 'implication' (or 'indication,' *lakṣaṇā*) is, in this case, of the kind 'which does not abandon the original sense of the word;' *i.e. jijñāsā* while indicating 'enquiry,' does not cease directly to denote 'knowledge.' It is because otherwise it could not originate the cognition of Brahman that *enquiry* must be held to have the Vedānta texts for its object; for we do not observe that men enquiring into other matters attain to that supreme cognition. And that the cognition of Brahman is the means of bringing about final release (*mokṣa, i.e.* that result which hitherto has been spoken up as 'Immortality') is proved thereby that otherwise such cognition would not have the character of the desired result. For what is desired by men qualified for entering on a line of action is the result, and in the case under consideration men qualified by possessing the four spiritual prerequisites desire nothing else but the total destruction of all pain and the enjoyment of supreme bliss, and the means to accomplish those ends. And as the knowledge of the highest Reality (*i.e.* Brahman) cannot in itself be the destruction of pain and the attainment of bliss, it can only be the *means* to accomplish those ends.

The full meaning of the first Sūtra therefore is as follows: 'He who is in possession of the four spiritual prerequisites must, since final Release is not to be attained through works, enter on a full enquiry into the meaning of the Vedānta texts, in order thereby to attain to that which *is* the means of final release, *viz.*, the cognition of Brahman.' The Sūtra thus expresses in a succinct form the whole purport of the Scriptural text.

[*Page 7*] That the need of an enquiry into the meaning of the Vedānta texts is the reason why the system of doctrine set forth in the Vedā nta Sūtras is undertaken is proved by positive and negative experience. For we observe in the case of the Jyotiṣṭoma sacrifice and similar activities, that men act when urged by an injunction with its three terms (object, result, person qualified); and, on the other hand, we observe that they do *not* act when some utterance addressed to them has no injunctive character (but is a mere statement of matter of fact), as when they are told that 'the earth consists of seven dvīpas (continents).' This necessity of undertaking an enquiry into the Vedānta texts—which constitutes the reason for the setting forth of the systematic body of doctrine embodied in the Vedānta Sūtras—the first Sūtra may be viewed as setting forth in the following technical form (implied in the Sūtra): 'The systematic body of doctrine in question must be begun because it has a possible object and a possible aim; just as, for example, the action of ploughing a field.' Nor must it be objected that since the Sūtra does not directly mention such an object and aim, these two factors cannot be considered as established by it. For although not directly named the two are *implied* in, or *suggested* by, the Sūtra; and '*suggestion*,' or implication, so far from being a defect must rather be viewed as constituting a positive beauty of a Sūtra. The 'object' (*viṣaya*) of the Vedānta texts, the meaning of which is investigated from Su-. I. 1.2 ('that from which there is the origination, etc., of this world') onwards, is the oneness of Brahman and the soul—as known from texts such as 'this Self indeed is Brahman.'* And this oneness is suggested in the first Sūtra itself by means of the word '*Brahman*' which denotes a Being of absolutely indivisible and homogeneous nature. The 'aim' (*prayojana*) on the other hand is the cutting short of all pain and the attaining to Brahman—as known from texts such as 'beyond all grief passes he who knows the Self,'** and 'He who knows Brahman reaches the Highest.'*** Now these two matters are suggested in the Sūtra insofar as the latter directly refers (by means of the word '*brahmajijñāsā*') to that knowledge of Brahman which is the means of the two being accomplished.

---

* Bri. Up. II. 5.19.

** Chhānd. Up. VII. 1.3.

*** Taitti. Up. II. 1.1.

IV

[The systematic enquiry into the meaning of the Vedānta texts which is carried on in the Vedānta-Sūtras can have its desired result only on the supposition of bondage—the opposite of Release—being not something real, but a mere figment of Nescience; for knowledge can put an end to non-knowledge only. The unreal nature of bondage is not indeed directly declared but at any rate suggested in the first Sūtra already.]

Nor does the Sūtra-writer only suggest the object and the aim of his enquiry, but he also undertakes implicitly to prove them by the wording of the Sūtra. For the Sūtra implies the following inference—'The body of doctrine in question has that possible object and aim, because it is antagonistic to bondage which is a mere thing of Nescience; in the same way as waking consciousness is antagonistic to dream-experience.' To this it must not be objected that the circumstance of bondage being a mere thing of Nescience is not actually suggested by the Sūtra. For, as a matter of fact this *is* suggested, in so far, namely, as the Sūtra implies the view of Bondage being something to be put an end to by Knowledge. To explain—In order to prove that the cognition of Brahman is a desirable result, the Sūtra-writer must maintain that such cognition puts an end to all pain whatsoever. Now it is nothing else but Bondage,—with whatever is implied therein, *viz.*, the Self appearing to itself as an individual cognizing subject, as a doer of actions, as experiencing the fruits of those actions and so forth,—which is the seed and root of all pain, and hence pain itself. The point then to be considered is whether this Bondage be something real or unreal. Now on the former alternative, bondage could not be terminated by the cognition of Brahman. There indeed are some of ours (*i.e.* some Vedāntins) who hold that knowledge may put an end to real things. But to them we address the following question: Does knowledge of a certain thing produce the effect termed *cessation* in the object of knowledge, or in its substrate? And, on the former alternative, is the object which it is supposed to put an end to, the Self insofar as implicated in the Samsāra (*i.e.*, the phenomenal individual Self); or only the attributes of that Self; or only those attributes which are opposed to the Self's absolute oneness and homogeneousness—such as the attribute of being an agent; or, lastly, only the attribute of non-knowledge residing in the Self? The three first alternatives are clearly inadmissible; for, to illustrate the matter by an analogous instance, in the case of a diverse-coloured fruit, *e.g.*, a mango, the cognition of the dark green part of it does not put an end either to its object (the dark part of the fruit), or the qualities of that part, its taste and so on; nor to the qualities opposed to those of the dark part, as *e.g.*, the yellow colour of another part of the fruit. The fourth alternative, on the other hand, agrees with our view (for we also hold that knowledge puts an end to non-knowledge; and this is an unreal object).

[*Page 8*] If, next, we consider the second main alternative (*viz.*, of knowledge producing the effect termed *cessation* in its own substrate, *i.e.*, in the knowing Self),—we again must ask whether that substrate itself is supposed to come to an end; or the qualities belonging to it; or certain attributes belonging to the substrate as well as to the object of cognition? The first alternative must be rejected, for it would imply a constant momentary perishing of the Self (in each act of cognition). The second alternative also is impossible; for, as a matter of fact, the qualities belonging to the Self—religious merit, etc.—are not put an end to by the cognition, *e.g.* of a jar. And the third alternative also is unacceptable; for the cognition,* on the part of the Self, of its body does not put an end to the connexion of Self and body. But, the opponent resumes, the Scriptural text 'Having known him he passes beyond death,'** (where Bondage is spoken of as 'death,' *i.e.*, something real) directly states that real bondage is put an end to by knowledge. Not so, we reply. The text quoted leaves it an entirely open question whether that bondage be real or unreal.

We on our part proceed in a different way; we assume bondage to be a mere thing of Nescience, *i.e.*, something unreal, in order thus rationally to justify the declarations made by Scripture. And this procedure is not essentially different from one adopted by yourself when you assume the so-called supersensuous result of the Jyotiṣṭoma and similar sacrifices in order to explain thereby what Scripture says as to those sacrifices being means of attaining to the heavenly world. "But," the opponent will perhaps reply, "what compels us to assume the *apūrva* is the undoubted truth that works such as sacrifices which perish as soon as performed cannot by themselves bring about results connected with a later time!" Well then, we reply, what compels us to view bondage as an unreal thing is the undoubted truth that knowledge can put an end to non-knowledge only! Nothing therefore remains but to acknowledge that Bondage is an unreal thing. What the Sūtra suggests then is that bondage, as being something to be terminated by knowledge, is a thing of Nescience.

---

* Read स्वदेहज्ञानेन

** Svet. Up. III.8

But, our opponent resumes, if this is so, the truth that bondage is a mere thing of Nescience should have been stated by the Sūtra-writer explicitly; for it is this which establishes the object of the enquiry (*viz.*, the oneness of the individual and the highest Self), and its final end (*viz.*, Release), and thus really is the cause of the entire systematic enquiry being undertaken. As long as this important truth is not directly stated, the entire drift of the enquiry will not be understood!

Well, we reply, the Sūtra-writer *has* stated that truth explicitly, *viz.* in the Sūtra II. 3-29. The purport of this Sūtra is as follows: The Sūtras immediately preceding had discussed those scriptural texts in which the Self is spoken of as departing from the body, going to the other world and again returning to this world; and the objection had been raised that with this *going* and *coming* the doctrine of the Self's essential omnipresence cannot be reconciled; to this the Sūtra quoted replies that, owing to an erroneous mutual identification* of the Self and the so-called internal organ (*buddhi*) there arises in the truly omnipresent Self the wrong conception of *going* and *coming*—which are attributes of the internal organ only—belonging to itself. Scripture makes statements based on this wrong conception, in order to guide thereby to insight into the true nature of the Self. But then, our opponent resumes, inasmuch as this Sūtra speaking of 'erroneous identification' would form a necessary 'introduction' to the whole enquiry, it should have been the *first* of the whole series of *Sūtras*; for the purpose of the 'introduction' consists in explaining certain details in connection with the main object of enquiry which is all along kept in view. Not so, we reply. The Sūtra-writer applying himself to the task of proving a certain theory cannot possibly begin with a Sūtra aiming at the refutation of objections. He who has to prove something at first directly states the matter to be proved, and after that sets forth the proving arguments. It therefore is quite in order that the first chapter of

* We here meet in the text for the first time with the term *adhyāsa*—literally meaning 'superimposition,' and in most cases best rendered by this latter term, heavy and scholastic as it may sound. As in what follows many pages will be devoted to a discussion of this *adhyāsa* — on which indeed the entire Vedāntic theory as conceived by Śaṅkara and his followers turns—it would be premature to attempt in this place a full explanation. We here say only so much, that *adhyāsa*, in its subjective aspect, is the wrong or mistaken identification of one thing with another, or else the wrong attribution to one thing of attributes of another; in its objective aspect, it is the process of Avidyā or Māyā, the principle of cosmic illusion, 'superimposing' itself upon things, and thereby deluding the individual mind. We shall claim the liberty of rendering the term in each place according to the exigencies of the context, and also of retaining the Sanskrit term wherever convenient.

the Vedānta-Sūtras should show that all the Vedānta texts refer to Brahman, and that only after this the refutation of objections— which tends to prove the writer's own view—should be undertaken. If the details as to the connexion of the Vedānta texts with Brahman were not explained first, the statement of objections and their refutation would be purportless.

But, our opponent once more resumes, if wrong super-imposition thus is not mentioned at the outset, the whole systematic enquiry really cannot be started, since neither an object nor a purpose for it have been established! Not so, we reply. We have shown above that the first Sūtra, although not directly stating wrong super-imposition, at any rate suggests it, and this affords a sufficient starting point for the enquiry.

V

[Against the fundamental Vedāntic tenet—asserting that the bondage of the Soul is due to the mutual 'super-imposition' (adhyāsa), *i.e.*, erroneous identification, of the Self and the Not-Self—, the opponent of the Vedāntin raises objections. The Self and the Not-Self of the Vedāntin are of totally contrary nature, just as light and darkness are: they hence cannot be erroneously identified in their full being; nor can even the attributes of either be ascribed to the other. In the case of this alleged Adhyāsa of Self and Not-Self none of the conditions which determine the adhyāsas of ordinary experience are present.]

[*Page 9*] But, an objection is raised, this adhyāsa, suggested though it be by the Sūtra, is incapable of rational proof. And this we show in the following way: (a) The Self and the Not-self cannot, through adhyāsa, be identified with each other, since they are absolutely destitute of any kind of identity; just as light and darkness are. Nor is the 'reason' in this argumentation (*i.e.*, the fact of the two being devoid of any identity) something not itself proved (and therefore incapable of functioning as a 'reason'); for we may argue—(b) 'the Self and the Not-self are destitute of all identity, because they are of contradictory nature; just as light and darkness are.' And here again the 'reason' is not itself non-proven; for we may argue—(c) 'the Self and the Not-self are of contradictory nature; for they fall within the spheres, respectively, of the ideas of the 'I' and the 'thou;' just as Devadatta and his opponent.' To this last inference the following objection might possibly be raised: Devadatta himself no doubt thinks of the aggregate consisting of his own body, sense-organs, etc., as 'I'; but his opponent thinks of the same as 'thou;' and thus there is no contradiction between 'I' and 'thou;' and the reverse holds good of Devadatta's opponent also (who thinks of himself as 'I' while Devadatta thinks of him as 'thou.') Hence the proving instance in the last inference ('just as Devadatta and his opponent') has no proving power. But this objection is ill-founded. What we bring forward as a proving instance is not two persons considered as the objects of ideas residing in two different minds, but two persons considered as the objects of two ideas residing in one and the same mind. In other words, the proving instance is constituted not by the two different aspects, (*i.e.*, Devadatta and his opponent, each of whom is 'I' to himself, and at the same time 'thou' to the other; without this giving rise to any contradiction); but by the one combined aspect which is constituted by the thought of Devadatta and the thought of his opponent (*both* appearing in the mind of Devadatta himself, or in that of the opponent).

Well, the Vedāntin may be supposed to resume, I drop the objection as to the invalidity of the 'reason' in your inference. But I now raise an objection with regard to the 'subject' of your inferences, the Self and the Not-self. Are the Self and the Not-self of your inferences the Self and Not-self of ordinary thought? or the Self and the Not-self as conceived by the followers of Prabhākara?* or the Self and the Not-self of the Vedāntins? The first alternative cannot be yours; for in that case the two first inferences would only prove what is proved already; (*i.e.*, admitted by us also); and the third inference again would be in opposition to actual experience. For according to ordinary thought the Self is an aggregate of factors, comprising the gross body etc., and also consciousness; while stones and the like are the Not-self. Now it is not either the oneness, or the wrong imputation of oneness, of these two classes of things which the Vedāntins maintain; and on the other hand, it is not a fact that the two are of totally contrary nature. Nor can you maintain the second alternative. For the followers of Prabhākara and others understand by the Self something in itself non-intelligent which is the substrate of certain

* The Prabhākara or Guru (whose followers are the Prābhākaras) is the founder of an important school of Mīmāmsakas who—apart from the more technical parts of the Mīmāmsa-theory—hold distinctive views of their own as to the nature of the cognizing Self, the processes of cognition, etc.

attributes or qualities such as *knowing, acting, enjoying*; while by the Not-self they understand the entire apparent world, including sense-organs, bodies, inanimate things and so on. Now, in the view of the Vedāntins it is the organ of egoity (Ahaṅkāra) which is the substrate of the attributes of *being a knowing subject, &c.*, and this Ahaṅkāra as well as its causal substance, *i.e.*, Nescience, fall both under the category 'Not-self.' Hence your reasoning is encountered by the same two objections as above; for since the 'Self' and 'Not-self' of the Prābhākaras both fall within what the Vedāntin considers to be 'Not-self,' it is neither the adhyāsa of the two, nor their identity, which is maintained by the Vedāntin (and hence the two first of the above inferences prove only what the Vedāntin does not call into doubt); and the two are not of contradictory nature (and hence the third inference is inadmissible).* Nor also is the third alternative open to you. For the Vedāntins understand by the 'Self' that which is mere knowledge (intelligence, consciousness), free from all fluctuation or instability, and by the 'Not-self' all things other than that. In what sense then do you take the *reason* in the (3rd) inference set forth above? Does the inference mean that the Self and the Not-self are of contradictory nature either because one of them is the object of both ideas,—*viz.*, of the idea 'I' and of the idea 'thou;'

---

* The Vedāntin objects to the two first alternatives on the same grounds. The Self and the Not-self of ordinary consciousness as well as of the Prābhākaras are not really distinct; for ordinary thought looks upon the Self as comprising the body, the sense organs, etc. also; and the Prābhākara views the Self as something in itself non-intelligent (just as the body and other material things are) of which *thought* is an attribute only. According to both views therefore there is absent that contrariety of nature, between Self and Not-self, without which it would have no sense to say that the two are wrongly identified.—According to the Prābhākaras the Self is the knowing, feeling, acting, etc. subject. This view is, of course, rejected by the Vedāntins, whose Self is universal non-personal intelligence (jñāna); all personality—which finds its expression in the self-affirmation of an *I*—falling within the sphere of the Non-real. The universal Self becomes an individual self only by its connexion with the so-called 'internal organ' (antah-karaṇa, manas etc.)—which itself is one of the manifold forms assumed by that unreal illusory principle (termed *avidyā* or *ajñāna*) through the association with which there arises the illusion of plurality—of a manifold world constituted by countless individual cognising minds and objects of cognition. Universal knowledge irradiates the internal organ, and thus there arise determinate individual cognitions, which differ according to the special form or modification (*vṛitti*) that the organ assumes or undergoes at the time. When assuming the '*I*—modification', the internal organ is called 'ahaṅkāra' (above translated by 'organ of egoity'). In the text the Vedāntin maintains (and rightly from his point of view) that what the Prābhākara calls the Self, is not the real Self, but only what the Vedāntins call the *ahaṅkāra* (*viz.* the ahaṅkāra insofar as irradiated and thus raised from the sphere of the Unconscious into that of the Conscious, by Universal Intelligence).

or because the Self is the object of the '*I*-idea' and the Not-self the object of the 'thou-idea'? In the former case you commit the mistake of employing a reason which is not present in the subject of the inference (since neither the Self nor the Not-self is the object of both those ideas, and the reason is not a 'reason' at all). And in the latter case your reasoning is vitiated by the fact that the reason employed is not present in the subject of the inference in its whole extent; for some Not-selfs,—*viz.*, the body, the sense-organs, the internal organ, the vital airs,—are not the object of the 'thou-idea.' "They may not be such in ordinary thought; but they *are* such according to the philosophic view of the Vedānta which defines the 'thou' as being everything that is (not self-luminous but) illumined by the light of intelligence (and such are the body, the sense-organs etc.,)" You may be right there, the Vedāntins reply; but all the same our objection to your inference remains valid, since according to the Vedāntins the Self is *not* the object of the 'I-idea'. It thus is evident that your inference cannot be established in whatever sense the Self and the Not-self are understood.

[*Page 10*] Against all this the opponent (who controverts the Vedāntic theory of adhyāsa) may now be supposed to argue as follows: My reasoning *is* valid as against the Vedāntin. It is not true that according to the Vedānta the Self is not the object of the 'I-idea;' for although the Self is self-luminous (and hence, properly speaking, not the object of any idea), yet since we are most clearly aware of it in the organ of egoity, it may itself, in a secondary or metaphorical sense, be designated as the object of the "I-idea.' Nor can it be urged against me that two individual consciousnesses, each of which is connected with a body, although standing *towards each other* in the relation of 'I' and 'thou,' are not really of contradictory nature; and that hence the inference that whatever is denoted by 'I' and 'thou' is of contradictory nature is fallacious. For consciousness can never be a 'thou' in the sense of being that which is illumined by (is the object of) consciousness; and it is only this philosophical, sense of the term 'thou' with which we are here concerned; not the unphilosophical sense in which the term is understood in ordinary life. But, a further objection is raised, the reasoning by which you thus undertake to prove the essential opposition of the Self and the Not-self proceeds after all by means of ideas only, not by means of the things themselves! Well, we then shall argue as follows: The Self and the Not-self are of contrary nature because the former is that for which objects exist (viṣayin), while the latter is the object (viṣaya); just as the eye and colour are. But, it is objected to this, we observe that the intelligent Self stands to the non-intelligent Not-self in a certain relation of agreement, in so far, namely, as the Self *establishes* the Not-self (which is known through the Self only). Now if two things are said to be contrary in nature, this means, either that one of them is destructive of the other, or that the two are incapable of abiding together—in both of which cases they are in complete disagreement or disharmony. The conclusion that the Self and Not-self are contradictory in nature thus would be in conflict with immediate experience; and for the same reason your proving instance also must be declared to be defective (for the eye proves colour, and hence the two cannot be of contradictory nature). There is no force in this objection also (the antagonist of the Vedāntin replies). For what we here understand by 'contrariety of nature' is the incapability on the part of two things of either being the Self of (*i.e.* becoming identical with) the other—such as *e.g.* the relation is between 'being' and 'not-being.' "But if you understand 'contrariety,' in this sense, how, can you, in the second of your inferences, employ *light* and *darkness* as a proving instance?—considering that those two things are well known to be contrary to each other in the sense of being incapable of abiding together?" Not so, the opponent replies. The fact rather is that in a faintly lighted room darkness *does* abide together with light; for otherwise things would be seen there as distinctly as in a locality well lit up. Nor may it be said that the terms 'darkness' and 'light' indicate shade (chhāyā) and sunlight (ātapa), which occupy the same space as light and darkness. For as a matter of fact we observe different degrees of heat in shade which in itself is of one and the same nature; and this conclusively indicates the presence of sunlight of which heat is a quality; and hence the abiding in the one place of brightness and shade cannot be denied. And thus even if, carrying the assumption of implied meanings one step further, we should assume that the terms 'light' and 'darkness' denote *heat* and *coldness*—which belong to sunlight and shade as attributes—we should have to admit that heat and coldness abide together; and from that it would follow that light and darkness abide together. The conclusion is that light and darkness are not capable of entering into a relation of identity of the same kind as that relation which connects the class-character (the jāti or *Universal*) and the individual; it is in this sense that light and darkness are of contrary nature.

But—a further objection is raised against the above reasoning of the opponent of *adhyāsa*—in the proving instance of light and darkness, what vitiates the proving power of the instance is that the two stand to each other in the relation of 'existence' and 'non-existence' (the one being the mere negation of the other).* For according to the Naiyāyikas *darkness* is nothing but *absence of light*; and according to the followers of Prabhākara it is absence of the perception of form and colour. The reply to this is that it is not so.** That which has the characteristic of being of different kinds according as it is more or less cannot possibly be a mere *non-existence*. And moreover the dark *colour* of darkness proves it to be a substance. "But if darkness is a positive entity, how is it that in a brightly illumined place a person whose eyes are closed perceives darkness (while there is no real darkness)? What we should expect in this case is that the abundant light would completely discard darkness. That the two abide together there only where there is a limited quantity of light we have remarked above already." The darkness perceived in that case, we reply, is the darkness within the sense-organ. Nor is there anything impossible in a man's apprehending something that is within the organ of sight; for it is a well-known experience that a person whose ears are shut apprehends an inward noise. Nor must it be said that the assumption of a sense-organ being capable of apprehending what is within it would imply that a man whose eyes are shut would perceive such things also as the ointment applied to the eye; for the law for the eye is that with the exception of darkness, it perceives coloured things only when it is assisted by light. But, a further objection is raised, if darkness were a substance, it would not, on the removal of light, arise instantaneously; for all effected substances originate gradually only by the successive formation of atoms, binary, ternary, and so on. Not so, we reply. Those who hold all origination to be a mere illusory appearance (*i.e.* the Vedāntins) do not allow any such gradual origination of substances, but recognise only one cause, *viz*., fundamental Nescience.*** Nor do we allow the objection that "darkness cannot be a substance which has colour for its quality, for the reason that it is not perceived by touch; just as ether (is not a coloured

* Light and Darkness have been put forward as two *things* of contrary nature, incapable of identification. An objection is here raised on the ground that as Darkness is nothing more than the mere *privation or negation of Light*, the two cannot be regarded as *two things*,—at any rate, not in the same way as 'Self' and 'Not-self.' Thus the proving force of the instance is vitiated.

** That *darkness* (tamas) is not the mere absence of light, but something substantial (dravya) is held not only by the Vedāntins, but also the Mīmāmsakas of the Bhattā-School, the Sāṇkhyas, and even some of the Naiyāyikas.

*** The material world, as it appears to our senses, originates, according to the Naiyāyikas, by the successive aggregation of the atoms, the ultimate constituents of matter, into larger and larger groups. According to the Vedāntin, any given material body arises by an instantaneous modification of the one fundamental substance of all phenomena—Nescience.

substance because it is not the object of touch)." For you might as well argue that air is not perceived by touch because it is devoid of colour; just as ether is. In both cases your argumentation would equally be in conflict with actual perception. Should it be said that the visual perception admits of being accounted for otherwise (than on the ground of darkness being a substance with colour for its quality),—*viz.*, on the ground that what is perceived is the dark blue colour which fictitiously superimposes itself on the absence of light,—we reply that all the same the above inference ('darkness is not a coloured substance because it is not the object of touch') remains inconclusive; for smoke, which decidedly is a coloured substance, is not an object of touch for any part of the body but the eye. And should this be met by the explanation that the quality of touch although actually existing in smoke is not manifested (anudbhūta, and hence not perceived),—we may say with equal justification that the quality of touch exists in darkness, but only in a non-manifest form. Nor could it be urged against this that it is impossible that something actually existing should be altogether non-manifest; for we observe that in gold as it comes from the mine the quality of brilliancy—whereby it illumines both itself and other things—, and the quality of warm touch (which both admittedly belong to gold as consisting of *light*)—are altogether non-manifest. It thus appears that the view of Darkness being a positive entity is free from all objections. But, the antagonist resumes, the same may be claimed for the view of darkness being a mere non-existence, *viz.*, the privation of light. The circumstance that there are different degrees of darkness may be accounted for as depending on the different degrees in which the counter-entity of darkness, *i.e.*, light, is present; and the dark blue colour actually perceived may be explained as super-imposed on the absence of light. We are unable, we reply, to admit this. For there are special difficulties in the way of Darkness being viewed as a mere negation. Is Darkness to be defined as the absence of light in general, or of some one light, or of all light? On the first and second alternatives it would be difficult to determine whether Darkness is the antecedent non-existence of light,* or the reciprocal non-existence, or the emergent non-existence, for in a place where there is sun-light there is no perception of Darkness either before the lighting of a lamp, or after it, or after the lamp has been extinguished. And the third alternative would imply that Darkness does not depart unless all light whatever be brought to bear on

* If Darkness cannot be shown to be any *one* of the three kinds of non-existence which the Naiyāyikas distinguish, it of course cannot be a non-existence at all.

it. Nor can Darkness be defined as the absence of the perception of colour and form. For a person within the dark inner room of a house perceives at the same time the colours and shapes of things outside the room, and the darkness within the room. From all this it follows that Darkness is not a mere non-existence or privation. And it cannot therefore be said that its force as a proving instance (in the inference 'The Self and the Not-self cannot be identified because they are of contrary nature, as light and darkness are') is vitiated by its being a mere negation.

All the same, the Vedāntin resumes, (against the opponent), your fundamental reason for rejecting the Vedāntic adhyāsa—*viz.*, the circumstance of the Self and the Not-self being altogether incapable of identification—has no proving force. For in the case of error, as exemplified by the cognition 'this (thing before me) is silver' two distinct things,—*viz.*, a piece of shell present to the sense and silver—although really quite incapable of identity, are nevertheless cognized as identical. Not so, the opponent of the Vedāntin replies. To the case quoted by you the reason (employed by me to prove the impossibility of adhyāsa) does not apply, because the capability of identification actually exists there. This capability follows from the fact that when real silver is perceived, we cognize the real identity of a thing present to the sense and of silver (which fact establishes the possibility of *something* present to the sense being viewed as silver). Nor may you, the Vedāntin, urge that the Self and the Not-self also may, in certain cases, be identical; and that owing to the possibility of such identity the reason in my inference is not established. For the fact is that a true identity of those two cannot be established in any case. For which of the two following alternatives would you be prepared to maintain—that the subject (draṣṭṛi-Self) identifies itself with the object (dṛishya)? or that the object identifies itself with the subject? On the former alternative, the identity cannot, in the first place, be one of essential nature; for in the subject which essentially is nothing but pure Intelligence there can be no objective element! If there were such an element, the alleged identity would not be between the agent (*i.e.*, the 'seer' or Self) and the object of the action (the *seen*, or Not-self) (but only between that objective element, and the object or Not-self). If, in the second place, that identity is (not essential but) only adventitious (*i.e.* accomplishing itself on certain conditions only),—does, we ask, the subject transform itself into something objective, by itself or owing to some extrinsic cause? Neither alternative is admissible, as the subject is not something made up of parts (and therefore cannot undergo any transformation). To quote an analogous instance, Ether, which is not made up of parts, never transforms itself into something made up of parts, either by itself or owing to some extrinsic cause. Analogous difficulties beset the second alternative:—*viz.*, the object's identifying itself with its counter-entity, the subject. If the alleged subjective aspect belonged to the object essentially, the objective character of the object would be forfeited. And should it be said that the subjective aspect also belongs to the object partially only (so that part of it would be object, part subject), we should have the contradiction of one and the same thing being *agent* (*i.e.* seeing or knowing subject) and *object of action*, *i.e.* thing seen or known. If, on the other hand, the subjective aspect of the object is adventitious merely, is the object to be viewed as itself transforming itself into something of an intelligent nature, or as receiving within itself the intelligence of the Self? Not the former certainly! for an effect of what is non-intelligent can never be of the nature of intelligence: we in no case observe that jars and such like things, which are shaped out of non-sentient clay, exhibit the characteristics of intelligence. Nor the latter, for the intelligence of the Self is essentially present everywhere,* and hence cannot be *imparted* to a thing. As thus we have shown that real identity of the Intelligent and the Non-intelligent is quite unproveable, the reason on which our second inference rests (*i.e.* the non-capability of those two to become identical) is well established, and hence the inference is sound. And as the second inference proves the original (first) one, the adhyāsa of the Vedāntins is proved to have no existence.

Well let it then, the Vedāntin resumes, be granted that the two substrates themselves are incapable of identity. All the same there may be a so-called *adhyāsa of connexion* (samsargādhyāsa); *i.e.* the qualities or attributes (dharma) of the Self may super-impose themselves on the Not-self. And against this it may not be urged that the Self as being mere intelligence possesses no attributes; for bliss (ānanda), the consciousness of objects, permanence, etc., are its attributes. These so-called attributes, indeed are at bottom not attributes, but constitute the very being of the Self, but they *appear* as several owing to the functions of the internal organ which acts as the limiting adjunct (to the universal absolutely non-differenced Self) and hence may, in a metaphorical sense, be termed 'attributes.' Nor can it be urged that there can be no adhyāsa of attributes, independently of their substrates. For when, owing to the nearness of the red Hibiscus flower, the crystal appears to us as red, we have an adhyāsa

* The universal Intelligence is present everywhere: it is the general substrate of whatever appears.

of a mere attribute, (*i.e.*, we hold the crystal to be red without identifying the crystal and the flower). But this theory also is groundless. Attributes cannot possibly be treated as something independent. What we perceive in the crystal is not *redness* by itself but redness belonging to the flower which is reflected in the crystal. So-called 'adhyāsa of attributes' apart form their substrates therefore does not exist. And as we thus have disposed of all adhyāsa of *things*, whether they be substrates of attributes or attributes, we have also disposed of *cognitional* adhyāsa which does not arise without the adhyāsa of things. The general conclusion therefore is that adhyāsa is something not capable of rational proof.

VI

[That of the adhyāsa of the Self and the Not-self no satisfactory rational account can be given, the Vedāntin replies, so far from upsetting our theory, fully confirms it. The phenomenal world is a mass of irrationality; it is throughout inexplicable, non-definable (anirvachanīya). Hence no objection can be taken to the view that that fundamental fact to which the whole phenomenal word is due, *viz.*, the adhyāsa of Self and Not-self, cannot be *rationally* explained. We however are able to assign a definite causal factor of that adhyāsa, *viz.*, the existence of a principle of illusion, termed 'Nescience' (ajñāna, 'avidyā') which as a matter of fact, though in an unaccountable way, is associated with what constitutes the reality of the world, *viz.*, Universal Intelligence.]

Against this we (Vedāntins) now finally reassert the validity of our adhyāsa theory, as follows: Do you, our opponent, on the ground of adhyā sa being contrary to reason, maintain that it is something unreal, or do you mean to deny that there is such a thing at all? If the former, there is no cause of disagreement; for we Vedāntins, who hold the theory of the inexplicability (anirvachanīyatā) of the apparent world, ourselves teach that adhyāsa is something unreal and contrary to all reason. We in fact hold the theory of the world's inexplicability, just because the adhyāsa of Self and Not-self is in contradiction to all reasoning; otherwise we should have to acknowledge it as something real.

But, our opponent here interposes, we altogether deny adhyāsa—there is no such thing as the adhyāsa of Self and Not-self. For there exist no causal or instrumental factors to bring about an adhyāsa in this case. In the adhyāsas of ordinary experience—as when a man mistakenly judges 'this thing before me (which in reality is a shell) is silver;' or 'this thing (which in reality is a piece of rope) is a snake,'—the required causal factor is supplied by the similarity, in point of qualities and constituent parts, between the substrates (*i.e.* the shell and the rope) on the one hand, and that which superimposes itself on them (*i.e.* the silver and the snake) on the other hand. But in the case of the alleged adhyāsa of Self and Not-self there is no such similarity; for the Self has neither qualities nor parts. Nor may you object to this on the ground that adhyāsa exists even in cases where such similarity is absent, as *e.g.* when redness superimposes itself upon the crystal. For as in this latter case the error is due to a conditioning adjunct, there is no need of similarity. The adjunct there is the red flower close by, to which the quality of redness really belongs; it is this which is the cause of the appearance of redness in the crystal. But why then, the Vedāntin asks, should not the organ of egoity (ahāṅkāra) which possesses certain qualities such as activity, etc., and moreover is in close contact with the Self, be acknowledged as that conditioning adjunct owing to which activity and other qualities may be superimposed upon the Self? Let us allow, the opponent replies, that attributes such as activity may super-impose themselves upon the Self; but for the adhyāsa upon the Self of *substrates* of attributes—such as the organ of Egoity itself, the body and so on—there is no conditioning adjunct; and hence such adhyāsa is not possible. For similarity also (which otherwise might take the place of an upādhi) is absent.

This also is groundless, the Vedāntin replies. The quality of smell (odour) has neither attributes nor parts, and yet we form judgments—such as 'the smell of a snake is similar to that of the ketaki-flower—proving that similarity may rest on the mere attribute of *odorousness*. Analogously similarity between the Self and the Not-self may be established on the basis of the Self possessing the attribute of being a 'thing' ('that which is the meaning of a word'—padārtha, just as the Not-self is). And, if to this argument you object on the ground that the Self which is nothing but mere intelligence in reality has no attributes whatever (not even that of being a padārtha), we finally remark that after all it is not necessary, in cases of error not due to conditioning adjuncts, to insist on similarity as the causal factor of the adhyāsa. For, as a matter of fact, there are instances of such error which do not depend on similarity; consider, *e.g.* the error 'the shell (which in reality is white) is yellow.' "But in this case there is present another causal factor through which the error establishes itself,—*viz.* the effusion in the eye of bile (caused by jaundice), or some other morbid affection of the organ of sight!" Well, we Vedāntins reply, in the case of the erroneous identification of the Self and the Not-self also, there exists a causal factor, *viz.* Nescience! "But as to this Nescience of yours people are not even agreed, whether it be the mere absence of knowledge (a mere negation), or some positive entity; would it then not be better to deny adhyāsa altogether than to assume Nescience as its basis?" This may not be, we reply. It is simply impossible to deny a beginningless (eternal) entity which immediate intuitive knowledge vouches for as something that, while depending on the existence of the inward Self, hides and obscures the intelligence and bliss of that Self. Were we to deny this, we should have to deny the inward Self as well!

"But adhyāsa being an effect cannot be held to be without a beginning!" Not so, we reply. Adhyāsa, in the case of the Self, means nothing else than the Self's being connected with the attributes of being an agent, having experiences of pleasure and pain, being liable to imperfections such as passion and desire, and so on. Now the adhyāsa of being a subject experiencing pleasures and pains pre-supposes the adhyāsa of being an agent; for he only who acts enjoys the fruits of his actions. Being an agent, again, pre-supposes the adhyāsa of being subject to passion and desire; for he who has no desire does not act. And desire, in its turn, pre-supposes experiences of pleasure and pain; for desire does not spring up in those who have had no such experiences. All these states thus constitute a beginningless chain, comparable to that formed by the seed which pre-supposes a plant, which again pre-supposes a seed, and so on *ad infinitum*. This reflexion also disposes of the objection that, as adhyāsa pre-supposes the consciousness of the world and that consciousness on its part pre-supposes adhyāsa, we are reasoning in a circle. For if, as we assert, adhyāsa is without beginning, the body, etc., as presented by the retrogressive chain of previous adhyāsas cause the subsequent adhyāyas through persisting in the form of impressions (samskāra; *i.e.* the impressions left on the cognising Self by previous adhyāsas give rise to the subsequent ones). Nor may it be objected that the body, etc., cannot be superimposed upon the Self because they are unreal. For as super-imposition can be established by mere consciousness, it is not real existence that determines the super-imposition of a thing upon something else.* In erroneous judgments of the type of 'this is silver' there is adhyāsa of identity between the shell which is real and the silver which is unreal. Nor can it be said that in the case of two trees which seen from a distance appear as one, there is adhyāsa of the identity of two real things. For there also an *unreal* attribute, *viz*., *oneness*, is superimposed on a real substrate, *viz*., the two trees. Were this not so (*i.e.*, where it not the unreal only that superimposes itself), it would follow that that identity also which holds good between a quality and the substrate of the quality—which are two real things—, is something merely 'superimposed.' Although in the case of the Self and Not-self the wrongly imagined identity is the same, viewed from either side (*i.e.*, the Self is erroneously held to be identical with the Not-self, and the Not-self to be identical with the Self); yet there is a certain difference, inasmuch as the Self superimposes itself on the Not-self not directly by itself, but only in the way of (saṃsarga) (which means that it is only the attributes of the Self which super-impose themselves on the Not-self), and hence is real; while the Not-self superimposes itself upon the Self in its entire essential nature (so that the entire Not-self is nothing but superimposition), and hence is unreal. Nor can it be argued that, if there were an identification of the Real ('Self') and the Unreal (Not-self') then just as in the case of a quality and the thing to which it belongs we perceive a difference as well as non-difference between them, and hence, have the notion 'the cloth has whiteness,'—so in the same manner, in the case of the real 'Self' and the unreal 'Not-self' (body, &c.) we should have the notion 'I have the body,' 'the body is mine,' and so forth (and not 'I am the body.)' This we say cannot be argued; for what constitutes adhyāsa is that either term should be the other in the sense of complete oneness. "But should it then not be said that there is an adhyāsa of *oneness* rather than of *identity*?" Not so, we reply. For after all ordinary thought and speech make a distinction expressing itself in forms such as 'the body is mine , analogous to the distinction expressing itself in the form 'the cloth has the quality of whiteness.' "But," it is objected, "adhyāsa must invariably be accompanied by non-apprehension of difference. And now you admit that ordinary thought and speech imply an apprehension of difference between Self and Not-self, and such apprehension destroys the non-apprehension of difference; hence adhyāsa itself is destroyed!" Not so, we reply. That apprehension of difference (which you say destroys adhyāsa) is not

---

* As mere subjective superimposition also is possible, it does not follow that because a certain thing is *superimposed*, it must have real existence.

really admitted by us. The fact is that ordinary people although verbally acknowledging the difference of Self and Not-self—in using forms of expression such as 'this body of mine'—do not really conceive a Self different from the body unless their minds be illumined by scriptural teaching. To their actual thought (which makes no distinction between the body and the Self) the term 'adhyāsa of oneness' may be applied, but with a view to their forms of speech it may be designated as an 'adhyāsa of identity.' The use of the term 'I' (as applied by ordinary people equally to the Self and the body) really implies non-difference of Self and Not-self; on the other hand, expressions such as 'this body of mine' seem to imply the difference of the two. Nor must it be said that identity (tādātmya) is neither more nor less than *oneness*. For by 'identity' we have to understand a relation of two things, contradictory to their mutual negation, and at the same time, implying difference as well as non-difference; while 'oneness' is simply contradictory to their difference; the two relations thus distinctly differ. The relation of Brahman and the individual soul (jīva) also in reality is that of *oneness*; but, with a view to the difference fictitiously established by Nescience it may be spoken of as 'identity.' Nor may it be said, that just as Brahman and the individual soul are really one, so the oneness of the Self and the body also—of which ordinary thought is directly conscious—is something real. For two entities which are absolutely distinct, inasmuch as the one is real and the other unreal, cannot be one in reality. Their 'oneness' therefore is something merely super-imposed.

VII

[Nescience, which is not mere 'absence of knowledge' but a positive entity, abides in, or has for its substrate, the Self.]

Of this adhyāsa the material cause (upādāna) is Nescience (ajñāna), which has the character of a positive entity (*i.e.*, is not a mere negation or privation), is without beginning and inexplicable (aniravachaniya). For where such Nescience exists, adhyāsa arises; where it does not exist, adhyāsa does not arise. "But," an objection is raised, "(there is no need of assuming Nescience as the cause of adhyāsa; for) the positive and negative instances quoted (*viz.*, the rise of adhyāsa where there is

Nescience, and its absence where Nescience is absent) may very well be explained on the ground of the absence of the knowledge of truth, which knowledge prevents adhyāsa." Not so, we reply. The knowledge of truth is not something that can be defined as being a preventive of adhyāsa. By a preventive thing or factor we understand that which arises in antagonism to the production of a certain effect, in cases where there is sufficient cause for the production of the effect. But the knowledge of truth arises where there is an absence of the sufficient causes of adhyāsa—such as morbid affections of the eye and the like (owing to which a white thing appears as yellow, or a piece of shell as silver, and the like). "But all the same, since the knowledge of truth is no doubt antagonistic to adhyāsa, the positive and negative instances above stated may be accounted for on the basis of the absence of that antagonistic factor (*i.e.*, the knowledge of truth)!" This also we cannot admit. In the case of any effect the first question that arises is that regarding the cause; after this only there arises the question as to the absence of antagonistic factors. In accordance, therefore, with the principle that what is intimately connected has greater force than what is remotely connected, it is proper to account for the stated positive and negative concomitances on the basis of what is intimately connected with them, *i.e.*, their material cause. "But may it not be said that, as in the case of emergent non-existence, here also there may be no need at all of a material cause?"The cases are not analogous, we reply. We must assign a cause for adhyāsa on account of the following inference—'Adhyāsa has a cause because it is a positive entity and at the same time an effect; just as a jar is.' "But," it is objected, "the reason in this inference has no general proving force, as shown *e.g.* by the instance of the colour which is a quality of a piece of cloth. That is a positive entity and also an effected thing; but it cannot possibly have a material cause. For what should be that cause? the piece of cloth? or some other substance? Not the former; for of two things that come into being at the same time (as, in the present case, the cloth and its colour), one cannot be the material cause of the other; not any more than one horn of a cow is the cause of the other horn. And on the second alternative the colour would belong to that other substance, and thus cease to be the colour of the cloth." By no means, we reply. Even according to the view of the Naiyāyikas* a substance when originating abides without qualities for one moment; hence, as the cloth and its colour do not come into being together, there is no reason not to accept the cloth as the material cause

* According to the Naiyāyika, the quality of a thing is produced one moment after the production of the thing itself.

of the colour. On the view of the Vedāntins, on the other hand, even if the threads (*i.e.* a substance other than the cloth) are viewed as the material cause, the colour would not on that account cease to be a quality of the cloth; for the Vedāntins hold cause and effect to be identical. Nor may it be said that, since the adhyāsa may be accounted for on the ground of morbid affections of the eye, etc., there is no need of our assuming an additional general cause, termed Nescience. For the adhyāsa and its material cause must have one and the same substrate; while in the instance adduced by you, the substrate of the adhyāsa is the Self, while the substrate of the morbid affection is the sense-organ. "But," it is objected, "the adhyāsa of silver has for its substrate the shell, while Nescience, which you hold to be the material cause of the adhyāsa, resides in the Self; it thus appears that even on your view the oneness of substrate for the adhyāsa and its cause cannot be established in all cases!" You are mistaken, we reply. As we shall prove later on, the adhyāsa also abides in the Self, and is only in contact with the shell.

Let us then say, the antagonist resumes, that Nescience constitutes the material cause of the *adhyāsa of things* (arthādhyāsa) only; while the Self and the internal organ constitute the material cause of the *adhyāsa of cognitions or ideas* (jñānādhyāsa). For in true (non-erroneous) cognitions one or other of these two, according to different theories, is the substrate of cognition! This also may not be, we reply. For as to the Self, it is incapable of change (and hence cannot be the cause of an effect). And as to the internal organ—this, for giving rise to cognitions, depends on connexion with the sense-organs (in the case of perception), or on some inferential sign (liṅga; in the case of inference). In the case of adhyāsa, however, no such connexion, etc., is possible. For as the false thing (*e.g.* the silver in the shell)—which has its being in the cognition only—does not exist previously to the cognition, wherewith should the sense organ enter into contact? The presence and absence of the sense organ's connexion with the thing are concerned with something else, *viz.*, the cognition of that which is the substrate of the erroneous cognition. Nor can it be said that the erroneous cognition originates just from this contact of the sense-organ with the real substrate; for in the absence of contact with a false thing the idea of that false thing (*i.e.* erroneous cognition) could not be accounted for. Nor again can it be said that the case of erroneous cognition is analogous to that of recognition—as when *e.g.* the Devadatta, whom we had seen on a former occasion is suggested to the mind through the impression he had left thereon, and then identified with the Devadatta now before us; for if the erroneous cognition were of this kind it could *not* be an erroneous one. Nor again can the erroneousness of the cognition be explained as due to the absence of contact of the sense-organ with the real substrate; for if that contact were absent, the false thing superimposed—which *as* false is not itself capable of contact with the organ—would not present itself as something immediately perceived. "But," our opponent argues, "in the case of false objects the internal organ in no way requires the co-operation of the sense; for we observe that dream cognitions arise without such co-operation!" Well, we reply, even if the internal organ were held to modify itself, without the co-operation of the sense-organ, so as to assume the form of the cognition of the false object, it yet would remain destitute of the character of *cognizing subject;* and hence the cognition of the false object could not accomplish itself (through the internal organ alone)! "Let us then assume that the internal organ, although not of the nature of intelligence, modifies itself at the time of cognition of the false object, so as to assume the form of cognizing subject; or else that the Self acts as the cognizing subject!" This also may not be, we reply. For as *erroneous cognition, true cognition, bondage* and *release* have necessarily to be viewed as abiding in the same substrate, it would follow from your theory that the internal organ, being the subject of erroneous cognition, must also be the subject of true cognition, bondage and release. But we hold that it is the Self that is the subject of erroneous cognition; and this is possible only if we assume that the material cause of error is Nescience abiding in the Self. There thus remains no alternative but to assume Nescience as the material cause of adhyāsa.

VIII

[That 'Nescience' ('non-knowledge') is something positive, not mere negation or absence of knowledge, is proved in the first place by direct intuitive consciousness. Whenever we are conscious of non-knowledge, there is not complete absence of knowledge (for if this were so, there would be no consciousness at all); there rather is cognition of the presence of something which interposes itself between the cognizing mind and the object of which we are conscious as not known—this something is positive ajñāna. The person who thinks or says 'I do not know this' is conscious of himself, of the *this,* and of ajñāna owing to which he is conscious of the thing as *not known*: of this ajñāna he is

conscious as directly as *e.g.* of pleasure or pain. In such a state of non-knowledge the light of impersonal consciousness illumines the cognizing individual Self, the object and Nescience. What takes place when an object previously not cognized comes to be cognized is that the internal organ begins to function (in the form of Perception, Inference and so on) and dispels Nescience.—The positive nature of ajñāna may further be proved in the way of inference: Cognition is of the nature of light which illumines what previously was obscured by (positive) darkness; it, therefore, must have for its antecedent a positive entity which obstructed cognition.]

Nor can the existence of such Nescience be called into doubt. For when our thought expresses itself in forms such as 'I am not-knowing,' 'I know neither myself nor others,' we are immediately conscious of a certain power of Nescience (avidyā-shakti) which is not of the nature of intelligence, and which, while having the Self for its abode, extends itself over all inward and outward things. "But why should we not hold that the object of that immediate consciousness is (not a positive entity termed Nescience) but mere non-knowledge (*i.e.*, absence of knowledge)?" Because, we reply, we are directly conscious of that Nescience, in the same way as we are directly conscious of pleasure and pain in cognitions such as 'I am pleased' and the like. Mere non-existence or absence of a thing, on the other hand, is known (not through direct, intuitive knowledge but) through the sixth means of knowledge.*

You deny that there is immediate intuitive knowledge of a positive ajñāna; but how then do you deal with judgments such as 'there is no knowledge in me' ('I have no knowledge')? If you admit that this judgment implies consciousness of the Self as a substrate of knowledge and of knowledge as an attribute of the Self, it would be absurd to say that there is immediate consciousness of the absence of knowledge. If, on the other hand, the knowledge of those two factors is not implied in that judgment, the immediate knowledge (expressing itself in the judgment) could not arise at all, since there would be no cause of it (*i.e.*, if we were not conscious of the Self and of knowledge, we could not form the judgment, 'there is no knowledge in me').

---

* According to the Vedāntin, as also according to the Mīmāṁsaka, there are *six* means of knowledge,—(1) Sense-perception, (2) Inference, (3) Words, (4) Analogy, (5) Presumption, and (6) Valid non-perception (anupalabdhi). It is this last that is here meant. The *absence* of a thing cannot be cognised by any of the first five means of knowledge,—it can be known only by the sixth, negation.

But [an objection is raised by the advocate of the view that we are, in these cases, conscious of the mere absence of knowledge], as practical activities (*viz.*, efforts either to take possession of something, or to avoid or abandon it) are the result of all knowledge, we accept them in all cases as evidence from which the presence of knowledge is inferred; and, *vice versa*, we infer from the absence of such evidence the absence of knowledge!

On this explanation also, we reply, there remain the difficulties pointed out above with regard to the case of substrate etc., of knowledge being known and to the case of their not being known.* The same difficulties also remain if, with the Bhatta (Kumārila) we should hold that the absence of knowledge is to be inferred through the sixth means of knowledge (*i.e.*, anupalabdhi, non-perception).**

Our view, on the other hand, is that the negation of knowledge in general (*i.e.*, the positive ajñāna of the Vedāntin) is known through 'witnessing' (sākṣin) consciousness; while the absence of cognition of particular things (such as a jar) is founded on non-perception (anupalabdhi) in accordance with the view of Bhaṭṭa which is accepted as true for all practical purposes.

If again, following the view of the Purāṇas, we should not allow any such thing as 'negation' or 'non-existence' (abhāva), explaining the destruction of a jar through a blow not as a case of 'emergent non-existence' of the jar, but merely as a new manifestation of the jar in the form of pieces of a jar; these again, if the blows are continued, appearing as a kind of powder, and the latter finally being reduced to atoms—; then of course the question of such negation being inferred from 'non-perception' would not arise at all.

But, the opponent resumes, as you also admit that Nescience, although not the mere negation of knowledge, is put an end to by knowledge, how can you account for the immediate consciousness of Nescience, expressing itself in the form 'I am not-knowing'—into which

---

* There is no pactical activity without an object (for all activity is either towards, or away from, some object). If then the object of a practical activity is not known, its negation or absence (abhāva) also cannot be known; for the cognition of the negation of something pre-supposes the cognition of the counterentity of that negation as well as its substrate. If, on the other hand, the object of the activity is held to be known, it would be self-contradictory to infer therefrom the absence of knowledge of the object.

** For in that case our judgment would have to be formulated as follows—'there is absence of cognition of *that* of which there is non-perception.' Now, if this *that* is known, there cannot be non-perception of it. If, on the other hand, it is not known, there again can be no non-perception, for all non-perception must be of something.

consciousness there enter as factors the knowledge of the substrate of cognition (the 'I'), and the object?* There is no real difficulty here, we reply. The substrate of cognition (the 'I'), its object and Nescience are all three of them illumined by (*i.e.*, are the objects of) the 'witnessing' consciousness (sākṣin). This witnessing consciousness, while proving the substrate and the object, in the same way proves Nescience also; it does *not* put an end to Nescience. What *does* put an end to Nescience, is a cognitional energy of the internal organ. And there is no cognition of the latter kind when we are conscious of 'not-knowing.' There is, therefore, nothing contradictory in our position.

But, a new objection is raised, in the judgment 'I do not know the jar' the jar which here defines Nescience (insofar as being the special object which is not known) cannot be the object of the witnessing consciousness which has no relation to that jar; for the knowledge of an external object depends on that special means of knowledge with which the object is connected. Nor is the jar, in the case under discussion, cognized by one of the means of valid knowledge; for those means put an end to Nescience (which the judgment asserts).

Quite true, we reply. The jar cannot by itself be the object of the witnessing consciousness. But insofar as possessing the attribute of *not being known* the jar does enter into relation to that consciousness—Nescience thus being the mediating factor—and in this way becomes its object. But, it may be said, if the jar by itself cannot be the object of the sākṣin-consciousness, the fact of its having the attribute of *not being known* cannot bring about the relation in question; for—to quote an analogous instance—a taste which by itself cannot be perceived by sight, does not become perceptible through the fact of its belonging to a substance that is visible! This again is inconclusive reasoning, we reply. For others hold that an atom, although not by itself an object of direct internal experience (*mānasa pratyakṣa*), yet becomes such by entering as a defining element into the cognitional act expressing itself as 'I know the atom'—which cognitional act itself *is* an object of internal experience. Ordinary experience supplies analogous instances; Rāhu, *e.g.*, although not perceptible by itself, becomes an object of perception as soon as it comes into contact with the moon which it obscures. And as we have explained above already, the view of others (*i.e.*, the Naiyāyikas) as to the judgment 'I do not know the jar' gives rise to insuperable difficulties,

* If knowledge puts an end to Nescience, how can Nescience—testified to by judgments such as 'I do not know such and such a thing'—co-exist with the cognition undoubtedly expressing itself in that judgment?

whether the jar which is the defining element of the absence of knowledge be said to be the object of consciousness or not.* The conclusion therefore is that all things are objects of witnessing consciousness, either as *known* or as *not known*. But, on this view, there will be no difference between objects known and objects not known; and this will imply the uselessness of the means of knowledge (through which things are *known*), and will allow no room for their positive and negative operation,—(*viz.*, that knowledge arises when the instruments of knowledge, Perception and the rest, are operative and does not arise when they are not operative). By no means, we reply. In the same way as Nescience imparts to its object (*i.e.*, the thing *not* known) the attribute of *not-being-known*, and thereby mediates the connexion of the object with witnessing consciousness,—so a means of knowledge imparts to *its* object the attribute of *being-known*, and in this way puts it in connexion with consciousness. This view entirely discards the objection raised. And we thus have shown that the immediate cognition 'I am not-knowing' proves the existence of Nescience as a positive entity.

For the sake of those, however, who are not to be pleased by anything but inferential reasoning, we in order to prove the positive nature of Nescience set forth the following argumentation, which in no way depends on the proof resting on immediate perceptive knowledge: 'Cognition (of the kind here under discussion) due to the recognised means of valid cognition must have for its antecedent some other positive entity which abides in the same place as the subsequent cognition; which is put an end to by the cognition; which obscures the object of cognition; and which is something other than the mere antecedent non-existence of cognition;—for cognition possesses the attribute of illumining an object previously non-illumined;—just as that attribute is possessed by the light of the first lamp lit in a dark place.' In this syllogistic argument Cognition is qualified as 'due to the recognised means of valid cognition,' because if the subject of the inference were cognition (or knowledge) in general (not thus qualified), it would comprise so called *anuvāda* knowledge also (*i.e.* knowledge not originated by one of the means of knowledge, but a mere repetition or re-statement of knowledge already gained), and with regard to such knowledge the reason in the syllogistic argument would

---

* The Naiyāyika holds that there is no knowledge without an object. Are we then to say that, in the case of the state of consciousness expressing itself in the form 'I do not know the jar,' the jar is an object of consciousness or not? On the second alternative, we cannot be conscious of the absence of knowledge *of the jar*; on the former alternative it would be contradictory to speak of absence of the knowledge of the jar.

have no proving force. The clause 'of the kind here under discussion' is introduced, in order to exclude so-called 'stream-cognition' (*dhārāvāhika jnāna*, which is constituted by a flow of cognitions each of which exactly reproduces the preceding one; so that each cognition is preceded not by Nescience but by another cognition). If instead of 'some other positive entity' the words 'positive entity' were used, these words might be taken as referring to the Self which is the substrate of all cognition; and then the inference would, superfluously, prove what is proved already (*viz.*, that all cognition pre-supposes the Self). Of the four clauses which qualify 'some other positive entity,' the first—'which abides in the same place etc.'—excludes any causal factors of the cognition which lie outside the substrate of cognition (*i.e.* the Self). The second clause—'which is put an end to, etc.'—excludes dharma (*i.e.* religious, or moral, merit) and the like. The third clause—'which obscures the object of cognition'—excludes previous cognitions. The fourth clause—'which is something other, etc.'—excludes previous non-existence of knowledge. By all this together there is established, as the antecedent condition of knowledge, positive Nescience which possesses all the stated qualifications. 'Not previously illumined' is added as a qualification of the object, in order to exclude 'stream-cognition' (where the second cognition illumines what is already illumined by the first); the 'lamp' is qualified as 'first' in order to preclude the 'stream of light,' issuing from the lamp, which is devoid of both (the character of illumining what is not already illumined and that of having for its antecedent some other positive entity, &c., &c.); the clause 'in a dark place' is added in order to preclude the case of the lamp lit in a place which is already lighted.

[*Page 18*]/ That this Nescience which we postulate as the material cause of adhyāsa is inexplicable (anirvachanīya) must necessarily be assumed; since otherwise the two-fold adhyāsa, itself inexplicable, of things and cognitions could not be accounted for. It cannot be accounted for otherwise; for if the material cause were real, it would follow that its effect also is real. Similarly we must assume Nescience, the material cause, to be without a beginning; for otherwise it would not be the fundamental (ultimate) cause. If it had a beginning we should have to assume an endless retrogressive series of material causes, and thus should never reach an ultimate cause.

We thus have conclusively established that the material cause of adhyāsa is Nescience which is a positive entity, has no beginning, and is of an inexplicable nature; and has the universal Self for its substrate and its object.

IX

[The 'obscuration,' 'concealment' due to Nescience, however, is an effect produced not upon the Not-self, but on the Self only. The effect of ajñāna upon the Not-self is that it throws over it a false appearance, an illusory projection (vikṣepa): upon the shell there superimposes itself the false appearance of silver. 'Obscured' in the proper sense of the term can be only that which is of the nature of light; and such of course is not the nature of the Not-self. When 'non-knowledge' of some part of the Not-self is put an end to by the energizing of the internal organ, the special illusory projection concerned is refunded in its causal substance—general 'Nescience;' while in the case of supreme cognition—the cognition of Brahman—general Nescience is put an end to.]

But—our opponent raises a new difficulty—does this Nescience conceal the Not-self in the same way as it conceals the Self? or does it not do so? The former alternative is inadmissible, since there is neither any proof of such concealment, nor any assignable purpose of it. For were there any means of proof for it, the result of that means would have to present itself in the following form—'this blue thing is concealed by Nescience;' and that such should be our state of consciousness is clearly impossible, either at the time when we perceive the blue thing (for then it evidently is not concealed); or at the time when we do not perceive it (for then we know nothing whatever about it). You perhaps will say that while concealment of the blue thing through Nescience indeed is impossible at the time when the thing is actually apprehended, such concealment is to be inferred for the previous time. But this we deny, for the reason that no basis for such an inference can be assigned. For, we ask, should the inference be based on the fact that the blue thing is apprehended now?* [or thereon that it is known *now only* and not ever *before*]? or thereon that otherwise the recognition 'this is that very same blue thing I knew before' could not be accounted for? or thereon that otherwise we

---

* In the text here there evidently is a lacuna. In the refutation of these alternatives, we have *four* alternatives, while here we find only three. The *first, third* and *fourth* refutations evidently pertain to the three alternatives found in the text; hence corresponding to the second refutation, there must be some such alternative as has been translated within square brackets.

could not account for the fact that in the interval between the original cognition and the recognition there is no remembrance of the thing cognized? The first alternative cannot be accepted; since in the case of so-called 'stream-cognition' the thing cognized in previous moments is cognized now also—which shows that cognition of something at the present moment does not depend on previous concealment of the thing. Nor can we accept the second alternative; as that would involve a "vicious circle": the idea that the thing is known now only being based upon the idea that it was concealed, and the idea that it was concealed being based upon the notion that it is known now only. The third alternative again is unacceptable; since it is not a general law that that only is recognized which, after having first been cognized, is forgotten during some time. For we observe that recognition takes place with regard to the Self also, of which we have a constant consciousness 'I am the same person I was.' Nor finally can we accept the fourth alternative. For we point out that there may be non-remembrance of such cognitions also as originated in the interval between the original cognition and the recognition, and at the time were clearly not concealed by Nescience. It is not a general law that whatever presents itself to consciousness is afterwards remembered. Nor can it be said that in judgments such as 'I do not know (understand) the matter stated by you' there is direct consciousness of Nescience connected with the object, and that, as the connexion of Nescience is discerned in the case of the Self to consist in *concealment*, the concealing quality of Nescience cannot be denied. For this case we explain as follows: what is immediately experienced by witnessing consciousness is Nescience, the object, and the relation of the two—all the three being super-imposed upon consciousness. The relation between Nescience and the object does not however consist therein that Nescience *conceals* and the object *is concealed*, but therein that Nescience is the cause and the object the effect. For what is superimposed cannot possibly be something concealed. As long as we are conscious of the thing super-imposed, it would be absurd to speak of it as concealed; and when we are not conscious of it, it does not exist; for a thing superimposed—such as a double moon—is nothing but thought (idea). If the superimposed thing also were concealed by Nescience, it would never present itself at all to consciousness; for as it is not an object of the means of true cognition, its concealment would never come to an end. Things which are the objects of the means of true cognition are real (in the relative sense) and as such persist even when not actually objects of consciousness; they therefore may in some way become concealed; a super-imposed thing, on the other hand, is put an end to by the means of true cognition; how then could it be concealed? From all this it follows that there is no means of knowledge to prove that the Not-self is concealed by Nescience.

Nor, in the second place, can any purpose of such concealment be shown to exist. For in all cases where concealment (or obscuration) exists, its purpose can be nothing else but counteraction (obstruction) of possible light or illumination. But how should light be possibly present in the Not-self?—through its own nature?—or owing to the means of true cognition?—or owing to Consciousness? The first alternative is clearly inadmissible; since the Not-self is essentially non-intelligent (non-luminous). Nor can the second alternative be maintained; for, since concealment is put an end to by the means of true cognition, it cannot be viewed as an obstruction to light depending on those very means. Nor can the third alternative be accepted; for, since the obstruction of that light which is shed upon the Not-self by Consciousness is fully accounted for by the concealment of the Self (which is one of the effects of Nescience) it would be useless to postulate a further concealment of the Not-self. At night time when the sun is hidden by Mount Meru nobody uses an umbrella to protect himself from the sun's rays. But, to quote a counter-instance, even when the sun is veiled by clouds, we *do* use umbrellas and the like in order to ward off those subtle rays which we call heat; and in the same way we may assume a separate concealment of Not-self by Nescience excluding those faint traces of light which may be due to consciousness although obscured by Nescience! This may not be, we reply. For do you mean to say that there is one Nescience only, abiding in the Self and concealing the Not-self? or that there is a special Nescience for each object? The first alternative is inadmissible. For as illumination (consciousness) of any object cannot take place without the destruction of the concealing factor, the cognition of even one thing would imply the total termination of all Nescience—in other words, instantaneous universal Release. Nor is the second alternative acceptable; since there is nothing to justify such an assumption. For we *do* hold that there is a faint illumination of the object due to consciousness although obscured by Nescience; as otherwise the actual thought 'this thing is not known' could not arise at all. The conclusion is that, since there is nothing to prove concealment of the Not-self, and since no purpose of such concealment can be assigned, the view of the Not-self being concealed by Nescience must be given up.

But, on the other hand, the second alternative (*viz.*, of the Not-self *not* being concealed by Nescience) is also inadmissible. For if there were no such concealment, there would be permanent consciousness of the Not-self in its entire extent.

To this we make the following reply. The first of the two alternatives discussed above we certainly do not accept. With regard to the second alternative, on the other hand, we ask you what you mean by saying that that alternative would imply permanent consciousness of the Not-self in its entire extent. Do you mean permanent consciousness of all things as known? or as not known? or of individual things as known at some times and not known at other times? We certainly do not hold the first of these alternatives; for the means of true knowledge—the effect of which it is to make things *known*—function at intervals only. Nor do we hold the second alternative; for there can be no question that that attribute of things which consists in their *not being known* is at times put an end to by the attribute of 'being known.' The third alternative, on the other hand, is just what we maintain. For above already (pp. 46-47) we have said that all things are objects of witnessing consciousness, either as known or as not-known. But it is objected, a thing being not known means its being the object of Nescience (ajñāna), and being an object means to be the abode of an effect produced by that of which it is the object;* but you do not allow that in the Not-self there exists obscuration (concealment), produced by ajñāna; how then can you say that the Not-self is not-known? That Nescience, we reply, which has for its substrate the consciousness particularized by the '*this*' element of the shell causes the superimposition, on the shell, of silver, and thus produces in the shell the effect which is called the appearance to consciousness (avabhāsa) of silver: it is in this way that the shell is not-known. Whenever some part of the Not-self is not-known, we have to understand this 'not-being-known' in the way defined, without acknowledging any 'concealment' of the Not-self. But, it is objected, while the shell is known, the *projection* (vikṣēpa) called 'silver' does not appear to consciousness; for the silver is put an end to by the shell being cognized as shell. And on the other hand, while the shell is not-known, how can the projection (the silver)—which you say

* 'Obscuration' is the 'effect' that is produced by the ajñāna; and in order that the Not-self may be the 'object' of this ajñāna the former must be the abode of the said 'obscuration.' But as you have already shown that this is not possible, how can the Not-self be spoken of as the *object of ajñāna* or 'ajñāta,' unknown'? It may be noted here that the text is not quite correct: *Viṣaya* (object) is never the *ādhāra* (abode) of the *atishaya* (effect) produced by the *viṣaya* (objecct) itself; the *viṣaya* rather is the abode of the effect produced by *that of which it is the object*; —hence instead of the word '*viṣaya*' in the compound 'viṣayakṛitātishayādhāratva,' we should read '*viṣayi* &c.'

is an effect on the shell,—be apprehended? Both these difficulties, we reply, vanish on a proper view of the case: what is *not* known (while the silver appears) is the shell-aspect of the thing before us; what *is* known, is the *this*-aspect of the thing.

But even if we accept the view that Nescience, abiding in the Self, is one only, and gives rise, in that which is non-intelligent (*i.e.* the Not-self) to a *projection* only, not to *concealment*, we are met by other difficulties. For, the question arises, does the cognition of the shell (first mistaken of silver) *as* shell merely refund the illusory projection into its causal substance (*i.e.* universal Nescience),—in the same way as the blow of a stick resolves the jar into its causal substance (*i.e.* clay)? Or does it put an end to the causal substance as well? On the former alternative even the cognition, by the individual mind, of Brahman, would do no more than resolve the illusory projection (of the phenomenal world) into its causal substance (*i.e.* general Nescience), and thus no Release could ever take place. On the second alternative general Nescience would be put an end to by the mere cognition of a shell, and thus universal Release would take place at once! And if, in order to escape from this latter consequence, you were to assume a separate Nescience for each object, or to view Adhyāsa as not having Nescience for its material cause, this would imply, on the one hand, an objectionable complication of hypothesis, and on the other hand the reality of Adhyāsa!

Not so, we reply. The former of the two alternatives is open to no objection. For we reason as follows: The cognition of Brahman puts an end to the illusory projection and its material cause, because, while being of a nature essentially contradictory to them, it is subsequent to them,—just as the cognition of the shell as shell puts an end to its own previous non-existence and to the illusory appearance of Silver.—And even the second alternative is not open to the objection raised by you. For, according to our view, it is merely the special forms of fundamental Nescience—constituting the special causal substances of illusory silver etc.—which are put an end to by the cognition of the shell etc. The view of Nescience not concealing non-intelligent things thus is vindicated from all objections. When, above, stating the formal inference that establishes the existence of *positive* Nescience we qualified the latter as concealing its *object,* the object meant was nothing else but the Self. In the case of non-intelligent objects such as shells, the special forms of Nescience which constitute the causal substance of silver etc. virtually conceal the objects, in so far, that is to say, as they interpose themselves between the objects and consciousness, but they do not conceal them in the full sense.

X

(*How* Nescience is capable of obscuring the Self—whose essential nature is to be non-obscurable light of Intelligence,—this is a matter of which no rational account can be given: Nescience and all its doings remain essentially inexplicable. But that the Self *is* so obscured is a fact guaranteed by everyday experience; men not enlightened by Vedic teaching quite fail to realize the existence of the Self. And even if this latter fact were to be accounted for by mere 'absence of knowledge'—without the co-operation of a positive ajñāna,— the assumption of the latter is required to explain that non-presentation or obscuration of the Self which is characteristic of deep dreamless sleep.]

But to return to the Self, what really do you mean by the so-called concealment of the Self by Nescience? Is it that Nescience destroys the light of the Self? or that Nescience obstructs that effect of the light of the Self which is termed the 'manifestedness' (prākaṭya) of the object? or that it renders that effect dependent on other co-operating factors? The first alternative is not possible, since light constitutes the very nature of Self-consciousness. Nor can we admit the second and third alternatives; for we do not allow that, apart from the light of consciousness as manifested by a special modification (vṛitti) of the internal organ, there exists in the object such a thing as so-called; 'manifestedness.' It thus appears that of the alleged concealment of the Self by Nescience no rational account can be given!

[*Page 21*], You are perfectly right, we reply! And it is just for this reason that we hold such concealment to be of the nature of *inexplicable* Nescience. That we are unable to give a satisfactory definition of it does not entitle us to deny it altogether. It in fact is fully proved by the following inference: Dull-minded people think—'That thing termed *Self*, which learned men believe in as something not subject to desire of food or any other imperfection, neither exists, nor does it shine forth;'—now such vulgar thought must have for its cause a concealment of the Self by some positive entity;—since it contradicts another conviction which has good reasons on its side, *viz.*, the self *does* exist and *does* shine forth;—where there is no such contradiction, no such cause need be assumed; as *e.g.* in the case of the thought 'the jar exists and shines forth.'—Nor may it be said that after all there is no good reason for believing in the Self; for truly no other proof is wanted here than eternally established self-illumined consciousness. And the vulgar thought characterized above cannot be accounted for otherwise (than by the concealment of the Self by Nescience); for a concealing factor different in nature from the one we assume—*e.g.* some material thing—cannot be assumed in the case of the Self which is not made up of parts and is infinite in extension. These considerations also help us to an adequate definition of the 'concealment' of the Self: The Self is concealed by that which renders possible with regard to it those vulgar conceptions above characterized.

But, a new objection is raised, if in *ā-jñāna* (non-knowledge; nescience) the *a* denotes *absence* or *privation,* the word signifies 'absence of knowledge;' if it conveys the idea of something contrary or opposite, the word signifies 'erroneous knowledge' (bhrānti-jñāna); if, lastly, it denotes *something other than knowledge* or *cognition,* then the word signifies only the impression left on the mind by erroneous knowledge.* The word then denotes 'absence of knowledge;' 'erroneous knowledge' and 'impression left by erroneous knowledge,'and why then should we not hold that it is these which, obstructing the cognition of the true nature of Brahman, give rise to the vulgar thought referred to above? What purpose would it serve to assume a concealment of the Self by a so-called positive entity termed 'Nescience'? There is a purpose, we reply; for without assuming obscuration of the Self by a positive entity, we should be unable to account for that non-presentation of the true Reality; *i.e.* Brahman, which is characteristic of deep dreamless sleep. For, tell me, how would *you* account for this non-presentation? Is it due to the nature of Brahman itself? or to Brahman being other than the cognizing individual soul? or to some obstructive agency? The first alternative clearly is inadmissible, since Brahman is self-luminous. Nor can the second alternative be accepted; since texts such as 'thou art that'** teach that Brahman and the individual soul are one. With regard to the third alternative, finally, we ask whether that obstructive agency is to be found in erroneous cognition, or in the impression left by erroneous cognition, or in the absence of cognition, or in 'Karman' (Destiny). The first cannot

* That which is not *right knowledge* (jñāna) must be either *non-knowledge*, or a *wrong knowledge*, or *an impression left on the mind by wrong knowledge*. Hence the word 'ajñāna' can mean one of these three only.

** Chhāndogya-Upa. VI.

be; since in deep sleep all cognition, including erroneous cognition, is arrested. Nor the second; for we do not observe that it is not the impression left by the erroneous cognition of silver that prevents the presentation to consciousness of the true nature of the shell. As to the third alternative that absence of essential cognition—which cognition is something eternal—is impossible, while the absence of other cognitions has no power to obstruct the consciousness of the self-luminous Brahman. Were this not so, the alleged obstruction would present itself even in the state of Release. On the fourth alternative, finally, the question would arise whether '*karman*' or destiny obstructs consciousness in its whole extent, or the whole with the exception of that part which illumines them? On the former view *karman* itself would not be established; since that which alone can establish it (*i.e.* consciousness) would be absent. And the latter view is objectionable, because it implies a 'half-assumption' for which there is no proof. Nor may it be pleaded that the same choice between two unacceptable alternatives presents itself in connexion with the theory of a concealing factor of a positive nature. For on that theory the 'half-assumption,' of consciousness being obstructed with the exception of one illumining part, must necessarily be made; since otherwise the direct consciousness presenting itself in the form 'I am not-knowing' could not be accounted for. On the other hand, there is no such direct consciousness of *karman*. And even if the mediate consciousness we have of *karman* were held to justify the assumption in question, yet '*karman*' is only an impression or effect (produced by the deeds of the agent); and as such, resembling the impression left by erroneous knowledge, it cannot have any obstructive force with regard to consciousness. "But may it not then finally be assumed that what obstructs consciousness is the element of darkness (tamo-guṇa),—in agreement with the Smṛiti-text 'Darkness concealing knowledge leads a man on to recklessness' (Bha. Gī. XIV. 9)?" This too we cannot admit. If darkness were not put an end to by the cognition of Brahman, no release could take place. If, on the other hand, it *is* put an end to, then the wrangling is about a mere name; for darkness also is a concealing factor of a positive nature. Hence even he who maintains the view of 'difference plus non-difference' will in the end have to overcome the perverse obstinacy prompting him to cling to the view, that in deep sleep it is the absence of knowledge only which causes the non-appearance to consciousness (Brahman),—and to accept *ajñāna* as a positive entity.

We now turn to another perverse doctrine held by the same people (*i.e.*, the bhedābheda-vādins = the Naiyāyikas), *viz.*, that what in the waking state and in the state of dream prevents the true nature of Brahman from presenting itself to consciousness is (not the *Nescience* of the Vedāntins but) merely a certain *erroneous* cognition, expressing itself in the form 'I am (not Brahman but) a human being.' This view also must be rejected, for it would be difficult for our adversary to show where error, in this case, comes in. You accept, we address him, as valid the relation of simultaneous difference and non-difference in cases such as expressed in the judgments 'the cow is broken-horned,' 'the cow is hornless'—the one class-character (or *Universal*) *cow* connecting itself in that way (*viz.*, of difference plus non-difference) with two individual animals. Why then do you not likewise allow that the relation of difference and non-difference is real and well-founded in the case of the two judgments 'I am a man' and 'I am Brahman'—which assert the connexion of one individual soul with a human body on the one, and with Brahman on the other hand? The judgment 'I am a man' which affirms the non-difference of the Self and the body thus must be viewed by you as a *valid*, not as an *erroneous* one. When subsequently the view enounced in this judgment is sublated by the negation, founded on Scripture, 'I am not a man but Brahman,' that is analogous to what happens within the sphere of ordinary thought when we form the judgment 'this is not a broken horned cow but a hornless one.' But, our opponent objects, in the same way as the judgment 'this is not silver' denies of the substrate *this* the silver erroneously imputed to it; so the judgment 'I am not a man' denies with regard to the substrate 'Self' ('I') the class-character *human being;* and hence the previous judgment which predicates human nature of the Self, is an erroneous judgment! By no means, we reply. For this your view would imply that, when we first view the substrate constituted by the class-character *cow* in its short-horned aspect 'the cow is not short-horned'—, and afterwards form the negative judgment 'that cow is not short-horned,' the idea of the short-horned cow would, on account of the subsequent negative judgment, have to be considered as erroneous (which it clearly is not). Nor may you plead that in this case the subsequent negative judgment denies short-hornedness with regard to an individual hornless cow only, but not with regard to the *Universal* 'cow.' For in the case of a hornless cow short-hornedness is not a given possibility and, therefore, cannot be denied. But, the opponent resumes, in the given case the substrate is the Universal *cow* in so far as specialized by a short-horned individual, and it is not of this that short-hornedness is denied: it *is* denied of the Universal in so far as especialized by a hornless individual! Well, we accept this. But let your reasoning be applied to the case under discussion also. When we form the judgment 'I am *not* a man,' the substrate to which the denial refers is not the Self as specialized by human nature, but the Self as specialized by Brahman-hood. In the same way as the two individual cows, the short-horned and the hornless one, are connected with the Universal *cow* which is present in both, the body and Brahman are connected with the Self which is present in both; hence the validity of the judgment 'I am a man' can be denied no more than that of the judgment 'the cow is short-horned.' And if you point out that the latter judgment must be admitted as valid in order not to cut short all practical thought and activity, we reply that, on your theory, the case of the former judgment does not differ. For according to your view there is even in the state of Final Release no cutting short of the practical identification with sense organs and bodies, on the part of the Jīva which in reality (as we Vedāntins prove) is omniscient and non-different from Brahman, the cause of all. But, our opponent rejoins, there are five relations only that determine the existence of simultaneous difference and non-difference, *viz.*, that of the Universal and the individual; that of cause and effect; that of quality and substrate of quality; that of distinguishing attribute (visheṣaṇa) and thing distinguished thereby; and that of part and whole. And as none of these relations holds good between the Self and the body, the alleged non-difference of the two can after all be error only! Not so, we reply. What determines 'simultaneous difference and non-difference' cannot be those five relations combined; for there are undoubted exceptions from this principle. And if any one of the five by itself possesses that determining power, you yourself thereby acknowledge the needlessness of the assumption of more than one determining cause, and why then should the relation between the body and that which is embodied not possess that power likewise? If you deny the power to this latter relation, it may be denied to the other relations also; the result of which will be that 'bhedābheda' can be established in no case. And even if, unwilling to extend the scope of that power too far, we limited it to the five relations aforementioned, it might be pleaded that the relation between the body and that which is embodied is at bottom identical with the relation between effect and cause; for the causal power of Brahman may in a secondary or metaphorical sense be ascribed to the soul also which, as being of the nature of intelligence, is *like* Brahman. But it is a real relation only (not a secondary or metaphorical one) that can claim determining power; and as no such relation exists in the case under discussion, the judgment 'I am a man' must after all be erroneous! What then, we ask is your view as to the nature of error? If you reply that it is a certain modification of the internal organ, then Nescience (*i.e.* error) would not reside in the Self !* And if, to escape from this difficulty, you maintain that that modification of the internal organ which constitutes error superimposes itself upon the Self (thus imparting error to the latter) we point out that according to your view of the process of superimposition—which view technically is called anyathākhyāti—there is no connexion whatever between the substrate of a superimposition and the things superimposed, and that hence, on this modified view also, there can be no connexion between the Self and Nescience! And if, on the other hand, you declare error to be a modification of the Self itself (not of the internal organ) we reject this on the ground of the Self being incapable of change. But we Naiyāyikas do not admit the unchangeableness of the Self! True, but you all the same acknowledge a Self in which permanent knowledge inheres as a quality; and thus your view comes to this that, while knowledge persists, there takes place in the Self that modification which is termed 'error.' And this is irrational, since in one and the same substance there cannot inhere two several indestructible** specific qualities of the same class. It certainly is not a matter of observation that two several white colours inhere at the same time in one piece of cloth.

The conclusion from all this is that in the waking and dreaming states also that which conceals Brahman is beginningless inexplicable Nescience. But does not the connexion of the Self with Nescience interfere with that freedom from all contact or relation which is claimed for the Self? By no means, we reply. That connexion, beginningless as it is, is like Nescience itself of an unreal (fictitious; kalpita) nature and hence, like the emanations*** or products of that connexion itself, does not infringe the Self's freedom from all relation.

The above discussion then justifies the following conclusion. Positive Nescience does not conceal or obscure the Not-self, it only produces upon it a projection or illusory appearance (vikṣepa); it, on the other hand, *does* obscure the Self and on it produces those adhyāsas which give rise to empirical thought expressing itself in forms such as 'I am this or that,' 'this is mine,' and the like.

---

* For a modification of the internal organ could never reside in anything except the internal organ itself.

** The Naiyāyika also regards the Ātman to be possessed of a quality that is eternal.

*** Just as the emanation of the fictitious connexion do not affect the nature of the Self so in the same manner the connexion also, being equally fictitious, cannot affect it.

XI

[Nor can it be maintained that in the case of the Not-self and the Self there can be no adhyāsa comparable to that of the silver on the shell. The body, the sense organs, the internal organ, and in the same way the entire so-called external world are mere fictitious superimpositions upon Universal Consciousness.]

But, another question is raised, by the 'I' we understand the intelligent Self which is not made up of parts and does not comprise within itself two different elements; judgments as above, therefore, differ in nature from the judgment 'this is silver,' and do not express an adhyāsa. The term 'this' again (in 'I am this') denotes the body which is apprehended by the senses that are sources of true knowledge, and, therefore, cannot be something 'fictitiously superimposed.' Moreover, if the body were nothing more than this, it would like Nescience be known by immediate intuition on the part of witnessing consciousness (while, as a matter of fact it is known through the senses). In the judgment 'I (am a) man' we no doubt are conscious of the relation between a substrate and something superimposed, so that a double aspect is present; but that relation is not a necessary one, for when the Self has passed out of the body, the latter is apprehended by itself. The superimposed silver, on the other hand, is not apprehended apart from its substrate, *i.e.*, the shell. Should you rejoin that the means of knowledge through which the body is apprehended lie within the sphere of mere empiric thought and do not impart real knowledge, we set forth another argument, *viz.*, if the body were a mere unreal superimposition, it would on death be absorbed into the Self. Scripture, however, gives a different account, *viz.*, that 'the body enters into earth.' The body is not, therefore, something merely superimposed upon the Self. Similarly, in the judgment 'This is mine' we are conscious of some real thing, other than the body, not comprised within the idea of the 'Ego,' but somehow connected with the Ego. Here also there is no trace of adhyāsa, *i.e.*, mere fictitious superimposition.

To all this we Vedāntins reply as follows. We shall show later on that into the idea of the 'I' there does enter a non-intelligent (non-subjective element; hence there is adhyāsa in that case. That the body is a mere thing of superimposition is proved by the fact that, like the internal organ and the sense organs, it is an object of cognition (dṛishya). As regards the internal organ and the sense organs, from the fact that they are never perceived to have an existence independent of the Self, it follows that they are superimposed upon it so as to be the immediate objects of witnessing consciousness. Nor must it be thought that this superimposition is one of 'contact' only (*i.e.*, one of attributes only) not of the things themselves. For Scripture ('his organs do not depart, they become merged in that itself') declares that, on the rise of the cognition of truth, the sense-organs completely merge themselves in the Self—which proves the adhyāsa to be one of the thing itself. What Scripture says as to the body being merged in earth must be understood to mean that it is merged in the Self through the mediation of earth. And if the individual soul together with the body, the sense organs etc., is a thing of superimposition, it of course follows *à fortiori* that the sum of external things—which is merely instrumental towards the soul's experiences—is likewise 'superimposed.' For if a person is a king (not in reality but merely) in the world of dreams or of magic, the paraphernalia also of his royal state are of course unreal.

All this clearly proves that the 'I,' the 'this' and the 'this is mine' are three cases of adhyāsa. Nor can there be any doubt as to the existence of an adhyāsa of mere attributes. For what is expressed, *e.g.*, in the judgment 'I am deaf,' is the superimposition on the Self of a mere attribute, *viz.*, deafness.

Having in this way proved the adhyāsa of things (arthādhyāsa) we need not specially prove the adhyāsa of cognitions (jñānādhyāsa), which never takes place apart from adhyāsa of the former kind. And we thus have completely established the conclusion that adhyāsa, guaranteed as it is by immediate consciousness, is an undeniable fact.

XII

[The preceding discussions make it possible for us to give a full definition of Adhyāsa, in its two aspects. Viewed as something objective (artha), adhyāsa is defined as something, similar to a thing remembered, which presents itself to consciousness as constituting the Self or true character of another thing. The apparent (unreal) silver (which is a special modification of the universal principle of all false appearance—Māyā or Avidyā) is on account of its similarity to previously perceived real silver, held by the observer—predisposed thereto by certain imperfections of his sense-organs and mental disposition—to constitute the true nature of what in reality is only a glittering shell. As a subjective process adhyāsa (to illustrate it at once by the quoted concrete instance) is the presentation to consciousness of silver as constituting the true nature of the thing before the observer (which in reality is a shell only); such presentation being similar in character to Remembrance.]

All scientific investigations are carried on between two sets of people—between the Teacher and the Pupil, or between two disputants. As regards the former the Teacher has, at the very outset, asserted the existence of Adhyāsa, for the benefit of the Pupil (who, confident in the wisdom of his Teacher, accepts it undoubtingly). Then as regards those who dispute the fact of Adhyāsa, we proceed to establish *Adhyāsa* by putting forward its definition, by showing the possibility of its existence, and by bringing forward proofs of its existence.

[*Page 25*] But, a new point is raised, it is in all cases the function of a definition to differentiate the thing to be defined from other things; the function of the demonstration of the thing's possibility (sambhāvanā) to dispel the idea of the thing being impossible with regard to its special conditions of time and place; and the function of the means of knowledge (pramāṇa) to establish the actual existence of the thing. Now in the present case the means of valid knowledge which will be set forth as establishing the existence of adhyāsa—*viz*. Perception, Inference, the practical demands of life, Presumption and Scriptural authority—while proving adhyāsa, at the same time effect its differentiation from all other things, and discard all suspicion of its intrinsic impossibility; for it clearly would not be feasible to prove the existence of an adhyāsa not differing from other things and not possible. The definition and the question of the possibility of the adhyāsa should not, therefore, be treated, separately from the proofs for it! Not so, we reply. Adhyāsa has a double character: it on the one hand consists in one thing presenting itself as another; and on the other hand it is something false (unreal). Now Perception and the other means of knowledge which enable us to establish the existence of adhyāsa in the former sense are incapable of bringing home to the mind its unreality; for in all cases of unreality—as *e.g.*, in the case of the notion 'this is silver' with regard to a piece of shell,—the *unreality* is proved* only by the fact that, otherwise, we could not explain the subsequent sublation of that notion (by the notion 'this is not silver'); and in the case in question there is no such sublating notion (that would imply unreality).

*The reading here apparently should be बाधान्यथानुपपत्ति and not बाधानुपपत्ति

But there *is*, our opponent says, for it is impossible to realise the idea of one thing appearing as another (*i.e.*, adhyāsa in the former sense) without discrimination of the one thing from the other, and such discrimination constitutes sublation!

By no means, we reply. There may be in that case sublation founded on reasoning, but that intuitive sublation which dispels erroneous presentation is absent, and hence no definite cognition of the unreality of the adhyāsa arises. It is for the sake of the definite realization of that unreality that the definition of adhyāsa requires to be given. Similarly as regards the *possibility* of adhyāsa. It happens in ordinary experience that the idea of a thing being *impossible* arises in spite of the thing being actually vouched for by a cognition of the validity of which there is no reason to doubt, so, *e.g.*, in the case of the portentous appearance of holes in the sun. In the same way there may arise the idea of the impossibility of adhyāsa of the Not-self on the Self, for the reason that we perceive the Self to possess attributes opposed to all adhyāsa, *viz.*, perfect non-objectivity, unrelatedness, non-similarity to any other thing, etc. Nor must you urge against this that as long as the Self is not cognized as non-objective, etc., the idea of the impossibility of adhyāsa does not arise; while after it has been so cognized adhyāsa does not persist (and that hence it is purposeless to show that the Self may be the substrate of adhyāsa). For what produces the idea of the impossibility of adhyāsa is mediate consciousness (founded on reasoning), and this does not put an end to the immediately presented adhyāsa. In order, therefore, to dispel the idea of the impossibility of adhyāsa, its possibility requires to be shown apart from the proof of its actual existence. Other teachers also have declared (in the following *Kārikās* quoted by Vāchaspati Mishra in *Bhāmatī*, Bibl. Ind. page 67) that the discussion of the proof of adhyāsa should be preceded by that of its definition and of its possibility.

'The establishing of the existence of the object is dependent upon Proofs or Means of knowing it; these latter are established only by means of definitions; and these last again depend upon the fact of the object being such as cannot be precluded, even by the gods, from the range of Perception and other Means of knowledge.'

'Only that position, the possibility of which is apparent, can be established by argument; you cannot save by reasoning that which is killed as soon as it rises from the ground.'

And the possibility again must be preceded by the definition. For it is only after the definition has placed before the mind something of a definite character that a discussion can be started as to the thing's possibility; without the definition the discussion would have no object. The definition, therefore, must be formulated first. We then formulate the definition of adhyāsa as follows. Adhyāsa has a double aspect: it is a thing (artha) particularized by a cognition (jñāna); and a cognition particularized by a thing. Of Adhyāsa viewed as *thing* the definition is as follows: 'adhyāsa is a thing, similar to some thing remembered, which presents itself to consciousness as constituting the Self of another thing.' And of adhyāsa viewed as cognition the definition is 'adhyāsa is the presentation to consciousness of one thing as constituting the Self of another—such presentation being similar to remembrance.'

XIII

[What we Vedāntins undertake to explain by our adhyāsa-theory; cannot be satisfactorily explained by the holders of the so-called akhyāti-vāda who, denying the existence of erroneous cognition as a special kind of cognition, maintain that all that really takes place in cognitions of which that of the shell silver may be taken as a type, is the non-discrimination of an actual perception (of the thing, the *this*, before us) from a remembrance (of, let us say, previously perceived silver which is suggested to the mind by the glitter of the shell). This theory fails to account for the fact that, as long as the mistake or illusion lasts, there is the actual presentation to consciousness, *not* the mere remembrance, of silver. It moreover is impossible to give a satisfactory account of that so-called *non-discrimination* on which the theory turns. Nor is the akhyāti-vādin able to explain the nature of that so-called 'obscuration of remembrance' (smṛiti-pramoṣa) which he has to assume in order to account for the fact that the person subject to the illusion is not conscious of remembering silver but rather of seeing it.]

[*Page 26*] Here an objection is raised by the adherents of the theory called the *akhyāti-vāda* (the theory of non-cognition). When, they say, we have the erroneous idea 'this (thing before me) is silver,' the sense of sight and the other means of true knowledge do not operate, and it, therefore, only remains to view the silver simply as *remembered* silver, not as 'similar to remembered silver.' By no means, we reply. For we are conscious of the silver as something here and now presented to us (not as something remembered). Nor can it be held that what so is presented to us is only *this thing,* not the silver. For the *this* and the silver are immediately presented to us in mutual combination; the case does not differ from that of correct judgments, such as 'this is silver,' 'this is a jar,' where the general and the particularizing notions present themselves in mutual combination. Should it be said that (in the case of the erroneously surmised silver) the general and the particularizing thing are viewed as combined because they are presented to consciousness in immediate succession, not because there is actual consciousness of their combination; we negative this on the ground that the case of erroneously surmised silver does not show any inferiority to that of a true presentation (inasmuch as in both cases the 'this' and the silver present themselves as combined in exactly the same way). But the inferiority of the case under discussion lies therein that the object before us is not really silver!—How, we ask, is the absence of silver ascertained—from the absence of immediate consciousness of silver; or from the (subsequent) sublative cognition 'this is not silver'? The former alternative is excluded; for the absence of immediate consciousness is just what we do not allow. And if the absence of such consciousness were said to follow from the absence of the thing we should reason in a circle. We, therefore, must admit on the ground of the existence of immediate consciousness, that silver exists before us. Nor must it be urged, in reversal of this process, that the ascertainment of the existence of consciousness rather depends on the ascertainment of the existence of the thing; for in that case the ascertainment of the existence of the thing would again depend on another ascertainment and so on and an infinite regress would result. The ascertainment of a state of consciousness rests on itself; while the existence of the thing depends on the existence of a state of consciousness. Nor can we accept the second alternative. For the latter cognition which contradicts the former one has no power to sublate it (for why should not the former cognition as well be held to sublate the latter?) But what then is the position of the latter cognition (if it is not be taken as sublating the former one)? It is the same, we reply, as that of the former cognition. You assume that in the case of the cognition 'this thing is silver' there is non-discrimination of the *this* and the *silver* (*not* cognition of the connexion of silver and the *this*); why then should you not similarly hold that also in the case of the negative cognition 'this is *not* silver,' there is mere non-discrimination (of absence of silver and the *this*) and not cognition of the absence of connexion (between silver and the *this*)?* It might be argued that—"from the fact

* From the expression निषेधसंसर्गसंवित् in the next sentence, it is clear that the reading here also is संसर्गसंवित् and not संसर्गासंवित्.

that the negative cognition is found to be corroborated by the practical activity of the person concerned, it is clear that there is cognition of the connexion of negation." But this view (which makes the authority of the cognition to depend on something else) contradicts the theory of the self-luminousness of cognitions! We put forward this reasoning, the opponent replies, against those who hold different views from ours; hence (in running counter to the view of Svataḥ-prāmāṇya of cognitions) we do not enter into contradiction with ourselves (for we Naiyāyikas do not hold the Svataḥ-prāmāṇya theory)! But in that case a *regressus ad infinitum* would be the inevitable result (each cognition in succession requiring a further cognition to validate it).

Nor can it be urged that after all, the non-existence of the silver before us is admitted by every one. For what we Vedāntins maintain in accordance with what actually appears to consciousness, is the presence of *unreal silver*, capable of being put an end to by the cognition of the shell. Nor may you object to this that this assumption of unreal silver is contradicted by the absolute negation 'this thing is not silver;' for the object of this negation is (not the unreal silver we assume but) real silver as met with in ordinary normal experience. Nor can it be urged that on this explanation the negation ('this thing is not silver') would refer to something to negate which there is no occasion. For as we observe that a person desirous of real silver stretches out his hand for the unreal one, it must be admitted that the presence of the *real silver* in the substrate of the characters common (to the shell and the silver) is given (or exists) as a possibility.

Were this not so, it would also be difficult to justify a negation such as 'there is no jar in this place;' for if there were a jar, the negation would be irrational, and if there were none, something would be denied which there is no occasion to deny. What actually is the case is that the presence of the jar,—though indeed not possible directly—is yet possible (or suspected) on the basis of such common factors as that of *time* and that of *place*; and exactly analogous would be the case with the presence of the real silver also.

On this view, moreover, there is justification for the two subsequent cognitions which actually do take place, *viz.*, (1) 'There is here no silver,' which refers to real silver and (2) 'Silver was falsely presented to me'—which refers to the unreal silver. On any other view either of these two judgments would have to be set aside. But, a further objection is raised, you assume a combined state of consciousness (in which the 'this' and the silver are equally present, because otherwise you cannot account for the immediate presentation of silver; and then, in order to justify your assumption, you complicate the matter by the further assumption of unreal silver. Now it certainly is simpler to dispense with that combined state of consciousness, and to account for the immediacy of the cognition of silver through non-discrimination of the cognition of the shell (from the remembrance of silver). Not so, we reply. For on your view such non-discrimination only would form the subject of thought at the time when discriminative knowledge has arisen, that is to say thought would present itself in the following form 'for such and such a time that silver was not discriminated by me.' This is not however the reflection which actually arises: it rather is the combined state of consciousness which is recognised in the following form 'for such and such a time this appeared to me as silver.' We, therefore, must accept the view of unreal silver being actually present. How otherwise would any one on perceiving a shell, put forth action with regard to silver? The silver thus is not silver remembered but silver similar to remembered silver. Such similarity is proved by the fact that the silver is apprehended through a cognition that depends on previous perception; for the erroneous cognition of silver is seen to take place on the part of those only who previously have actually perceived silver.—The adhyāsa of cognition (jñānādhyāsa) is similarly to be viewed as having the character of remembrance, since it is produced by the mental impression left by previous perception. Nor may you counter-argue this latter assertion in the following way 'the thing under discussion *i.e.*, the subjective adhyāsa is not due to a mental impression; for it is a cognition other than remembrance, as perception is.' For the condition to make such reasoning valid is that the cognition in question should be produced by contact of the sense-organ (and this condition is absent in the case of shell-silver).

Against this reasoning of the Vedāntin the upholder of the view of non-discrimination (akhyāti) now re-states his case. The states of consciousness under discussion (such as the cognition of silver in the shell) are true, because they are states of consciousness, just like those states which are generally admitted to be true. And all cognition belongs to either of two classes—it either is knowledge directly resulting from the operation of one of the recognised means of knowledge; or it is remembrance (representative knowledge). And thus the cognition of silver also is not an adhyāsa, as the Vedāntins hold, but nothing else but a remembrance; for like other remembrances it is merely a product of previous impressions. Nor is there any weight in the question why, if the apprehension of silver in the shell is a mere remembrance, we do not instead of silver remember other shells rather to which the shell before us bears a greater resemblance than to silver. For the fact is that in the given case additional causes are at work, *viz.*, the desire for silver on the part of the person who sees the shell, and certain other imperfections: causes which (while suggesting silver) do not suggest other shells. It is these very imperfections which obscure the consciousness of remembrance, so that the remembrance of silver is not recognised as such. And as these imperfections at the same time obstruct the realization in consciousness of the special features of the shell actually seen, its dark colour and other attributes do not present themselves to consciousness. And as in this way apprehension and remembrance are not discriminated, the result is that the man desirous of silver stretches out his hand for the shell before him. But, it may be asked, what in the given case is it that moves the man to action, is it the actual apprehension and the remembrance together or either of the two? And do, in the former case, the two elements of consciousness operate together, or in succession? The former of these two latter alternatives is inadmissible since the apprehension and the remembrance (as being distinct mental acts) cannot take place at the same moment. Nor can the latter alternative be accepted; for if the two cognitions are successive, the former can have no causal power with regard to the man's action since the latter interposes itself between the two. Nor also can it be said that either cognition by itself moves the person to action; for the practical action which as a matter of fact results from the cognition is a particularized one (*i.e.*, proceeds on the supposition of the thing before us being silver). For these reasons, in order to account for the particularized action, we must after all assume a composite mental state (*i.e.*, an immediate apprehension of *this* and the silver). Not so, the akhyātivādin replies, what really moves the person to action is the rise in consciousness, in immediate succession, of direct apprehension and remembrance.

But, we recognise a composite state of consciousness, when later on we judge 'this thing appeared to us as silver!' This, the opponent replies, is a mere matter of practical experience (and need not be regarded as strictly true). As to the case of the new-born baby which spits out the (sweet) milk it had sucked from its mother's breast—wherefrom it may be inferred that the milk appears to it bitter,—here also we have no composite mental state, of the nature of error, but merely the remembrance of bitter tastes experienced in a previous state of existence; as for the *sweetness* that should be actually experienced now, and the idea of *that* which ought to be present in reference to the *bitterness* experienced in previous states of existence, and remembered now,—that these two do not appear in consciousness at the time is due to some bilious disorder.

The statement made by the author of the Bhāshya that 'the experiences of previous states of existence are not remembered' refers only to the generality of cases. For if the baby did not remember by what means desired objects are attained, it would not take to its mother's breast. And even on the Vedāntin's error-theory the experiences made in former states of existence have to be admitted as causes determining the experiences of the present state of existence; otherwise, if every experience alike were an entirely new one, there would be no reason why a seventh kind of taste should not erroneously present itself (in addition to the six kinds of taste actually experienced).

And if you say that the propounder of the system himself when saying 'the cognition of the real in the unreal,' declares error to depend on a composite state of consciousness; we reply that that declaration refers only to what is found to be the case in ordinary practical experience.

But in all non-erroneous cognitions it invariably is a composite state of consciousness that moves to action; why then should this hypothesis be abandoned in the case of error?—Because it introduces a needless complication! Even he who holds the error-theory must needs assume, as the cause of error, a non-distinction of apprehension and remembrance. And as such non-distinction, acknowledged by both parties alike, suffices to account for action, why assume a further composite cognition? The theory of non-discrimination thus evidently is the only rational one.

Against this restatement of the akhyāti-view we Vedāntins now finally argue as follows: What, we ask, do you understand by *ā-khyāti*? Absence of cognition in general? Or such cognition as causes a man desirous of one thing to engage in action with regard to another thing? Or the cognition of several things as non-discriminated?—On the first alternative there should be error in the state of deep sleep, not in the waking and dreaming states.—On the second alternative error would be absent in those cases where, owing either to instantaneous sublation of the error or to indolence, action is not actually entered upon.—As to the third alternative, we ask for your definition of 'discrimination'—the counter-entity of non-discrimination' (on which term your definition turns). Does it mean 'apprehension of difference,' or non-apprehension of non-difference, or the cognition of the mutual non-existence of things, such cognition being particularized by number such as *two* and so on? The first definition does not suit your case; for the judgment 'this is silver' causes the remembrance of two separate and non-tautological words, *viz., this* and *silver;* there thus is the apprehension of the difference of a general and a particularizing element, and hence no 'non-discrimination' in the sense of the first definition. Nor will the second definition meet your case. For since, in the way explained, there is (in the case of erroneous judgments like 'this is silver') apprehension of difference, there also is non-apprehension of what is contradictorily opposed to difference, *viz.*, non-difference, and how then could it be shown that there is present non-discrimination which negatives such non-apprehension? And as to the third definition we ask whether discrimination as there defined implies immediate cognition of a number, such as *two;* or whether an eventual cognition suffices. The former alternative would imply that when a person says 'Drive the cow to this place with a stick' there is non-discrimination of the cow and the stick, because the person does not at the time explicitly realize that there are *two* things. And on the latter alternative non-discrimination would be absent in the case of the silver before us; for the two-ness of the *this* and the silver may of course be cognized eventually. Well then, if non-discrimination cannot be defined on the basis of its counter-notion (discrimination), let us define it by means of the things of which it is an attribute! This also, we reply, cannot be done. For there can be no non-discrimination of two things presented to consciousness, for (*as* two) they clearly present themselves as not tautological (*i.e.*, as distinct). And if you say that there is non-discrimination of things *not* presented to consciousness, there would be error even in the case of deep sleep (in which as a matter of fact error does not arise since there is no cognition at all).

Listen then (the akhyāti-vādin says) to the following definition of non-discrimination. Non-discrimination means non-apprehension of non-connexion (asaṃsarga). And such non-apprehension is present in the case of the *this* and the silver being present to consciousness, because at the time there is no consciousness of the following form 'the *this* and the silver are *not* combined.' But, we reply, what do you really understand by the non-apprehension of non-connexion? Do you mean the non-connexion of apprehension and remembrance only; or of any two things; or of such things only regarding which there is no cognition of connexion?—The first alternative would imply that the state of consciousness 'I am a man' is not an error, for here both the terms non-discriminated are directly apprehended (*i.e.*, this is not a case where the non-connexion of direct apprehension and remembrance is not apprehended).

On the second alternative judgments such as 'the cow is short-horned,' "the cloth is white' would be erroneous; since they do not imply a consciousness of non-connexion (between the cloth and the whiteness etc.) And on the third alternative the same difficulty arises. For in the case of the judgments last quoted no cognition of connexion (saṃsarga) is possible, since the true object of such cognition, *viz.*, oneness (aikya) is absent. And that oneness really is the object of the cognition of connexion (saṃsarga) we learn from recognition (of the silver, as perceived elsewhere, in the shell).

Should it be said that the object of the cognition of saṃsarga is not oneness but relations such as that subsisting between quality and substrate; then, we point out, the relation of similarity also, which is expressed in the judgment 'this is silver,' may be held to be the object of such cognition of saṃsarga, and that consciousness of saṃsarga (as implied in that judgment) cannot be denied. But the cognition in question is sublated by the cognition of non-connexion (*asaṃsarga*) which is implied in the subsequent judgment 'this is *not* silver,' and hence the connexion and the consciousness of it are not possible! But, we reply, on your view, in the case of quality and substrate also there is cognition of non-connexion which in that case is called cognition of mutual non-existence (we no doubt judge 'the cloth is white;' but at the same time we cognize the cloth not to be whiteness, and whiteness not to be the cloth); and as thus there is neither connexion nor consciousness of it; it follows that those judgments also (*i.e.* the judgments affirming relations of quality and substrate) are erroneous! (which you of course do not mean to admit). The conclusion, therefore, is that non-discrimination (which, according to you, constitutes error) cannot be defined as non-apprehension of non-connexion.

But, the holder of the akhyāti-view retorts, if you reject my theory of non-discrimination, you on your part are bound to show that what constitutes the discriminating agency in the judgments under discussion. The perception certainly does not discriminate its own object from the thing remembered, since its power to present to consciousness particulars is, at the time, obstructed by imperfections. Nor also is remembrance capable of discriminating its own object from the object of perception; for the consciousness of remembrance as such is obscured at the time. This is not so, we reply. The discriminative power of both may easily be proved.

[*Page 30*] And first with regard to perception; if you say that the perception is incapable to distinguish its object from the thing remembered, do you hold the difference between the *this*- aspect and the *silver*-aspect to be between those things regarded *as individuals belonging to particular classes*, or between themselves only (regarded, independently of all other conditions)? You cannot hold the first alternative; for as in the given case, the *this*-aspect and *silver*-aspect are not cognised as individuals belonging to particular classes, there is no difference between them; and hence as they are *one*, what would arise under the circumstances is that combined state of consciousness which you deny.

And as to the second alternative we ask whether you understand the process of cognition to accomplish itself in that way that the first cognition apprehends the thing only, the second apprehends it as possessing characters distinguishing it from the other thing; and the third only the difference; or whether you hold the difference to be apprehended at once, together with the thing. The former alternative would imply that all cognitions whatever are erroneous; for all of them alike would, in the stages previous to the apprehension of difference, imply non-discrimination. On the second alternative, on the other hand, since the apprehension of difference would immediately result from the apprehension of *this-ness*, that particularizing content which is required for the cognition of difference would present itself to consciousness at once; and this of course amounts to the admission that the apprehension (perception) possesses discriminative power.

Analogously remembrance also may be shown to be discriminative. You (the holder of the akhyāti-vāda) are unable to give a satisfactory account of that so-called 'consciousness of remembrance' (smaraṇābhimāna) to the obscuration of which you ascribe the want of discrimination on the part of remembrance. What, we ask, do you understand by 'consciousness of remembrance'? Is it, firstly, nothing else than remembrance; or secondly, something other than remembrance; or, thirdly, an attribute of remembrance; or, fourthly, the mental apprehension of something as distinguished by previous perception; or, fifthly, some special feature of remembrance depending on remembrance itself only; or sixthly, a special feature depending on an object different from that of the previous perception; or, in the seventh place, the quality of producing a difference in the resultant activity (due to the two) or, in the eighth place, the immediate consciousness 'I remember'? There is no room for the first alternative; for if remembrance (which, according to the definition, is the same as 'consciousness of remembrance) is itself obscured, the cognition of silver (which you say *is* remembrance) cannot rise at all. The second alternative is equally inadmissible; for why should remembrance become non-discriminative on something else being obscured? The third alternative cannot be accepted because no such attribute is known to exist. To the fourth alternative there is the following objection. In the case of errors of recognition—as when we mistakenly think 'This man is that same Devadatta whom I met on a previous occasion'—a previous perception enters into our state of consciousness, and thus there is non-discrimination (as envinced by the mistaken recognition) *without* that obscuration (on which you say non-discrimination depends). But our definition was meant for simple remembrance only, not for recognition! Even with this limitation we reply, your definition cannot be upheld. For, we ask, does the previous perception constitute as its object itself also (*i.e.,* the perception), or only the thing perceived? The former cannot be; as it is not possible for a thing to operate upon itself. And, on the latter alternative, it is the thing only which in the act of remembrance, is represented in consciousness; not the perception itself which was *not* the object of perception (and therefore cannot be remembered). But, when our thought has the following form 'the jar was perceived by me,' we clearly remember a thing as qualified by a previous perception! Not so, we reply. The remembrance to which you refer is a different remembrance due to what the Naiyāyikas call 'secondary' or 'supervening' cognition (anuvyavasāya) or to an inference. Such remembrance is other than that which is due to the 'primary' cognition (vyavasāya) which has for its object the jar only (not the perceptionn of the jar). Of remembrance of the former kind you may not even say that its object is that previous cognition, termed anuvyavasāya, which gives rise to it (the remembrance); its object rather is the jar as cognized in the anuvyavasāya cognition and distinguished by the vyavasāya cognition. We, therefore, may argue as follows. 'The remembrance under discussion does not apprehend the thing as characterized by the cognition on which it (the remembrance) rests; for it is a (mere) remembrance; just like the remembrance of things denoted by words.' For words give rise to the remembrance of the things with which they are associated.

[*Page 31*] At this place, unwilling to admit the proving force of the last instance, the Buddha philosopher interposes.

It is irrational, he contends, to ascribe to words the power of reminding one of the things associated with them, since things and words clearly cannot be viewed as connected with each other either in the way of conjunction (saṁyoga) or of any other form of connexion. If it be said that the connexion lies therein that words possess the power of producing knowledge (bodha, *viz.*, of things); we ask what you understand by knowledge—whether immediate intuitive knowledge (anubhava), on remembrance (representative knowledge). The former cannot be the case; for although words combined so as to form a sentence produce an immediate cognition of the sense of the sentence, each by itself does not give rise to an analogous cognition of the thing it denotes. At the time when the meaning of a word is first learned, the thing denoted by it is apprehended by some other means of knowledge (Perception and the rest); as has been declared: The word also, not affording the cognition of anything now, cannot be regarded as different from what causes remembrance.'

On the second alternative we shall have to say that the 'power' of the word when producing its effect is either known or unknown. The latter cannot be; for as a matter of fact, Remembrance has its cause always known. Nor is the former alternative possible; for since a power is known through its effects only, we here entangle ourselves in reasoning in a circle—'words give rise to the remembrance of things because they possess the power of doing so;' and 'we infer that power belonging to words from the fact that they do give rise to the remembrance of things.' But, it may be objected, the way in which we come to know the power of words is as follows. The child inferring from the actions of the older people around him the ideas which give rise to the actions ascertains from the fact that those ideas and actions immediately follow on certain words, that the words have the power of originating those ideas: they thus ascertain the power of words, at the very first time when they come to learn their meaning, from actions such as bringing and lifting, and hence the charge of reasoning in a circle is baseless. But even granting this, the Bauddha resumes, there arises a further question, does that power (of originating ideas; which you say is originally ascertained in the manner described above) belong to the mere words or to the words as connected with certain definite things? To the former alternative there lies the objection that on it, it could not be shown at all why each individual word is connected with one definite idea only. On the second alternative, again, we should have to search for a further connexion determining the connexion called 'power' (*i.e.*, the connexion consisting therein that a certain word has the power to express a certain idea, and that connexion again would require a further connexion to explain it, and so on *ad infinitum*. If against this you were to urge the principle that 'the power establishes itself as well as other things,' we ask the further question, 'Is the thing, at the moment of remembrance, remembered owing to the auditory perception of the mere word; or owing to the perception of the word as possessing 'power' with regard to the thing; or owing to the mental impression due to the cognition of that power together with the perception of the word? The first alternative is unacceptable for the reason that it leaves unexplained why definite words are connected with definite ideas. On the second alternative the thing also would be immediately known at the very time when the word is heard, and it thus would be purposeless to assume a remembrance (of the thing) produced by the word. Nor can we accept the third alternative. For we observe that in other cases of remembrance there are certain other definite relations between the thing remembered and that which suggests the remembrance—such as similarity, contrariety (contrast; virodha), the relation of cause and effect, etc.; while there is no such relation to connect the thing and the word. That words possess reminding (suggestive) power and that the sentence is a means of valid knowledge, we, therefore, hold to be a mere baseless theory of the followers of the Veda.

Against this Bauddha view we Vedāntins now argue as follows. No valid objection lies against the theory that the remembrance of a thing is produced by the auditory perception of the word together with the impression left on the mind by the cognition of the power of the word. What the Bauddha asserts on this point ('in other cases etc.') is unfounded. Does he mean that as in other cases so in the case of words also similarity or the like has to be admitted? Or that, as in the case of words, there should be in other cases also power, and not similarity or the like? Or that, since in the case of words there are absent such fundamental relations as similarity and so on, words do *not* give rise to remembrance in spite of their *power* to do so? The first alternative is inadmissible; for we do not observe any similarity between words and the things they denote, and we have no right to make assumptions not resting on actual observation. In those *other* cases, on the other hand, similarity and certain other relations are actually observed and, therefore, need not to be assumed. The second alternative is likewise inadmissible; for what is actually experienced cannot be denied. Nor can the third alternative be accepted; for it is irrational to maintain that a thing possessing a certain power does not produce its effect. Our conclusion, therefore, is that words inasmuch as possessing a specific power *do* give rise to the remembrance of things. The original perceptions are *not* remembered together with the thing. For, if they were so remembered, it would follow therefrom that the words denote not only the things but also those original perceptions (and this is clearly not the case).

After this digression we now proceed with the refutation of the remaining definitions of 'consciousness of remembrance' (smaraṇābhimāna) (noticed on page 76). The fifth definition also is inadmissible. For apart from the special circumstances of cause, object *etc.* (of cognitions, remembrance), we observe no special characteristics of cognitional states themselves.

Nor can we accept the sixth and seventh definitions; for remembrance has no object and no resulting cognition other than the object of, and the cognition resulting from, the original perception. Nor finally can we accept the eighth definition. If it were by other means that the immediate consciousness expressing itself in the form 'I remember' possesses discriminative power, it might perhaps be said that it loses that discriminative power through obscuration, for the consciousness in question arises in intimate connexion with the word denoting remembrance ('I remember'), the word denoting perception ('I perceive') being shut out from consciousness. How then could such consciousness (which implies discrimination of perception and remembrance) arise at all, unless there were an initial discrimination of perception and remembrance? The acceptance of the definition thus would involve us in circular reasoning 'if there is discrimination, there is consciousness of remembrance,' and, on the other hand, 'if there is consciousness of remembrance, there is discrimination.'

As it thus appears that no rational account can be given of that so called 'consciousness of remembrance' by means of the obscuration of which the akhyāti-vādin undertakes to explain error, it follows that remembrance *does* possess discriminative power.

But, the opponent objects, if both the perception and the remembrance had for their object nothing but the single thing, it would follow that the two do not differ in any way; and hence you must admit after all that what constitutes the specific object of remembrance is the thing *as qualified by the previous perception,* and this is what we understand by the 'consciousness of remembrance.' Not so, we reply. A difference between remembrance and perception is established by the difference of their respective causes. On your view, there would be no difference between an act of remembrance, and an act of inference that has for its object a previous perception; since both have the same object. There would be a difference, the opponent replies. What distinguishes an act of remembrance from an act of inference that has for its object a thing previously perceived, is that character or aspect of remembrance which is expressed by the pronoun 'that' (the remembrance expressing itself, in the form 'this thing now before my mind is *that* thing). But what, we ask in reply, *is* that aspect or character which is expressed by *that*? Does *that* denote what is distinguished by non-present place and time? Or what is connected with a previous perception? Or what is produced by an impression left on the mind by a previous perception? The first alterative does not suit; since from it it would follow that the act of inference also is recollection (for an inference also may be expressed in the form 'this fire which I now infer from smoke is *that* fire which I perceived on previous occasions.') Nor is the second meaning acceptable; for the inferential cognition also presents itself to the mind as connected with a previous direct apprehension. And the third alternative clearly implies a view the same as ours, *viz.*, that the difference between perception and remembrance is one of *cause* (the remembrance only being caused by a mental impression). Very well, the opponent resumes, let us then say that in the case in question also (*i.e.*, the erroneous cognition of silver) there is *remembrance* of silver, due to an impression left on the mind by the previous perception of silver! Are you not aware, we reply, that of this view we have already disposed by pointing out that the silver presents itself to consciousness as actually present, not as remembered? Nor may you say that such presentation is the effect of non-discrimination; for it is not non-discrimination that determines error. What, indeed, should it be that is non-discriminated—two things perceived? or one perceived and one remembered? or two things remembered? The first alternative is inadmissible; for it would imply that there is no error in the dreaming state. For in that state the only thing immediately apprehended is the Self; hence your condition of error, *i.e.*, the presence of *two* apprehended things which are not discriminated, is absent. From the second alternative it would follow that the dreaming soul has states of consciousness of the following form 'I am something blue or the like.' (For in dream there is erroneous cognition, and according to the definition error consists in the non-discrimination of a thing apprehended and a thing remembered. Now the only thing immediately apprehended in dream is the Self; hence judgments of the above kind would arise). And on the third alternative, *anything* not directly apprehended (but previously apprehended) should present itself in erroneous cognition; for all such things alike may be remembered. We, therefore, are justified in maintaining that the inference that the silver before us is (not false but merely) remembered silver is invalid; for the condition of its validity, *viz.*, the silver appearing to consciousness as something not directly perceived, is absent. As regards the reasoning in support of reality, we meet that with the following counter-reasoning: "The cognitions in question are not real, because they are sublated, like all activity due to wrong conception." From all this it follows that you should give up your hankering after the double character of cognitions, and accept the fact that the cognition in question is an *error*.

XIV

[Nor can the solution of the difficulty be found in the so-called *anyathā-khyāti* theory, according to which the object of the erroneous cognition, let us say of silver, is other silver *i.e.*, real silver, observed at some other time and place, the remembrance of which, due to the glitter of the shell, imparts to the shell before us the character of silver. For of this latter process no intelligible account can be given.]

[*Page 33*] Another opponent here comes forward. I agree, he says, that the *akhyāti* theory is not able to account for Error. And instead of it I propose the theory of *anyathā-khyāti i.e.*, 'cognition *otherwise*'. According to this theory the organ of sight suffering from some defect (which obstructs clear non-erroneous perception), on coming into contact with the shell, apprehends silver which (does not exist where the shell now is, but) exists at some other place or time—as constituting the self of the shell. Nor must you object that on this view of the process anything not actually perceived at the time might be apprehended by the defective organ (*i.e.*, that the shell might be mistaken not only for silver but for any other thing also); for similarity (between the shell and the silver, which both are glittering things), or some other circumstance of the kind, restricts and determines the actual apprehension.

But this theory also we Vedāntins declare to be unsound. For to what does the *otherwise-ness* you maintain, actually belong?—to the cognitional energy?—or to its result (*i.e.*, the state of consciousness resulting from the cognitional energy)? or to the thing? The first alternative is impossible; for the state of things, on that assumption, would have to be expressed as follows: 'A cognition which has the form of silver has the shell for its basis.' Now the shell's being the *basis* of the cognition could mean only either that the shell imparts its own form to the cognition, or that the shell is the object of such practical thought, speech and action (*vyavahāra*), as are caused by the cognition. The former alternative is not possible since the shell cannot impart its own form to a cognition engrossed by the form of silver. And the second alternative is likewise inadmissible; for from it it would follow that swords, spears and darts—which are the objects of energies, cognitional or practical, that are caused by the sight of a tiger or similar wild beast—are the basis of the cognition of the tiger or other wild beast. Nor in the second place, can the *otherwise-ness* belong to the result of the cognition; for the result *i.e.*, the presentation to consciousness does not essentially differ, whether the case be one of error or one of true cognition. In the third place, in what sense could you speak of the thing as being *otherwise*? Do you mean that the shell identifies itself with the silver?—or that it transforms itself into the form or shape of silver?

On the former alternative, do you view the shell and the silver as absolutely distinct and different? or as standing to each other in the *bhedābheda* relation *i.e.*, as being different and non-different at the same time? You cannot hold the former view, since things absolutely different cannot identify themselves in all *real* way; and the 'inexplicability' of the *Vedāntins* (which alone could meet such cases) is not acknowledged by you. If, on the other hand, the identity intended by you is of the nature of the *void* (*i.e.*, a non-entity), we point out that also the relation which exists between a quality and its substrate is *identity* in that sense, and that hence such relation also would have to be considered erroneous. For the *samavāya* relation which is acknowledged by one philosophical system only (*viz.*, the Nyāya system, which teaches that a substance is connected with its qualities by the relation termed *samavāya*) in no way differs from the relation of identity (*tādātmya*). On the view, on the other hand, of the shell and the silver being different as well as non-different, it would have to be held that also judgments such as 'the cow is short-horned' (where admittedly we have a case of such combined difference and non-difference) are erroneous (which of course they are not).

As to the second alternative,—*viz.*, the thing undergoing a transformation (which is the object of cognition),—this would mean that there would be no subsequent sublation of the error by the judgment ('this thing is not silver but a shell'): the proper reasoning in that case rather would be 'the cognition of silver is not liable to sublation; for it is the (valid) cognition of a real change, just like the cognition of curds—which are a changed form of milk. Like the milk, the shell would, subsequently to the change, not be perceived again.' But, the Naiyāyika retorts, we actually observe that on the departure of the sun-light which had caused the lotus bud to unfold, the bud closes again; analogously we may suppose that the shell may again become a shell as soon as the special defect which had caused it to change into silver is removed. The two cases, we reply, are not analogous. We are conscious of the expanded flower *having been* a bud; we are not conscious of the silver presenting itself to us having been a shell. And even, if somehow we had that consciousness, the theory of change could not rationally be maintained. For if the shell actually transformed itself, for the time, into silver, the silver would be perceived by those also who do not suffer from any defect. We do not observe that the same milk appears to one person to have turned into curds, and to another person to have remained milk. The *anyathā-khyāti* theory thus shows itself incapable of being stated in any rational form.

XV

[Equally unprofitable is the *ātma-khyāti* theory of the Bauddhas, according to which the silver seen in the shell is a mere idea which, like other ideas, in due time emerges from one of those individual 'streams of ideas' which constitute all reality. For generally the Bauddha fails to show how presentative cognitions can arise from mere 'streams of ideas.']

[*Page 34*] Let us then accept the theory of *ātmakhyāti* (consciousness or cognition of the self). The silver in question, it is argued, is of the nature of an idea; since it is something immediately presented to the mind, without any contact of the sense-organ with the object, as ideas generally are. But, the Vedāntin objects, according to the view of the Bauddhas (who are the supporters of the *ātma-khyāti* view) mind (*chitta*) and mental things (*chaitta*) originate in dependence on causes of four different kinds. Now the silver in question cannot, in the first place, originate from the cause called *sahakāri-pratyaya i.e.*, co-operating cause, which, in the given case, would be light; for light is the cause of the *distinctness* of the perception only. Nor can it, in the second place, originate from the so-called *adhipatipratyaya i.e.*, ruling or defining cause—which in the present case is constituted by the eye; for that cause operates only in so far as to define the object (as a *visual* one, in the given case). Nor, in the third place, can the silver originate from the *samanantarapratyaya*, or immediate cause *i.e.*, the immediately preceding cognition; for we observe that the erroneous cognition of silver may arise immediately after a cognition of an entirely different kind, as *e.g.*, that of a jar. Nor, in the fourth place, can it originate from the so-called *ālambana* cause *i.e.*, the external thing; for the Vijñāna-vādin (*i.e.*, the adherent of the theory that ideas only exist, not external things) does not admit the existence of external things. As thus none of your four causes are applicable in the given case, how do you, Bauddhas, account for the cognition of silver? On the basis of a mental impression, the Bauddha replies. But, if impressions are lasting, this contradicts one of your own fundamental tenets, *viz.*, the merely momentary existence of all things. And even if you admit the momentariness of the impression, it is an *object of cognition*, and this implies an abandonment of your main theory, *viz.*, that there are cognitions (ideas) only. Not so, the Bauddha replies. By the impression (*saṃskāra*) from which the idea of silver originates, we understand a previous idea of silver which at some time or other, had arisen in the beginningless series of cognitions; such an impression produces, at some time, an idea of the same kind as itself, although many ideas of a different kind may intervene between the impression and the idea. The case is analogous to that of a grain of wheat which in the end gives rise to another grain of the same kind, although the sprout and several other effects of a different kind intervene between the first and the second grain. Should you urge that according to our view of the matter what gives rise to the ultimate grain is not the original grain but the intervening series constituted by the sprout etc., we have no objection: we are ready to define the 'impression,' as the 'series of ideas which were produced by the previous idea of silver.' This previous idea again was in its turn produced by a yet earlier idea. What really exists, therefore, is only an idea having the form or character of silver which is the result of a beginningless series of impressions. And owing to error (*bhrānti*) this idea appears to consciousness as something external.

Against this Bauddha theory we Vedāntins argue as follows: Is that silver (which appears in the shell), on account of its *extraordinary* nature, devoid of origination?—or does it originate as ordinary silver does? On the former view it would not be of the nature of a rising cognition (which it actually is). On the second view it must originate either from a cognition or a thing. The latter alternative is excluded, since you Bauddhas do not admit the existence of external things. On the former alternative it cannot be pure (*vishuddha*) cognition that originates the idea of silver; for pure cognition constitutes final release. If on the other hand what originates the silver is a cognition (not pure but) itself due to a vitiated cause, is it that same originating cognition which apprehends the silver?—or is it a cognition other than that? The former alternative is not possible; for since the originating and the originated cognition are both 'momentary' and hence occupy different moments of time, the consciousness of immediately presented silver would thus not come about at all. If, in the second place, it is another cognition that apprehends the silver, it cannot be a cognition produced by a non-vitiated cause; for this would be too wide an assumption (inasmuch as there would be no reason why such a cognition should specially apprehend silver). If, on the other hand, the cognition (which apprehends the silver) is produced by a *vitiated* cause, that cause either is silver or it is not silver. In the former case you ascribe to silver causal efficiency; and this means that the cause *is* (has *being*); you thus acknowledge the silver as a real external thing. If the cause is not silver, silver cannot be the object of the cognition; for you admit yourself that the object is the cause which imparts its form to the cognition. It thus is evident that on the *ātmakhyāti* view the cognition of silver could not come about at all.

XVI

[We are thus led back to the Vedānta theory which explains cognitions such as that of shell-silver as belonging to a special class of 'erroneous cognition' due to a special cause, *viz.*, Māyā or one of the particular forms of Māyā. In this way only we can account for the presentative character of those cognitions, and for their being put an end to by the cognition of truth.]

But, a final objection is raised against the Vedāntin, you also must after all accept either the *akhyāti* view, if, namely, the cognition of the shell-silver is of the nature of *Remembrance;* or either the *anyathā-khyāti* or the *ātmakhyāti* view, if that cognition is of the nature of Direct Apprehension (*anubhava*). And as no third kind of cognition is possible, the cognition of the silver must be either *Remembrance* or *Direct Apprehension.*

Not so, we reply. What, we ask, should be the cause of this alleged impossibility of a third kind of cognition? Is it that for such cognition no special causal apparatus can be assigned?—or no special character?—or no special object? The first alternative cannot be admitted; since the contact of the sense-organ with the object, together with a certain mental impression and certain defects, *does* supply the required causal apparatus. Nor must it be said that those defects, being of a merely obstructive nature, may indeed cause the *non-origination* of the ordinary effects, but not the *origination* of altogether new effects (such as the alleged shell-silver). For 'non-origination' really is nothing else but so-called previous non-existence, which is something beginningless (existing from all eternity), and hence cannot be the result of special defects. Moreover, to quote an analogous instance, we *do* observe that certain bodily defects such as excess of wind and bile do produce altogether extraordinary effects. Nor must it be said that the operation of such defects exhausts itself in resuscitating the mental impression; for such resuscitation is a merely intermediary effect of the defects. What the axe directly effects is indeed no more than the movements of rising and falling; but it cannot be said that on that account it is not, likewise, the cause of the action of cutting the wood.

But, considering that the contact of the sense-organ with the object exhausts itself in giving rise to the mere idea of the *this*,—and that although the mental impression (of previously perceived silver) is capable of giving rise to remembrance, you do not in the present case admit the rise of remembrance,—and that the defects cannot by themselves cause cognition,—how do you Vedāntins account for the actual presentation to consciousness of silver? As follows, we reply. In the first place the sense-organ, which (when there arises what is ordinarily called 'erroneous cognition') must be held to be impaired by a certain defect, gives rise (on coming into contact with the shell) to a certain modification (*or* function, *vṛitti*) of the internal organ which has for its object *this-ness* only.* Next consciousness manifests or reveals itself with regard to the *this-ness* and the modification of the internal organ which apprehends it. At the same time that (part of general) Nescience which has for its substrate (or locus) consciousness as manifested or determined in the manner described, is thrown into a state of agitation, owing to the influence of the defect (which, in all cases of so-called error is present). (And a further distinction has here to be noted). On being agitated, that Nescience which has for its abode Consciousness defined by the *this*-element, owing to the assistance (co-operation) which it receives from the impression left behind by previously perceived silver—which impression on the present occasion is resuscitated by similarity (between silver and the glittering shell)—illusorily manifests itself (*vivarttate*) in the form of silver. That Nescience on the other hand which has for its substrate consciousness as defined by the *vṛitti* (function) of the internal organ, being co-operated with by the impression left behind by the original *vṛitli* by which silver was apprehended, illusorily modifies itself into the form of that *vṛitli*. Finally those two illusory modifications (or projections),—*viz.*, that of silver and that of the *vṛitti*— are irradiated by witnessing consciousness which constitutes their substrate, and thus there arises the cognition of silver. There indeed really are two cognitions, *viz.*, the *vṛitti* of the internal organ and the *vṛitti* of Nescience; but the object of the two becomes one in so far as the real and the unreal element (*i.e.*, the *this* and the silver)

* *i.e.*, the internal organ which, apart from consciousness, belongs to the sphere of the non-intelligent, material, modifies itself so as to assume the form of a *this*.

mutually identify themselves; and as hence the result determined by the object (*i.e.,* the cognition) also becomes one, oneness of cognition may be allowed in a figurative sense.

Nor again is there any force in the second and third of the objections (above raised, text p. 35, 1.8-9); for we are fully able to give a satisfactory definition of false cognition and a false object. Although, no doubt, the contact of the sense-organ with the object and the mental impression left behind by previous apprehension) are capable of giving rise, independently of each other, to true direct cognition on the one and to remembrance on the other hand, yet the mere origination, in immediate succession, of direct true cognition and of remembrance would not result in activity (such as *e.g.,* effort to take possession of the presumed silver); and we, therefore, must assume *one* false cognition which results from present sense-contact and mental impression combined. The assumption is analogous to one made by yourself (the Logician). The cognitions produced by the several letters of a word pronounced in immediate succession are not simultaneous and hence cannot give rise to the cognition of the sense of the word; yet the latter cognition as a matter of fact arises; and hence to account for it, you assume *one* cognition of the last letter combined with the impressions left behind by all the preceding letters of the word.

[*Page 36*] But, an objection is raised, the cognition under discussion (*false* cognition) is *not* one, for the reason that it is the effect of several causes—just as the cognitions of colour and taste are. This argumentation, we reply, is refuted by the cases of inferential cognition and of Recognition; for in the case of both of these there is acknowledged to be one authoritative cognition only which contains within itself an element of *remembrance;* while the *cause* of the cognition is in the case of Inference the mental impression of the Vyāpti (*i.e.,* the invariable concomitance of middle and major terms), *and* the actual perception of the middle term; and, in the case of Recognition, the contact of the sense-organ with a present object *and* a mental impression. Nor may it be said that the cause of the inferential cognition is the *remembrance* of the Vyāpti *and* the perception of the middle term; *not* the impression. For two cognitions (of which the *remembrance* would be one) cannot take place simultaneously. And although the same objection would not lie against Remembrance being accepted as a cause of Recognition (in which case the full cause would be contact of the sense-organ with the object, *plus* remembrance), yet in any case the resuscitation of the impression would have to be admitted as the cause of remembrance; and as such resuscitation suffices to account for Recognition, Remembrance—which does not occur by itself (apart from the revival of the impression) and the introduction of which only complicates the case—need not be assumed as a cause. "But," it is objected, "we may reason as follows: 'the cognition of silver is not due to several independent causes; for it is a (simple) cognition like the cognition of a jar.' "

This, we reply has no force; for we can easily oppose to it a counter-argument, *viz.*, 'the cognition of silver *is* due to the mentioned causes, because it is different in nature from simple cognition and valid remembrance; just as recognition is.' Nor will this entitle you to argue in the following way: 'the cognition of silver is a valid cognition; because it is due to a cause which is co-operated with by an impression; just as inferential cognition, is.' For there is a special condition for all valid cognition, *viz.*, that it should be direct cognition (*anubhava*) not due to a defect (a condition not present in your *probans* or middle term). 'But,' it is objected, 'it is contrary to reason to maintain the non-reality of silver which is cognized as real, specially when no incongruity is found in the cognition.' Not so, we reply; what we maintain is the connexion of the real existence of the shell with the (imaginary) silver;—similar to the connexion between the *silver* and the notion of 'this.' 'Well then, if that connexion is perceived as really existing, it is irrational to maintain its unreality.' Let us then say that there is existence (or being) of three different kinds—*real (pāramārthika)* existence which belongs to Brahman; *empirical* (or conventional; *vyāvahārika*) existence which is conditioned by Māyā, and belongs to ether etc., (*i.e.* to the so-called real things of ordinary normal experience); and *apparent* (*prātibhāsika*) existence which is conditioned by Nescience and belongs to shell-silver and the like.* That the latter two kinds of existence which are not real in the true sense (*pāramārthika*) should be called 'unreal' or 'false,' is in no way irrational. Nor is the hypothesis of such falseness devoid of proof; for the subsequent judgment 'silver falsely appeared to me' expresses the recognition of the unreality of the silver and its cognition. It hence appears that our theory is not, like other theories, open to the charge of contradicting facts of consciousness and of involving baseless assumptions. The *akhyāti* theory on the other hand is irrational, because it declares something immediately presented to consciousness to be something remembered; and it involves several baseless assumptions;—*viz.*, that of the cognition of silver being not immediate but remembrance, and that of

* Though in what follows Māyā and Avidyā (Nescience) are proved to be one and the same, yet there is some diference between the two recognised in ordinary speech. This difference is pointed out later on (page 11 of this proof).

the obscuration of the consciousness of remembrance. Similar objections lie against the other theories also. The general conclusion, therefore, is that our theory (of Error) according to which the silver is the product of Māyā, is the only one that can be accepted.

XVII

[The objection that what is put an end to by knowledge can be the product of Avidyā only, and not of Māyā, has no force since Māyā and Avidyā are fundamentally one.]

[*Page 37*] But an objection is raised, as you hold the silver to be put an end to by cognition of the truth, it must be the product of Nescience, not of Māyā. Nor can it be said that Nescience is nothing else but Māyā; for the definitions of the two as well as their ordinarily received meanings show them to be different. Māyā is something which does not bewilder the mind in which it abides and is governed by the will of the agent; while Nescience is of a contrary nature. For in everyday speech the term 'Māyā' only is applied to things such as elephants, horses, chariots, etc., if produced by extraordinary (magical) power; not the term 'Nescience.'

To this we reply as follows: The definition—'that which, while itself of an inexplicable nature, is the cause of the obstruction of the presentation to consciousness of truth, and of the presentation of error'—is valid for Māyā and Avidyā alike. Nor must it be said that the term 'Māyā' properly denotes real things, as such *mantras* (formulas of incantation and the like), drugs and the like (through which so called 'magical' effects are produced). To such things the term 'Māyā' is, as a matter of fact, not applied; the spectators call 'Māyā' the magical illusion only which they actually see, not unseen things such as *mantras*. The presence and absence of *mantras* constitute instrumental causes only; just like some morbid affection of the eye (which acts as the instrumental cause of the perception of shell-silver and the like). Inexplicable magical things (*indrajāla*)—which we call 'Māyā'—cannot have for their material cause real things such as *mantras* and drugs. We, therefore, must assume for them some inexplicable material cause which is without a beginning; for if it had a beginning, some further cause would have to be postulated, and so on *in infinitum*. And that this cause also should be called 'Māyā' is justified by the non-difference of the material cause from its effects. Now this same Māyā which we have to postulate as the material cause of magical things, may also be assumed to constitute the cause of all *adhyāsa* — of silver and the like; and hence there is no need of a separate Avidyā. That Māyā is the universal cause, Scripture, moreover, confirms: 'Know Māyā to be Prakṛiti.'* It thus appears the simpler hypothesis to take Māyā and Avidyā as one. Nor is it an established truth that Māyā possesses no bewildering power with regard to its substrate; Viṣṇu in his *avatāra* as Rāma, was deluded by the Māyā abiding within himself. Nor again does Avidyā, on its part, necessarily delude the mind in which it abides. For we know that *e.g.*, with regard to trees on the banks of a sheet of water which are 'superimposed' ('illusorily projected', *adhyasta*) on the surface of the water with their tops downwards, the beholder is *not* bewildered, but knows the tops (really) to be above. Should you object to this that the absence of delusion in this case is due to the discriminative knowledge produced by the sight of the trees on the bank, while Avidyā in itself has a delusive quality;—we reply that the Magician also is not himself deluded (by the magical shows he produces), since he possesses true insight antagonistic to such delusion; that on the other hand, the magic show (Māyā) in itself is delusive, since we observe that all who behold it are deluded thereby. When however the spectators possess the antagonistic insight they also are not deluded; it, therefore, is not the circumstance of not being the abode of Māyā which determines its delusive power. Nor again is it a fact that Māyā is governed by the will of the agent. For the Magician is free only with regard to the instrumental causes he employs, such as *mantras*, drugs and the like. And this kind of dependence on the will of the agent is observed to occur in the case of Avidyā also; for by pressing the eyeball with a finger we can at will produce the appearance of a double moon. And if it be said that the agent has no power over Avidyā itself (but only over certain conditions of it), we point out that such is the case of Māyā also. The scriptural use of terms also proves the two not to be different. In the passage 'and in the end there is the cessation of all Māyā,'** the word 'Māyā' denotes Avidyā which is put an end to by perfect knowledge. And the Smṛiti passage—'He on whose entrance the Yogin passes beyond the Avidyā stretched out in the heart—the Māyā—, to him who transcends all knowledge, whose self is knowledge, be reverence!'—directly states Māyā and Avidyā to be one. The distinction made in ordinary speech is justified by the principle that different terms may be applied to one and the same thing according to the point of view taken: We speak of 'Māyā' when we have in view its power of producing extraordinary effects and its being subject to the will of the agent; of 'Avidyā,' on the other hand, we speak when having in mind its

* Śvetā. Upa. IV.10.

** Śvetā. Upa. I. 10.

obscuring power and its independence. We have thus finally established the theory that the shell-silver is the product of Māyā.

XVIII

[The Nescience and its effects to which the illusion of shell-silver and the like is due, is destroyed by sublative (or destructive) cognition (*bādha*); of which a fully satisfactory account may be given.]

[*Page 38*] 'But why all this trouble to prove that the silver is the product of Māyā? Why not rather admit that the silver is just as what it presents itself to consciousness, *i.e.*, a real thing?' If it were real, we reply, it would be perceived by those also who do not suffer from any imperfection; just as jars and similar objects are perceived by all men alike. If defects had causal efficiency with regard to the apprehension of real things also, nothing whatever would present itself to those free from defects; while on the Māyā theory it is the defects which account for the limitation of the appearance of silver. It cannot be argued that the silver is apprehended by all, for the reason that it belongs to the *this* aspect of the shell; just as the white colour of the cloth is perceived by all. For the condition for the validity of this argumentation would be that the silver should belong to the *mere this*-aspect of the shell. The Māyā-silver, however, super-imposes itself upon consciousness as determined by the *this*-aspect of the shell and manifested by a cognition that is due to a defect; this is the reason why it is not perceived by those who are free from defects. For the cognition of one person is not perceived by other persons. Against this the advocate of the reality of the silver will perhaps plead that the thing seen in some way determines and limits the perception of silver (owing to which it is perceived by some men only). But how then, we ask, will he get over the subsequent sublative cognition that expresses itself in the form 'this is not silver,' and implies the absolute non-existence of silver in the substrate in which it had been cognized? On the theory of the silver's unreality, on the other hand, that sublative cognition is just what we expect; for the Unreal (*mithyā*) is defined as that which is the counter-entity to absolute non-existence (*i.e.*, as that which is absolutely non-existent) in the substrate in which it is (erroneously) cognised. That this negation does not pertain to the *unreal* silver we have proved above (p. 70), on the basis of the Recognition that one has in the case, in the form—'this falsely appeared as silver.' On the *anyathākhyāti* theory, on the other hand, and on the *ātmakhyāti* theory, the subsequent reflection should be, not 'this falsely appeared to me as silver,' but '*this* is not silver, but *that* is,' or 'this is (*not* a thing, but) a mere idea.' Hence for the reason that the silver is not perceived by people who are free from defects, and on account of the subsequent sublation and reflection, we must hold to the view that the silver is unreal, not real.

"But what really is that so-called *sublation* (or refutation, *bādha*), on the strength of which you determine the silver to be unreal? Is it (1) the cessation of activity, with regard to a certain thing on the part of a person desirous of another thing? or (2) the destruction of the person's capability of such action? or (3) the discrimination of what was previously cognized as non-discriminated? or (4) the cognition of the mutual difference of things first cognized as identical?, or (5) the destruction of erroneous cognition?, or (6), the destruction of the object of such cognition? or (7) the destruction of defects and the like? The first alternative is inadmissible; for it would imply that there is no sublation in the case of him who, free from all desire, does not act at all.* "Let then the definition be narrowed as follows: 'Sublation is the cessation of activity preceded by desire!'" From this, we reply, it would follow that 'sublation' takes place in the case of a man who having seen at a distance (the appearance of) water due to a Fata Morgana has set out towards it but stops halfway because he finds robbers or a snake or some other dangerous thing in his way. But, as a matter of fact, sublative cognition does not arise in that man's mind, since the idea of water remains for him unrefuted. The second alternative also is inadmissible; for since at some subsequent time the error and the action due to it may again occur with regard to the very same shell even, the man's capability of such action is not destroyed. As to the third alternative, we ask whether the difference (which is apprehended on discrimination) is an attribute of the things, and as such is apprehended after the things have been apprehended; or constitutes the essential nature of things, and as such is apprehended in and with them. On the former view all cognition of difference would be sublative of the cognition of things; since the latter would have for its object that which is non-discriminated. On the latter view there never would be non-discrimination of things once apprehended. The fourth alternative would imply—whether we hold the view of *absolute difference* or the *bhedābheda*-view (of simultaneous difference and non-difference)—that the *prima facie* judgment of identity 'the cloth is white' would be 'sublated' by the subsequent judgment of difference 'whiteness belongs to the cloth.' The

* *i.e.*, the definition would not apply to the case of the man who while mistaking the shell for silver, does not actively exert himself to take possession of the silver.

fifth definition is purposeless; since all cognition, being in its very nature momentary, perishes of itself. The sixth and seventh definitions finally must be rejected, because objects and defects—both of which are *realities*—cannot be destroyed by cognitions. On the other hand, we cannot deny the existence of sublation; for it is something fully well known from ordinary experience. We hence do not know exactly what to think of 'sublation.' "

We solve the difficulty by the following definition: "Sublation is the termination, by means of the cognition of truth, of Nescience (non-knowledge) together with its effects whether present or passed away." It is in this sense, of 'termination of non-knowledge,' that the term is generally understood. "But, this being so, the mere cognition of the shell would be 'sublative;' for it puts an end to the unreal silver and its material cause (the *ajñāna*)!" Such indeed is the wonderful fact. Since however, for him who is moved to action by the idea of real silver, the cognition of the absence of silver (apart from the cognition of the shell) suffices to cut short the impulse to action, the cognition 'this is not silver' is also designated as *sublative*. It thus appears that the unreality of a thing is ascertained through 'sublation.'

XIX

> [Nor is there any essential difference between the illusory shell-silver, and the illusory things seen in a dream; the difference merely is that in a dream the internal organ functions independently of contact with an external object. Nor finally, is there any essential difference between illusory silver and dream-images on the one hand, and on the other hand, the things perceived in the waking state. In all cases alike Nescience or Māyā effects an illusory projection of unreal things on the substrate of Universal Consciousness.]

"Well then, let us admit that the cognition of unreal silver is to be classed as error (*bhrama*). But what about the cognition of things seen in dreams? Such cognition is not true knowledge; for it is sublated (by the cognitions of the waking state). Nor is it remembrance; for it is of the nature of immediate presentation. Nor is it Error; for the characteristic features of error are absent in dreams. To dreams we cannot, in the first place, apply the definition of Error—*viz.*, that it is that which is produced by the triad of causes (contact of the sense-organ with the object;

impression left on the mind by previous experiences; defect); for while there no doubt is a defect, *viz.*, the dull drowsy condition of the sleeper's mind; and while there also are previous mental impressions which are resuscitated by the unseen principle (adṛiṣṭa); the third cause, *viz.*, contact to the sense-organs with their objects, is absent. Nor does the *essential* definition of Error, 'the presentation to consciousness of one thing in, or on, another,' suit the case of dreams, in which that abode or substrate which in the above definition is referred to in the words 'in another' is absent. What place then do you assign to dream-cognitions?"

Our theory on this point is as follows: In the waking state the contact of the sense-organ with the external object produces a modification of the internal organ which has for its object the external *this*-element of the shell and the like; for the internal organ has no independent energy outside the body. In dreams, on the other hand, the internal organ—which within the body is independent—may function on its own account, and is not, therefore, dependent on contact with external objects. The third cause, *i.e.*, the modification of the internal organ, thus is present in dreams no less than in the waking state. The substrate also is in both cases the same *viz.*, Consciousness circumscribed by the modification of the internal organ. (But in the case of *bhrama*) the *shell* and the *this*-aspect are what bring about the contact of the sense-organ, eye and the rest; as in the absence of these, no contact,—for which an object is always necessary—would be possible; for the simple reason that such contact is the qualifying adjunct to *something* that circumscribes or characterises the substrate—consciousness. The two cases, therefore, stand as follows: In the waking state that Nescience, which has for its substrate Consciousness as manifested by that modification of the internal organ which is due to the contact of sense-organ and object, and as defined by the *this*-element of the shell, illusorily projects itself in the form of silver; analogously, in the state of dream, there is concerned that Nescience which has for its substrate Consciousness as defined or circumscribed by a certain modification of the internal organ—which modification originates within the body (independently of external objects) and is influenced by the defect of drowsiness and so on—; and as defined by that modification; this Nescience, being at the same time co-operated with by the mental impressions left behind by previous perceptions—which at the time are revived by the unseen principle—illusorily projects itself in the form of the world of things that are seen by the dreaming person.

[*Page 40*] "But," it is objected, "if Consciousness, or the Self, is the substrate of the dream-illusion, the consciousness of the dreamer should express itself in a form in which the Self and the dream-image superimposed upon it would appear grammatically co-ordinated—that is to say, just as in the waking state our thought expresses itself in forms such as 'this is silver,' 'this is a snake,' the dreamer's thought should assume forms such as 'I am blue' 'I am yellow;' and should not (as it actually does) present blue and yellow colour as belonging to some place outside the dreamer's mind. And as that place also is super-imposed on consciousness, it should likewise appear as something internal, in the form 'I am that place.' Perhaps you will say that this objection of ours does not go far enough and should properly be extended to the waking state also; since in that state also Consciousness is the sole substrate. Well, we reply, let this be done; we are quite ready to urge the point with regard to the waking state also."

To this we reply as follows: Do you (in urging that on our theory dream-consciousness should express itself in forms such as '*I* am blue') mean that those inward ideas (of blue colour, etc.,) should appear in co-ordination with (as co-existent with) the 'organ of egoity' (*Ahaṅkāra*) which is circumscribed by the body, or with Consciousness? The former alternative is impossible, since the organ of egoity can never be the substrate (of any cognition). And the latter alternative you need not advocate against us, since it represents our own view. For otherwise, the things super-imposed, which in themselves are of an absolutely non-intelligent nature,would not shine forth to thought at all. The I-consciousness (*aham-ullekha*) on the other hand, depends on the organ of Egoity (the *Ahaṅkāra*), and is not produced in *mere* consciousness. But, it is objected, things (real in the ordinary sense) such as jars and the like, also present themselves only in connection with consciousness, just as (so-called illusory) things, such as shell-silver! Well, we reply, we then have to assume that they also are super-imposed upon Consciousness. Nor must it be said that the manifestation to consciousness of jars and the like is produced by the operation of the so-called means of cognition (*pramāṇa*), and is not of the nature of the self (Consciousness). For the thing under discussion, *i.e.*, Consciousness as defined by an object, is in reality not different from the consciousness circumscribed by the *Ahaṅkāra*; since no difference manifests itself apart from reflexion on the respective limiting adjuncts; just as the universal ether is not in reality different from the ether circumscribed by a jar. We, therefore, viewing the distinction of the *within* and the *without* as relative to the body, must conceive the correct distinction of the Self and the Not-self—as expressed by the notions and terms 'I' and 'Not-I'—as depending on the limiting adjunct constituted by the *Ahaṅkāra*. That the one Consciousness should be alike present *within* and *without,* explains itself from its infinity. For Consciousness cannot, on the one hand, be of atomic extent (*aṇu*); for it is perceived to be present throughout the body. Nor, on the other hand, can that which does not consist of parts, be held, apart from a limiting adjunct, to be of intermediate size (intermediate, that is to say, between atomic size and infinite extension). The entire world of the waking state thus must be viewed as super-imposed on omnipresent Consciousness as its substrate, with the false appearance of reality; and it follows *a fortiori* that the world of the dreamer also rests on the same substrate.

"But," a new objection is raised, "scriptural texts such as* 'He is to meditate on name as Brahman,' enjoin the super-imposition of the cognition of Brahman on *name* and the like. How can, in these cases, the erroneous cognition (of *name* viewed as Brahman) be accounted for, considering that no defect is present in the cause of such cognitions?"** What is enjoined in statements of this kind, we reply, is not erroneous knowledge, but only a certain mental activity; for knowledge is something not depending on man's will and, therefore, cannot be enjoined. Nor may you say that since the representation to the mind of *e.g.*, some divinity, and the dismissal from the mind of *e.g.*, the image of a naked woman or the like, depend on the will of man, cognition in general is subject to will. What in the instances adduced really *is* under the control of man's will, is no more than, on the one hand, that concentration of mind which results in remembrance, and on the other hand that diversion of the mind towards other objects which results in the dismissal of a given idea. If the power of man extended further, he might, on his mere wish and without lengthy study, remember subjects which he has read once only as *e.g.*, the Veda; and on the other hand at once forget what he would be glad to forget, *e.g.*, the death of a son. Erroneous cognition hence cannot be enjoined, and the conclusion is that the definition of Error as that which is produced by the triad of causes holds good. Against the other definition according to which it is the 'presentation to consciousness of one thing in another thing' nobody has anything to say. For the adherent of the *akhyāti*-theory also in order to account for actual mixed empirical thought, must needs acknowledge a combined cognition or combined misconception. And other theorists, although disagreeing as to the nature, place and time of substrate and thing superimposed, are at one with us as to the general nature of erroneous cognition.

---

* Chhā. Upa. VII. i.5

** For the cause of these cognitions is Scripture.

XX

[Without this real substrate, on the other hand, no cognition of any kind would be possible; we therefore must reject the view of the Nihilist (*Shūnyavādin*) who holds that this apparent world has for its substrate, not Universal real Consciousness, but the absolute Void or Nought.]

However, the *Shūnyavādin* (*i.e.*, he who holds that there is nothing real, but that whatever appears to be is fundamentally void *i.e.*, unsubstantial, unreal) forms an exception. He rejects our view of error, for he will not allow the existence of a real substrate as implied in the 'in another thing' of our definition; and he maintains that erroneous cognitions, as of the shell-silver, arise on the void, owing to the power of Saṃvṛiti. I do not admit, he says, that Error is not possible apart from a real substrate. For according to your view also, the illusion called 'the tuft of hair'* and the illusion called 'the town of the Gandharvas' *are* of that nature, *i.e.*, have no real substrate. Nor also is it a fact that there can be no non-limited (*niravadhika*) negation (*i.e.*, negation which does not imply a positive assertion). For when the erroneous conception of a man, who in the dark mistakes a rope for a snake, is sublated by the assertion made by a competent and trustworthy person '(there is here) no snake,' this assertion is a case of pure negation.

All this is baseless reasoning, we reply. The so-called illusion called 'the tuft of hair' *has* a real substrate, *viz.*, the visual rays which, on the corner of the eye being pressed with the finger, become obstructed (and circumscribed); and Ether is the *real* substrate of the 'town of the Gandharvas.' Otherwise (*i.e.*, if erroneous cognitions were those which rest on the void) it would follow that your cognition of the void also is an error, and then your whole theory of the void could not be established. And if you should say that the erroneous cognition and the erroneous object of cognition have each other for substrate, you would implicate yourself in a vicious logical interdependence; for the substrate must in each case be viewed as something antecedent. And if you should say that cognitions and objects of cognition succeed one another in an endless series, analogous to the endless succession of seeds and plants,—we point

* On closing the eyes a person sometimes fancies that he *sees* tufts of hair, and looking at the evening sky, one notices fanciful shapes among the drifting clouds,—sometimes appearing like palaces, &c. This latter is called the 'town of the Gandharvas.' [Vide *Nyāyamañjari*, Vol. I, page 185.]

out that in the case of seeds and plants there is a permanent element which persists through the whole series, *viz.*, the earthy matter (of which seeds and plants consist), and that, in order to render the analogy fruitful, a similar persistent element would have to be acknowledged as maintaining itself in the series of cognitions and objects of cognition. Were no such element admitted and, instead, the action of the *unseen* principle (adṛiṣṭa) appealed to, we should have a clear case of the blind leading the blind. Nor further, do we allow that the affirmation made by a competent person '(there is here) no snake' is a *mere* negation; for it leads up to and is defined by the positive affirmation 'but a rope.' And even if the affirmation is made in the form 'There is nothing *there*, your fear is groundless' the place which is indicated by 'there' constitutes a positive limitation. And it also is evident that sublative enunciations such as 'the Pradhāna which some hold to be the material cause of the world does not exist' do *not* sublate *some* general cause of the world, for such a cause is admitted by all. And in other cases also—as of elephants, horses chariots etc., illusorily projected by the magical power (Māyā) of a magician—which you hold to be cases of error without any substrate and of subsequent limitless (mere) sublation (or negation), there at bottom *is* a substrate and a limit, *viz.*, witnessing Consciousness which brings about both error and sublation. Nor again may you say that that Consciousness itself is liable to sublation, for there is nothing that could effect such sublation, everything else but Consciousness being of a non-intelligent (jaḍa) nature. Nor may you say that the *Void* is the substrate (demanded by me for all erroneous cognition); for it is not the Void that persists (is uniformly present) in the things erroneously super-imposed. If the Void were so present, Consciousness, at the time of error, would deliver itself in the form '*the Void* is the silver,' not '*this* is silver' (which is the actual delivery of Consciousness at the time). And if you say—'that which we are conscious of as *this* is the Void'—our quarrel is about a mere name. Nor also can the 'Void' constitute the positive limit (*avadhi*) in sublative cognition; for we are not conscious of it in any such case. Or if we *are* conscious of it, it is nothing else but Consciousness that is denoted by the term 'the Void.' Nor again can the Void be that which is erroneously superimposed upon the substrate. For were it such, it would follow that the thing superimposed would not be immediately perceived (for it would be =0). But this is just what is acceptable to the Shūnyavādin whose aim it is to disestablish all presentations whatever to Consciousness! Then, we reply such disestablishment also would not present itself to Consciousness! But, the Nihilist resumes, you Vedāntins also hold the thing superimposed to be void! By no means, we reply. In order to establish (on the part of the thing superimposed) that character which is the counter-entity of subsequent sublation, (*i.e.*, is that which subsequently is sublated) we assume that the thing superimposed, as long as it presents itself to Consciousness, is different in character from that which *is* as well as that which *is not* (neither truly *is* nor is absolutely non-being). Subsequently to sublation it indeed is *void*: nobody will contest that what has perished is nought.

To those again who hold that the silver which is sublated (by the cognition 'there is no silver here') exists elsewhere (*i.e.* the Naiyāyikas who hold the *anyathā-khyāti* view) we address the question—'what is it that, as you allege, makes one apprehend the existence of silver elsewhere?—is it the sublative cognition itself, or the impossibility of sublation here (without reference to the existence of silver elsewhere)?'—The former alternative is inadmissible since perception does *not* deliver itself in the form 'This here is not silver, but there is silver elsewhere, or in the mind.' And the affirmation on the part of a competent person also intimates the absence of silver only, not the existence of silver in some other place. The second alternative again—*viz.*, the impossibility of sublation with regard to the present place,—is not established by any of the different theories in question. For the *Anyathākhyāti* theory assumes (as shown above) sublation of 'Connexion' and the *Ātmakhyāti* theory, sublation of the externality of the silver, without reference, in either case, to the existence of silver elsewhere. And on the *Akhyāti* view also what is negatived (by the sublative cognition) is the false cognition of silver in the shell, in this place only, without assuming the existence of silver elsewhere.

Nor also is such impossibility established by ordinary thought; for when a jar is broken *here*, we deny its existence without reference to the existence of jars in other places. Let it then be said that as in the case of the jar, so in the case of the shell-silver also there is existence of silver, dependent on difference of time! This also is inadmissible. In the case of the jar, no doubt, we judge 'formerly there was a jar here, now there is none'; but in the case of the silver our denial (of the existence of the silver) is not dependent on difference of time. Non-limited negation, in the case of the silver, is possible because there is voidness, *i.e.*, nought-ness, of real silver at all time. This nought-ness is intimated through the subsequent reflexion 'The silver *falsely* appeared to me': were there no such absolute nought-ness, the form of the reflexion would be 'real silver *was* presented to me.' That, at the time of the erroneous cognition, the man was conscious of silver is sufficiently accounted for by the mere false silver.

It is this false silver which, together with its material cause, (*i.e.*, Avidyā) is sublated by the cognition of the real nature of the shell. That the sublative cognition should establish the existence of silver elsewhere, cannot enter one's thought even. Although, therefore, subsequently to sublation, the superimposed thing is nought, the Nihilist also must admit that before sublation, a false thing presented itself to Consciousness as abiding in a real substrate.

XXI

[The Antagonist, while allowing that shell-silver and the like may be accounted for by the *adhyāsa* theory, refuses to admit an undue extension of this theory. The illusion of shell-silver can be traced to the presence of certain defects in the individual mind and organism, and the substrate of the superimposition; but when we come to consider the great fundamental superimpositions assumed by the Vedāntin—that of a material world upon the Universal Self, and the distinction of many individual Selfs—we miss all those conditions on which ordinary *adhyāsa* depends; for the Universal Self is free from all distinctions and defects whatsoever.]

[*Page 43*] A new objection is here raised against the view of the Vedāntin. You have, the opponent says, given two definitions of Error (*bhrama*); the *non-essential** or *accidental* definition according to which it is that which is produced by the three causes, *viz.*, the apprehension of a substrate, a mental impression and a defect (or group of defects); and the *essential* definition according to which it is what is produced through the presentation to Consciousness of a real substrate in a false character. Now we are willing to admit Error thus defined in the cases of 'this thing is silver,' 'there are two moons' and the like. But how will you account for the error which consists in the superimposition on the Self of the 'organ of egoity' and so forth (*i.e.*, the entire aggregate of things constituting the Non-self)? or the error of *difference* (*bheda*) which consists in viewing the one Self as differentiated into the individual soul (*jīva*) and Brahman, and the jīva again into many *jīvas*? To these cases your definitions do not

* In Indian Philosophy, there are two kinds of definitions of things: (1) the *Taṭastha-lakṣaṇa*—that which serves to distinguish the thing defined, though it does not subsist in it always; and (2) the *Svarūpa-lakṣaṇa*—which is inseparable from the defined thing.

apply. In the case of the shell-silver we have in the object the defect of similarity, (*i.e.*, the misleading similarity of the shell to the silver), in the sense-organ the defect of a morbid affection (*timira*—which dulls the discerning power of the eye); and in the seeing person the defect of desire (which renders him apt to mistake the shell for the silver he covets). In those cases, on the other hand, where the Self is concerned, the Self alone occupies the place of object, sense-organ and seeing subject, for everything else belongs to the category of that which is superimposed. But in the Self, which is without a second (is the only reality), and which is essentially free from all blemish, the mentioned defects cannot possibly exist—neither through itself nor through anything else. The unreal defect, termed 'Nescience,' may indeed somehow exist in the Self; but all the same the presentation to Consciousness of what is superimposed on it, *viz.*, the organ of egoity and the rest, cannot be *produced* by the triad of causes. For such presentation is of the nature of Consciousness (*chaitanya*), and that is eternal (and hence *non*-produced). The presentation to Consciousness of the shell-silver also no doubt at bottom is nothing but Consciousness; but Consciousness in this case has limiting adjuncts (the internal organ etc.), and hence may, in a metaphorical way, be spoken of as *originated*. In the cases under discussion on the other hand, the limiting adjuncts also fall under the category of the superimposed; and how then can that, which is without limiting adjuncts, be said to be produced? For these reasons the aforesaid *non-essential* definition of Error does not fit the cases under discussion. Nor does the so-called *essential* definition fit them. The Self no doubt is real, but it cannot be the substrate of a false appearance. In order that a thing may constitute the substrate of an error, it must be apprehended in its general character but non-apprehended in its specific character (as when the shell is apprehended as *this* but not as *shell*); how then can the Self to which the distinction of general and specific character does not apply constitute a substrate? But why should we not reason as follows: 'The Self is a substrate, because it is a real thing, just as a shell is'? Not so, our antagonist replies. The reason in that inference has proving power only if qualified by the condition of the real thing being one illumined by something else (*i.e.* being an object of consciousness, not Consciousness itself). Let us then, with the *Siddhānta-rahasya*, argue as follows: 'The Self is the substance of error, because it is of the nature of intelligence; like the consciousness defined by a shell.'

Not so, the opponent replies. The consciousness which is defined by the *this*-element and the shell-element is made up of parts, and hence capable of being apprehended in its general character, and *not* apprehended in its specific character; but this is not possible in the case of the Self which is not made up of parts. And if you should retort that the Self, although not made up of parts, does, like ether, not present itself to Consciousness in its entirety;—we reply that which is self-illumined must present itself to Consciousness to the whole extent of its being. And that the Self is self-illumined is proved by the scriptural text 'That person is self-illumined,. . . the Self only is its light.'*

But a question here presents itself with regard to the meaning of the word '*light*' in the Vedic passage just quoted. Does it denote light as a quality, or the substance which is the substrate of the quality? The former alternative is inadmissible, for it would imply that the Self which there is termed 'light' is a quality (and that, of course, is impossible). On the latter alternative, on the other hand, there is nothing to be objected to in what the text says about the Self being light, while at the same time cognition (jñāna,—which may be called *light* insofar as light is a mere quality) may be viewed as something originated (non-eternal; non-permanent). It hence follows that the Self does not necessarily manifest itself to Consciousness in its full extent at all times (but only when *cognition* of the Self arises). Not so, the Antagonist replies. The term 'light' denotes Consciousness pure and simple, and the scriptural text means to say neither more nor less than that the Self is of the nature of pure Consciousness. Otherwise the qualifications conveyed by the term 'self' (in *svayaṃ-jyotis* = self-light, self-luminous), and by the 'only' (*eva*) in the second clause, would be unmeaning. To explain in detail. Are those two qualifications meant to preclude what, on the analogy of the cognition of jars and the like things, would seem to be *prima facie* established with regard to the Self also, *viz.*, that the apprehending cognition is different from the apprehended object? or are they meant to preclude the difference (from the 'light,' the 'self') of that which produces cognition? On the former alternative the scriptural text is meant to establish the oneness of the object apprehended and that which apprehends *i.e.*, the Self and its cognition. But this would imply that the Self is a quality and cognition a substance! This does not matter; for the logical distinctions of 'quality,' 'substance' and the rest, which have been invented by the Logicians, do not avail to produce contradictions in the things themselves. The second alternative is inadmissible, because it implies an abandonment of what the scriptural text directly states, and an assumption of what it does not

* Bṛi. Upa. IV. 3. 6-9.

state. For you *assume* the meaning of the text to be 'it (the light) itself produces cognition; the Self only produces cognition; there is nothing else to produce it'; but what the text actually says is 'It is self-illumined; the Self only is light; there is no other light but that.' Nor can it be pleaded that as some factor producing knowledge is absolutely required, we must construe the words of the text as defining such a factor. For, on the Vedānta view, knowledge is eternal and hence requires no factor to produce it. But is not the following inference valid—'the cognition under discussion is *produced,* because it is cognition; like the cognition of jars and similar things?' It is not; since the Vedāntins do not allow the validity of the proving instances. According to them, in the cognition of a jar also the properly intellectual or conscious element (*sphuraṇa-aṁsha*) is nothing else but pure Consciousness; while that element which consists in the modification of the internal organ is (non-intellectual) Nescience to which the term 'knowledge' is applied in a figurative sense only. Nor is your inference a purely *negative* one (whereby it would be free from the necessity of proving instances); because there are other substrates also where your *probandum,* (the character of being a product) is present. According to the opinion of others (Non-Vedāntins) indeed, the cognition of a jar does constitute a valid proving instance; but even thus the conclusion cannot be established. For is this knowledge of which—as these people hold—the Self is the substrate, a substantial thing of which light (*prakāsha*) is a quality; or is it the *quality* 'light?' On the former view the substantial thing Knowledge being *light* (*jyotis*), owing to its having light for its quality, the character of *light* of which Scripture speaks cannot belong to the Self. On the second alternative a question arises—does knowledge, the quality, originate together with the substance in which it abides? or does Knowledge only originate? Clearly not the former; since the substance Self is eternal. Nor the latter; for we have to reason as follows: "the knowledge under discussion is not produced in its substance, apart from the origination of that substance itself; for it is of the nature of 'illumination' or 'light,' like the light of the flame of a lamp." In the latter case the light of the flame originates only together with the substance *flame,* not apart from the latter; the instance, therefore, has proving force. Nor can you quote against the above argumentation the instance of the mirror (in which it might be urged the quality 'light' or 'brightness' is produced, apart from the production of the substance, *i.e.,* the mirror); for in reality the quality *brightness,* exists already in the mirror : it is not produced, but only manifested, by the polishing of the mirror's surface. Nor again can the reason given by us be said to fail, in regard to the 'light of the internal organ' (which it may be said is *produced,* even though it is of the nature of 'illumination'). For according to the *Pariṇāmavāda* theory of Vedānta, what is produced as the 'cognition of a jar' is, not indeed the light of the internal organ, but the internal organ itself which is qualified by that light; and according to the *Ārambhavāda* theory also, 'light' is not a quality of the internal organ at all. The conclusion thus is that, since knowledge is not something that originates, and hence pre-supposes no originating factor, the scriptural text must mean that the Self only is light and that there is no other light beside it. It, of course, has further to be understood that what the text means by light is the light of intelligence, not non-sentient (physical) light; this is proved by other scriptural texts such as 'pre-eminent knowledge (*prajñāna*) is Brahman.'* We cannot allow that, in this latter passage, the term *prajñāna*) denotes the attribute or quality of being a knowing subject (*jñātri*); for this would be contrary to the received meaning of *jñāna* as denoting a *state*. But the term may, in agreement with the rules of grammar, be analysed as 'that the knowledge of which is pre-eminent,' and then it does denote a knowing subject! All the same, it is said in reply, it would be a needlessly complicated hypothesis to view the Self as something in which at each moment a new cognition springs up. But again, if this latter assumption is not made, the shining forth of the Self is not accounted for; and yet as a matter of fact the Self does shine forth constantly. We thus are led back to the tenet that the Self—the nature of which is self-illumined Consciousness—manifests itself in its full extent at all times.

But, it is objected, that in the Self a certain specific character is *not* apprehended, is a fact of immediate experience; for the Brahman-aspect of the Self is as a matter of fact not apprehended! Not so, the opponent replies. Brahman either is different or non-different from the individual soul. If it is different, the non-manifestation (of things), as also misconception, would have for their substrate Brahman itself, and not the individual soul. As for its being non-different, there can be no proof for it. The proof might be put forward in the following words—"Such scriptural texts as 'this Self is Brahman'** must refer to a single undifferentiated thing (Brahman),—because they express co-ordination, but do not speak of substances bearing the relation of cause and effect—like the sentence 'this is Devadatta'." But in that case, Brahman could never be *unknown*; because any manifestation of knowledge or

* Ait. Upa. V. 3.

** *Bṛi. Upa.* II. 5. 19.

cognition would be contrary to its nature, and also because there would be absolutely no difference between the 'substrate' and the 'object' (of knowledge). The conclusion, therefore, is that the internal organ, etc., (*i.e.*, the body, and the external world) cannot be viewed as merely superimposed upon the Self; for as we have shown, the Self cannot form the substrate of a superimposition, and is free from all imperfections.

XXII

[The answer to this is that to the Universal Self also a certain permanent 'imperfection' attaches itself, *viz.*, *Nescience*—which, although of an unreal nature, suffices to bring about those *Adhyāsas* of which the Self is the substrate.]

[*Page 45*] Against all this the Vedāntin now states his case as follows: That even in the Self—though it constitutes the only reality and in itself is free from all blemish—there is a certain defect, of an unreal nature, termed Nescience,—this is the direct teaching of Scripture as well as implied in the teaching of Scripture. 'As men who do not know the place, walk again and again over a gold treasure hidden in the earth and do not find it, thus do all these creatures go day after day into the Brahman-world and yet do not find it, for they are covered by the Untrue'*—this scriptural passage teaches that at the time of deep sleep the consciousness of Brahman does not present itself to all these living creatures because they are covered by unreal Nescience. And that this covering by Nescience is unreal in nature, and different from mere false knowledge and the impressions it leaves behind, as well as from mere absence of knowledge, and from Karman, we have shown in the section treating of 'concealment' (*āvaraṇa*; Sec., X, p. 55). Nescience in the second place is *implied* in the teaching of Scripture; for the declaration that the release from bondage is accomplished through the cognition of Brahman implies that, previous to such cognition, there is in Brahman a want of true knowledge which constitutes a defect and is the cause of *adhyāsa* and bondage. Nor must it be suspected that Nescience, because apprehended through the legitimate means of right knowledge, is on that account something *real*. For we avail ourselves of those means of proof only to refute those who maintain that there is no such thing as *inexplicable* Nescience. Nescience itself is directly proved by witnessing consciousness only.

---

* *Chhā. Upa.* VIII. 3. 2.

We now turn to the assertion, above made by our opponent, that the view of the individual soul and Brahman being non-different, implies that Brahman cannot be *not-known*. Do you mean, we ask, that non-knowledge (*ajñāna*), because pre-supposing a difference of substrate and object, cannot be related to one thing only? or, secondly, that being so related, it is in contradiction with the oneness of its substrate? or, thirdly, that it is contrary to reason that that the nature of which is *light* should be the substrate of *Avidyā*? or, fourthly, that Brahman being the substrate of *Avidyā* implies its not being omniscient?

The first alternative is untenable. For we argue in the following way: 'the *ajñāna* under discussion does not pre-suppose the difference of substrate and object; for it is not of the nature of action; just as jars and the like are (not of the nature of action);' or again, we may argue, 'the *ajñāna* under discussion abides in, and at the same time, obscures one and the same object; for it is of obscuring nature, as *e.g.*, the darkness abiding within the inner room of a house',—arguments which prove that one thing may stand in a two-fold relation, without this implying any difference. But our antagonist objects, *a-jñāna* (non-knowledge) actually pre-supposes a difference of substrate and object, just as knowledge does. For just as we say, '*I* (substrate) know *this* (object),' we also say '*I* do *not* know *this*.' Not so, we reply. This notion (of *ajñāna* also requiring difference of substrate and object) is due merely to the use of the term *ajñāna* which (also) denotes the mere absence of knowledge. The latter no doubt demands those two things (*viz.*, substrate and object). When, on the other hand, we employ the term *Māyā* (instead of *ajñāna* in the Vedāntic sense), the question does not arise. The case of analogous to that of our using, instead of the word *sthiti* (standing, rest), the term *a-gamana* (non-motion); while the former term requires no object, the latter immediately suggests the question 'who or what is not moving,' and in relation to what object?

The second alternative is disposed of by the argumentation— 'the *ajñāna* under discussion is not in conflict with the oneness of its substrate; for it has obscuring quality, just as darkness has (which obscures the very space in which it abides).'

Nor can be accept the third alternative. For, we ask, is the alleged irrationality,—*viz.*, of something the nature of which is light being the substrate of *ajñāna*—a matter of immediate consciousness or of inference? Not the former certainly; for that the witnessing consciousness which proves *ajñāna is* the substrate of *ajñāna* is immediately realised in the consciousness 'I am not-knowing.' As regards the latter alternative we should like to hear how you propose to formulate the inference. Is it as follows: 'the Self is not the substrate of *ajñāna* because it appears to consciousness, just like the jar placed before us?'—or as follows—'the Self is of a nature antagonistic to *ajñāna*; for it is of the nature of light; just as the modifications of the internal organ are?'—or as follows—'the Self is contradictorily opposed to all connexion with *ajñāna*; for it is self-luminous; just as states of consciousness are in the opinion of the followers of Prabhākara?' The first alternative is inadmissible, as it is contradicted by (universally accepted) facts; inasmuch as others (*i.e.*, non-Vedāntins) also, according to whom the Self is presented to consciousness by a cognition which originates (is non-eternal), have to acknowledge that the Self *is* the substrate of *ajñāna*; for otherwise omniscience of the Self would result at the moment when the Self is presented to consciousness. The second inference must be rejected; for it goes astray in the case of that act of consciousness which presents *ajñāna*. Nor may it be said that the existence of such an act is just what is not proved; for others also (who do not hold the Vedāntic view of *ajñāna*) could not speak of *ajñāna*—as acknowledged by them—if there were no consciousness of such *ajñāna*. The third inference also is invalid, because there really are no instances to prove it; the so-called self-luminous states of consciousness (which the Prābhākaras bring forward) are either more nor less than just the Self.

Nor finally can we admit the fourth of the original alternatives, (on page 112)—*viz.*, that from the Self being the substrate of *ajñāna* it would follow that Brahman is not omniscient. Although the thing reflected in the mirror and the reflected image are in reality one, yet the indistinctness of outline, which owing to the mirror's dimness superimposes itself on the image, in no way detracts from the distinctness of the object reflected. Analogously we argue that although the individual Self is the substrate of *Avidyā*, the omniscience of Brahman is not thereby impaired. Moreover, if in order to disprove *Avidyā* you bring forward either the oneness of Brahman and the individual soul, or Brahman's self-luminousness, or its omniscience,—each of these facts will merely disprove that *Avidyā* consists in the absence of apprehension, and on the other hand prove that it is a positive entity. For if there were no obscuring factor of a positive nature, it could not be explained why such attributes as omniscience and the like, and Brahman to which they belong, do not appear to consciousness. Mere absence of apprehension might account for the fact that, among the things different from the individual soul, jars and similar things—which are non-intelligent and not all-knowing—should not appear to consciousness; but not for the fact that Brahman which is of an altogether contrary nature does not so appear.

XXIII

[The chief of these *adhyāsas* is the distinction between Brahman and the individual soul (*jīva*). Nescience at first produces this fictitious distinction and then, somehow clinging more pronouncedly to the individual soul than to the Universal Self, produces for the former the whole phenomenon of a multiple world.]

[*Page 47*] But, an objection is raised, if it be held that the individual Self is the substrate of *Avidyā* while Brahman is omniscient, it follows that the individual Self and Brahman are different entities! Is, we ask in reply, that resulting difference real or the effect of *Avidyā*? And, on the former view, does the difference result from a limitation due to the internal organ; or from a *redundancy* or *excess* (*atireka*) inhering in the very nature of the Self;* or from the relation of whole and parts inhering in the nature of the Self?

The first alternative is inadmissible; since the internal organ which is a thing that has a beginning cannot determine a distinction which has existed from all eternity. That the internal organ is not a thing without a beginning is proved by its non-existence in deep sleep and similar states. "But we hold that it *does* exist in deep sleep also, although indeed in a subtle form only!" What, we ask, do you understand by this existence in a subtle form? Does the internal organ pass over into a condition in which it does not consist of parts? or do its parts decrease in number only? or does it then exist in its causal condition only? or does there remain nothing of it but an impression (*saṃskāra*)? The first alternative is impossible; for that a thing consisting of parts should pass into the condition of having no parts would mean nothing else but that it perishes utterly. Nor can the second alternative be accepted; as in that case, that *whole* (compounded of parts) left after the decrease of a number of parts, being deprived of the character of an *effect* (as during *suṣupti* there is no active efficient cause for it), it could not cease to exist at any time (and thus this suitable form should continue also after the *suṣupti*, in the waking state); and if, in order to avoid this difficulty, the *whole of reduced parts* were regarded as the *effect of the whole with all its parts,* then its operations during *suṣupti* would have to be exactly like those during the *waking* state. On the third

* *i.e.* from the fact of the Self possessing qualities over and above the 'pure consciousness' of Brahman.

alternative, do you mean that the internal organ, at the time of deep sleep, exists in its causal condition only, or *also* as an effect? If the former, it ceases to exist at all. If the latter, the entire empirical world which is present to the waking consciousness should be present to the sleeping soul also. Nor finally is the fourth alternative possible. For since a mere *impression* cannot be the material cause of limitation, the soul would in deep sleep be altogether non-limited and hence attain to final release.

"Let us then assume that, that which is limited (lit. 'cut off') is the material cause of limitation, just as in the case of the cutting of wood it is the wood, which is the material cause of the 'cutting;' while the internal organ is merely the efficient (operative) cause; just as the axe is in the act of cutting!"

In this way, we reply, the limitation could not be accomplished at all. For consciousness not being made up of parts cannot, like wood, really constitute the material substrate of any division. According to us, Vedāntins, it is Nescience only which is the material cause of all limitation and determination. Division also really belongs to *Avidyā* and is only falsely superimposed upon the Self. The internal organ also—which is a product of Nescience—limits and determines the Self through Nescience only, not directly. On this our view nothing remains unexplained.

Nor can we accept the second alternative,—*viz.*, of the distinction of Brahman and individual soul being due to *redundancy* or *excess* (*atireka*). For since that distinction may be accounted for on the basis of Nescience which is something actually given, there is no occasion for the assumption of a *redundancy* (*atireka*). Nor may you object that since Nescience must be defined as that which belongs to the individual soul and has Brahman for its object, it rests itself on the distinction of the two and hence cannot be the cause of the distinction. For we observe that, even though the conception of a certain thing being the '*pratiyogin*' (the object of distinction, or negation), is due to its being actually so distinct, yet what causes that distinction is that same character of '*pratiyogin.*' Were it not so, your assumption of an *atireka* also would be impossible, for that *atireka* means something which distinguishes Brahman from the individual soul, and hence presupposes the distinction of the two; and how then could it be the cause of that same distinction? Moreover, we have proved above already that Nescience does not demand difference of substrate and object.

Nor finally is the third alternative admissible. For that which is absolutely without parts cannot by itself enter into the condition of a whole consisting of parts.

There thus remains the second main alternative only,—*viz.*, that the distinction of Brahman and the individual soul is due to nothing else but Nescience; and this, of course, is just the view we Vedāntins hold. This Nescience indeed is really connected with pure Consciousness, and in this way brings about the division between Brahman and the individual soul; yet it may be viewed as somehow disregarding Brahman and leaning towards the individual soul, and thus to produce the phenomenal world; just as a mirror of other reflecting surface which really has a connexion with the face only (*i.e.*, the real face), after having once brought about the distinction of face and reflected face, produces effects (such as dimness of outline and colour) in the reflected face only. But consider the judgment, '*I* am not knowing'—does not Nescience therein present itself as abiding in the Self as particularized by the *ahaṅkāra* (*i.e.*, the organ of egoity or self-consciousness), and not in pure (universal non-personal) Consciousness? Not so, we reply. Of a red hot lump of iron we say 'the iron burns,' *i.e.*, the iron and the quality of burning present themselves to our mind in co-ordination, since both are connected with the fire (which really is what burns); in the same way Nescience and the internal organ present themselves to our mind as co-ordinated (as they do in the judgment '*I* do not know'), because they are both connected with one and the same Self, and because the internal organ is the real substrate of Nescience. Otherwise our reasoning would move in a vicious circle—'the internal organ is due to the connexion of the Self with Nescience' and 'the Self is connected with Nescience, insofar as it (the Self) is particularized by the internal organ.' Nor can it be said that the Self is never observed to be connected with Nescience—apart from the internal organ; for such connexion is actually admitted to exist in the state of deep sleep (in which the internal organ ceases to exist). "But, since Consciousness, which in its very nature is unrelated (*asaṅga*), cannot be the substrate of Nescience, we must needs assume that that substrate is to be found in something particularized!" Well, what could that 'something particularized' be but the internal organ, Consciousness and the connexion of the two. So in the end Consciousness again will be the substrate! "But the 'something particularized' may be a thing different from those just mentioned!" Then, we reply, it could be only something of a non-intelligent (*jaḍa*) nature; and such a thing cannot be the substrate of Nescience. For if it were such, it would follow that also erroneous cognition, true cognition and release—which necessarily have the same substrate as Nescience—abide in what is non-intelligent, unconscious! (and this of course is absurd). Nor, we remark finally, is there any contradiction implied in our holding that Consciousness is *in reality* absolutely non-related, and at the same time *fictitiously* the substrate of Nescience. The final conclusion then is that Nescience has for its substrate pure Consciousness but as it has a learning towards the individual Self, is spoken of as having the latter for its substrate.

XXIV

[The theory, held by some Neo-Vedāntins, that Nescience abides not in the Self, but in the internal organ, cannot be accepted. If the Self were free from Nescience, it would be permanently omniscient; for its consciousness could not be limited by Nescience not abiding in itself. Nescience is without beginning, and hence the cause of the beginningless world-process. The power of Nescience, and its relation to the self, are not indeed matters to be rationally accounted for; to be non-rational is just the characteristic feature of Nescience.]

Bhāskara* indeed teaches that it is the internal organ that is the substrate of Nescience. But in that case the Self would be *permanently* omniscient, and this is contradicted by consciousness. He, on the other hand, who holds the Self not to be omniscient, must admit that there inheres in the Self Nescience expressing itself in the form 'now and then the Self does not know this or that.' Let us then say that while non-cognition (*i.e.*, absence of cognition) and false cognition abide in the Self, *ajñāna* conceived as a *positive* entity abides in the internal organ! This also will not avail. For if we understand by '*ajñāna*' (non-knowledge), that which is other than knowledge, even such diseases of the eye as the '*kācha*' (an affection of the optic nerve causing dimness of vision) and '*kāmala*' (jaundice) would have to be regarded as '*ajñāna*.' Let us then understand by *ajñāna* that which is contradictorily opposed to knowledge! This also will not avail. For to knowledge which admittedly resides in the Self, there cannot be contradictorily opposed a non-

* Author of the *Bhāskarabhāṣya* on the *Brāhmasūtras*; published in the Chaukhambhā Sanskrit Series, Benares.

knowledge residing in the internal organ. Knowledge of some object that resides in Devadatta does not put an end to non-knowledge, regarding the same object, which resides in Yajñadatta! But although we admit that in other cases there can be no real opposition between knowledge and non-knowledge if abiding in different substrates, yet the *ajñāna* abiding in the instrument of knowledge may be in opposition to the knowledge abiding in the knowing subject! Not so, we reply. When Devadatta makes the inference,—'This Yajñadatta does not discern the cause of the resolution (in general Nescience) of his internal organ; owing to that internal organ being resolved in deep sleep,'—this cognition on the part of Devadatta does not put an end to the *ajñāna* abiding in the internal organ of the sleeping Yajñadatta, although that organ is the instrument in the inferene made by Devadatta. But an end is put to the *ajñāna* abiding in the internal organ of the knowing agent (Devadatta)! This reasoning also, we reply, does not avail; for there is no proof to show that *ajñāna* abides in the internal organ at all! There is such proof. For we may argue—'the *ajñāna* under discussion abides in the internal organ; since it is a defect giving rise to error; just like the affection of the eye called *kāçhaka*.' Then, we reply, the *ajñāna* should reside in the eye and the other sense-organs! But these, being things that have a beginning, cannot be abodes of the beginningless *ajñāna*! The internal organ also, we reply, has a beginning. "But, as you hold the *satkārya*-view, the internal organ cannot be conceived as having a beginning!"*

This reasoning holds good with regard to the eye and the other sense-organs also! And the conclusion thus is that Nescience does *not* reside in the internal organ, but in the Self. This view is thus set forth, in answer to an objection, by Vishvarūpāchārya:—

Q.'But how does Nescience approach the Self that is self-illumined, absolutely unchanging, the sole reality?'

*A.*As darkness approaches the sun with his thousand rays!'

'Nescience cannot be denied! For every one is conscious of it; it does not exist apart from the Self; nor does the Self exist apart from it.'

And that this Nescience is the cause of the distinction of Brahman and the individual soul, the (Viṣṇu) Purāṇa declares—

---

* The '*Satkārya* view' is that every effect that is brought about by a cause is *sat*, ever existent; even before it is *produced*, it exists in its cause, in a latent form; and all that the so-called 'production' does is to render *manifest* the effect which had hitherto existed only in an *unmanifested* state in the cause. According to this view then, nothing, whether a cause or effect, can be said to have a beginning. This is the theory of 'Cause and Effect' accepted by the Saṅkhya and the Vedāntin. (Vide *Saṅkhyakārikā*, 9 and Brahmasūtrā II-i—14.)

'When *ajñāna*, which gives rise to distinction, has utterly perished, what then will bring about the unreal distinction of the individual Self and Brahman?'

As Nescience is eternal, there is nothing irrational in our viewing it as the cause of a beginningless distinction. And that Nescience is without beginning *Smṛiti* expressly declares*—'know *Prakṛiti* and the soul to be both without a beginning.' That *Prakṛiti* is the same as *Māyā* follows from the scriptural text—'know *Prakṛiti* to be *Māyā*.'** And the identity of *Māyā* and *Avidyā* we have already set forth.

But an objection is raised, admitting that the self-illumined Self is the *substrate* of Nescience, it cannot be its *object*; for it everlastingly reveals itself to consciousness. A person to whose consciousness a jar clearly presents itself, does not express himself as if the jar were an object of *ajñāna*, and say 'I do not cognize the jar.' Nor may you plead against this that, forms of expression, such as 'I do not know (understand) the matter stated by you,' show that we do speak even of such things as are present to consciousness as being objects of *ajñāna* in so far as defining it; for in the instance quoted the object of *ajñāna* is (not the matter stated in itself) but only some special aspect of the matter which is not comprehended. If it be argued that that which is not comprehended cannot rightly be regarded as *defining* (or differentiating) anything,—our reply is that, in that case, it is for you to supply us with an explanation of such well-known instances as—'I do not understand the matter stated by you.'

Our answer to the above objection is that it is only such matter as is illumined (made cognizable) by a valid means of knowledge that cannot be an object of *ajñāna*; since it is the very nature and function of those means of knowledge to put an end to *ajñāna*. On the other hand, there is not any objection to the view that something known by immediate intuition, whether it be a jar and the like or Consciousness, is the object of *ajñāna*. For, as we have explained before, witnessing consciousness does not put an end to *ajñāna*; it rather is that which establishes or proves it. By what other means, indeed, could *ajñāna* be proved or established, considering that it is contradicted and opposed by all means of knowledge and all rational arguments? It has been said—

'This error, devoid of foundation, in conflict with all logical arguments, can stand rational enquiry no more than darkness can stand the light of the sun.'

---

* Bhag. Gi. XIII—19.
** Shevetā Upa. I—10.

And this incapability of standing rational enquiry indeed is the characteristic feature and beauty of *Avidyā*. This also has been declared, in the following stanza:

'That it cannot stand rational enquiry,—it is just this which constitutes the characteristic feature of *Avidyā;* were it not so, *Avidyā* would be a reality.'

Nor must it be imagined that *Avidyā,* the beauty of which consists in its evading all rational enquiry, has no power of obscuring the Self; for on this point also we have the following authoritative saying:

'Nothing truly may surpass the audacity (or impudence) of *Avidyā*; in contempt of all valid means of knowledge and all reality, it attaches itself to the highest Self!'

Nor can those who put their whole trust in ratiocination (which contradicts *Avidyā*) set aside intuitive knowledge; for ratiocination itself rests on intuitive knowledge, and without it, it would have no foundation. And intuitive cognition manifests to us the fact that, although the soul is self-luminous, its radical difference and separation from the body and the rest is obscured by *ajñāna*.

XXV

[That the Self is the substrate of Error is proved by our ordinary 'I-consciousness,' which by its very nature is a composite cognition in which a *real* element (the Self) and an *unreal* one (the body) are confounded.—The Self, though nothing but pure consciousness and free from all diversity, thus has a diversity of aspects superimposed upon itself, owing to false conceit; and to this superimposition both the aforesaid definitions of *adhyāsa* are applicable.]

But, it is objected, also in that consciousness of the Self which expresses itself in the word 'I' we are conscious of the distinction of the Self from the body and the rest,—this distinction being of the nature of a positive entity (and as such cognisable by direct intuition). Nor may you say that this distinction is again obscured by the false conceit of the Self being identical with the body, which expresses itself in the judgment 'I am a man.' For since this notion of oneness can be explained as being of a metaphorical character—so as not come into real conflict with the consciousness of difference—, there is no occasion to view it as *false* and thus contradicting the consciousness of difference. If the I-consciousness, on account of the *I* presenting itself in co-ordination with the body, did not imply the apprehension of the Self as something different from the body, this separation could not be established at all; for there would be no valid means of knowing it, scriptural teaching and inference themselves losing their authoritative power if in conflict with the meaning of the I-consciousness. Nor may it be said that there is no such conflict, since, like the cognition of a double moon and the like, the *I*-consciousness is something false (unreal). For this would implicate us in circular reasoning—'the I-consciousness is false if scripture and inference are held to be authoritative,' and—'if the I-consciousness is false, scripture and inference are authoritative.' The case of the cognition of a double moon and the like really is not analogous. Cognitions of this latter kind are proved to be false, at once, previously to any formal consideration of the relative strength of the several means of knowledge concerned in each case. In the case under discussion, on the other hand, the relative strength of the means of cognition would have to be considered, and by reason of the non-appearance of any contrary cognition (that could sublate it), the I-consciousness would show itself to be the stronger; and hence scriptural teaching and inference which are in conflict with that consciousness would not avail to prove the difference of the Self from the body. As, therefore, the mere I-consciousness does establish the difference of the Self from the body, we hold that the thought which expresses itself in the judgment 'I am a man' is of a metaphorical character (and is *not* false).

All this, we reply, is devoid of foundation. For, we ask,— do you hold that the I-consciousness has for its object a Self different from the body, on the ground that such difference actually exists? or on the ground that it appears to consciousness? The former is not a tenable view; since it is not the actual existence of difference that causes us to judge that the judgment of non-difference is a merely metaphorical one. For as a matter of fact, it is the mere *consciousness* of difference that gives to judgments such as 'Devadatta is a lion (*i.e.*, as brave as a lion)' their metaphorical character. Were it otherwise (*i.e.*, if '*gauṇatva*' depended on the reality of the difference) also judgments such as 'this (shell) is silver, would have to be classed as 'metaphorical,' not as *erroneous*, since in those cases there exists actual difference. As to the second alternative we ask—does the I-consciousness manifest the difference of the Self from the body, *before* reflexion (*vichāra*) has taken place, or after that? The first alternative is inadmissible because it would imply the uselessness of philosophical reflexion. And the second alternative is in admissible; because (in that case) what manifests the difference would be the *reflexion* itself (and not the I-consciousness); as what reflexion does is to distinguish between what is *proved* (established) and what is *not proved*. But by *reflexion* we understand a mental review and examination of arguments (*yukti*); and arguments do not by themselves produce knowledge, but only in so far as co-operating with one of the recognised means of knowledge. In the case under discussion arguments enable us to discriminate the fact that the I-consciousness which is the true means of knowledge—has for its object the Self so far as distinct from the body. Not so, we reply. Is it, we ask, the function of arguments to determine the sphere of a given means of knowledge as comprising certain objects only—'so much only is to be apprehended by thee, neither more nor less!'? Or does their function consist in removing eventual obstacles that may beset the operation of the means of knowledge which has already begun to apprehend a certain object given to it by its own nature? The former alternative cannot be accepted; for—since the minds of men are of the most diverse kind and hence their reasonings follow no definite law—it would imply that there is no fixed rule as to what objects fall within the sphere of each means of knowledge. But this consequence is just what it ought to be; for if the means of knowledge had their fixed several objects, there could be no diversity of opinion between the different philosophical schools! Not so, we reply. Wherever there is a disputed matter, every one clings to his own view as authoritative, and not to any other view. If there was no fixed law as to the objects of the several means of knowledge, every one would have to treat the views of others also as authoritative. Not even many strong arguments combined avail to determine the sphere and scope of a means of knowledge. A thousand arguments even, devised by minds fortified by the knowledge of all *shāstras,* would be unavailing to constitute sound as the object of the eye, and to break the connexion between the eye and colour. With regard to the second alternative we ask the following question—what constitutes the self-established object of the I-consciousness? Is it the distinction of the Self from the body and whatever else is contrary to the Self? or the Self only? From the former alternative it would follow that also materialists and ordinary (non-thinking) people would distinguish between Self and body (which as a matter of fact they do not do). And if against this you urge that in the case of those people discrimination does not emerge because they fail to remove the obstacles to true knowledge by means of philosophic arguments,—we reply that *you* who do understand the theory of those matters could not on any account ever formulate the judgment '*I* am distinct from the body' and so on; for as (on the alternative in question) the mere term *I* would by itself express that distinction, it would be an idle tautology to form the complete judgment 'I am different from the body.' If, on the other hand, the I-consciousness (does not by itself imply the distinction of Self and body but) has for its object the Self only,—well then, arguments may possibly do so much as to remove obstacles in the way of the Self being apprehended in the *I*-consciousness, but they will *not* avail to get rid of what immediate consciousness suggests, *viz.*, that the body also is the object of the *I*-consciousness. But on this view the judgment 'I am a man' does neither more nor less than apprehend its own, appropriate, object, and hence cannot be erroneous! Not so, we reply. Our tenet is—not that such cognitions as apprehend their own object are valid, and such as do not apprehend their objects are invalid,—but that a cognition is valid if it apprehends what is true (real), and invalid if it apprehends the real and unreal together. Now the *I-consciousness* confounds a real element, *viz.*, the Self, and an unreal one, *viz.*, the body, and apprehends this composite object; it, therefore, must be classed as *error*. Nor must it be said that no error is possible with regard to the Self which is self-luminous and admits of no distinction of parts, since in the case of a being of this kind it is impossible that some part should not be apprehended (and hence error arises). Consider the case of letters. Letters such as *a, i,* etc., are without parts, and are on each occasion apprehended in their totality; all the same there are superimposed upon them certain characters, such as *length* and *shortness,* which really belong to the *letter-sound.* Length and shortness are not attributes of the letters, as appears from the fact each letter (whether short or long) is always recognised as the same 'this is the letter *a,*' etc.; all the same even those who are aware of this fundamental identity do not ordinarily give their mind to the arguments proving it, and hence are under the erroneous impression of the letter itself being short or long. Analogously the identity of the Self with the body which is vouched for by the immediate consciousness of all human beings, learned men no less than villagers and children, remains practically unrefuted unless the teaching of scripture produce an insight into the identity of the Self with Brahman, and thus constitutes a universal unavoidable error. The view that the judgment 'I am a man' is a merely metaphorical one will be refuted in our comments on Sūtra 4.

The conclusion from what precedes is as follows: The Self indeed is self-luminous and devoid of parts, but a diversity of aspect is introduced into it thereby that it is obscured by false conceit and hence *not* apprehended in its Brahman-aspect; owing to this diversity of aspect there arises the possibility of its being apprehended in its general nature only while special features remain non-apprehended, and hence there is nothing irrational in our viewing it as the substrate of error. We, therefore, can in this case also give the *essential* definition of *adhyāsa*,—*viz.*, that 'it is the presentation to consciousness of the connexion of an unreal thing with a real substrate,' which thus holds good with regard to the great (cosmic) *adhyāsa* also which has the universal Self for its substrate. And it is equally evident that the *secondary* or *accidental* definition also holds good ('*adhyāsa* is that which is produced by the triad of causes'); for it has been shown that to the Self—which must be viewed as by itself occupying the place of the triad—*object, knowing subject* and *instrument*—there clings the great imperfection called *Nescience*; inasmuch as it is the intelligence of the Self itself which cognises (is the means of cognising) the substrate (of error). And during the beginningless cosmic process (*saṁsāra*) an endless chain of previous *adhyāsas* may be postulated without any difficulty. Although in the case under discussion, owing to the oneness of the substrate and that which is superimposed upon it, illuminating consciousness is not really originated, yet there is nothing wrong in viewing it as originated *in a certain aspect*,—*viz.*, insofar as it is affected by a particular object. We further remark that, applying the previous definition of *adhyāsa* to the present case, we have to understand by the 'similarity (of *adhyāsa*) to remembrance' the circumstance of its being produced by the mentioned triad of causes. And the 'presentation to consciousness of one thing as constituting the self of another' we have to explain as meaning the presentation of the Real mixed up with the False. We thus have fully proved that to the erroneous identification of the internal organ, body and the rest with the Self, and to the erroneous view of difference as depending on conditioning adjuncts, the general definitions of *adhyāsa*, previously given, may be applied.

[*Page 53*]—But a further difficulty here presents itself. How is it *possible* that anything should be superimposed upon the inward Self (*Pratyagātman*)? We observe that in all recognised cases of superimposition the substrate is an object of the same kind of sense-perception as the thing superimposed. But this is not so in the case of the Self into the idea of which nothing whatever of *objectivity* enters.

What alone, we reply, is required for *adhyāsa* is that the substrate and the thing superimposed should present themselves to consciousness as fused in one act of cognition. It is not required that the substrate should be an object; for we cannot point to any negative concomitance proving this (*i.e.*, it is not a rule that the absence of objectivity invariably goes together with the absence of *adhyāsa*). Now in the case under consideration, (*viz.*, of superimposition on the Self) there *is* one cognition which presents a fusion of the Self and the Not-self *viz.*, the cognition of the *I*. Of this cognition the Self indeed is not the object, neither in part, nor in its totality; for the Self is without parts, and is essentially not an object. But what presents itself in the form of the Ego-consciousness is the internal organ which is superimposed upon the Self and impregnated with the reflection of the Self—comparable to a mirror which is impregnated with the reflection of the universal ether. This ego-*adhyāsa* possesses a double aspect, just as the *adhyāsa* '*this* thing before me is *silver*.' For as in the judgment 'the iron burns,' two elements are presented to consciousness,—*viz.*, fire possessing burning quality, and iron; thus also in the judgment 'I perceive' or 'I know,' two elements are presented,—*viz.*, a Self that possesses perceiving or knowing quality and an internal organ. That element of which we are conscious as liable to pain and change, as non-intelligent and distinguished from other objective existences such as the sense-organs, their objects and so on, is the internal organ. That element, on the other hand, of which we are conscious as the abode of delight, as absolutely unchanging, as a mere witness or spectator, unaffected by what he witnesses, and as consciousness constantly present to all objective existences—sense-organs, their objects and so on—is the Self. The Ego-consciousness thus contains an objective (*idam*) and a non-objective (*an-idam*) element.

XXVI

[The view of the composite character of the *I* is not indeed admitted by the Prābhākara who holds that the *I* is nothing else but the cognizing Self, free from any objective element; and that every act of cognition reveals the *I* or Self to be the *substrate* of cognition. We may accept as valid the criticisms to which the Prābhākara, on the basis of this his view, subjects the theories of the Self, and the ways in which it is known, held by the Sānkhyas, the Naiyāyikas, the Sautrāntikas, the Vijñānavādins, and the Bhāṭṭas respectively.]

Now this view of the nature of the Ego the followers of Prabhākara refuse to accept. For, they maintain, the self-luminous cognition 'I know the jar' manifests the jar as the object and the Self as the substrate (subject) of cognition. What appears as the *I* is the Self only; the *I* contains no objective element whatever. Nor is there any force in the alleged analogy,—*viz.*, that, as in the cognition 'the iron burns' the quality of burning is something different from the iron, so in the cognition 'I know' the knowing subject is something 'different from the Ego. For, as to the former case, we sometimes observe the two elements in separation—on the one hand, the cold lump of iron, and on the other hand, apart from the iron, fire; but the Ego and the knowing subject are never cognised apart from each other. The Ego thus is neither more nor less than the Self; of which we are immediately conscious as the substrate (subject) of cognition.

[*Page 54*] The Sāṅkhya indeed (denying this immediate consciousness of the Self) claims to arrive at the existence of the Self by means of the following inference: 'the reflexion of consciousness in the non-intelligent internal organ presupposes a thing which is reflected, of a similar nature; for it is a reflexion, like the reflexion of a face in a mirror.' And others also hold the theory, in various forms, of the Self being known through inference only. But all these theories, the Prābhākara holds, are in conflict with the evident fact that in the Ego-consciousness the Self is directly presented. The different forms of inference, however, have a use insofar as they may convince others (materialists and the like) of the existence of the Self.

Nor is there, the Prābhākara continues, any truth in the doctrine of the Logicians who maintain that the Self is the object of internal perception (the instrument of which is the *manas*); for there is nothing to prove that view. The presence and absence of the *manas* constitutes a necessary causal condition with regard to the cognition of objects (which are known when the *manas* functions, and not known when it does not function). And as the Self is proved through the relation of its being the abode of this cognition of objects (*i.e.*, as the Self, in each cognition of objects, at once presents itself immediately as the abode of that cognition), it is needless to assume another cognition (*i.e.*, the abovementioned *mānasa pratyakṣā*.) through which the Self should be known.

Let us then, it might here be said, accept the view of the followers of Bhaṭṭa (Kumārila.) They argue as follows: The Self is an object of cognition, since it is directly perceived; as a jar is. That (on this view) the Self is both the object of knowledge and the knowing subject, implies no contradiction; for we distinguish in the Self a substantial (*dravya*) element which is the object of cognition, and a conscious (*bodha*) element which is the subject of cognition. Nor does any contradiction arise here on the ground that the object of an action is the main factor (*pradhāna*) and the agent a mere secondary factor (*guṇa*) (and that one and the same thing cannot be *pradhāna* and *guṇa* as well). For we may view that element in the Self which is object as *pradhāna*, and that element which is subject of cognition as *guṇa*. This view also the *Prābhākara* rejoins, is untenable. For what you call the *substantial* element in the Self is non-intelligent, and hence cannot be a *Self* at all. There thus remains the *conscious* element only; and if you view this as an object of cognition, you cannot rid your view of the two contradictions stated. Nor can it be said that that conscious element is capable of undergoing a change so as to have simultaneously the character of object and of subject of knowledge; for it is not made up of parts (and hence cannot undergo any change). And if, to escape from this difficulty, it were assumed somehow to undergo changes, like the fundamental matter (*pradhāna*) of the Sāṅkhyas, the cognising element would either not be apprehended as self-luminous and the abode of knowledge, and this would be contradictory to the Bhāṭṭa view of the cognising agent; or it would be apprehended as the object (*viṣaya*) of cognition; and this would imply that it is a Not-self, like the jar. It, therefore, must be held (and this leads us back to the Prābhākara view) that the Self is immediately known (*pratyaksa*) as the substrate of cognition, while jars and the like are immediately known as objects of cognition.

The Sautrāntika (Bauddha) will not allow this latter point,—*viz.*, jars and the like being immediately perceived; but proposes the following inference: 'the presentation to consciousness, in the several acts of cognition, of the images (*pratibimba*) of objects has for its antecedent original things (*bimba*) of the same kind, for it is a presentation of something in something else, just like the presentation of the face in the mirror.' But him we meet in the following way: In this cognitional act of inference, the original things either appear to consciousness directly, apart from the images, or they do not. On the former alternative, your *probans* would fail in this very case (this being a case of presentation of something in something else, and yet appearing directly, apart from the image). On the second alternative, since the thing to be established,—*i.e.*, that the antecedent of the images is the real objects,—does not present itself to consciousness, the inferential cognition could not arise at all (the *appearing to consciousness* being non-existent, and this being the *subject* of your inference). We, therefore, maintain it as an undeniable fact that there is an *immediate consciousness* of objects (not an *inference* of them.)

Nor can we accept the view of the Vijñānavādin who holds that things are directly known only on account of their being (not external things, but) ideas. For it is a fact that the externality of things—which is *not* of the nature of an idea—is also immediately known. If this 'externality' were of the nature of *idea,* then its cognition would not be as liable to sublation as the cognition of silver in a shell [as according to the Vijñānavādin, it is only things other than *ideas* that are unreal, and as such liable to sublation, like the wrong cognition of silver].

We (the Prābhākaras) therefore hold that whatever *is* known—such as jars and the like—is immediately perceived, because it is an object. On the other hand, the cognition (*pramiti*) is not perceived, because it is (not an object but) self-luminous.

[*Page 55*] We, on this occasion, must declare against the views held by the Logicians and the Bhāṭṭas, respectively, as to the nature of knowledge (*pramiti*). The former teach that knowledge—inhering through the co-called *samavāya* relation in the Self which through conjunction (*saṁyoga*) is connected with the internal organ (the *manas*)—is itself immediately cognized (*pratyakṣa*) through another cognition—the relation between the two being the one of '*Saṃyukta-samavāya.*' The Bhāṭṭas on the other hand hold cognition to be something that abides in the object known—and as such is denoted by the technical term *prākaṭya* (manifested-ness) and itself is the object of another cognition. But both these theories are untenable. For the view that one cognition is the object of another cognition would imply that two moments of time exist together.

To this the Logician might rejoin: 'You also accept the simultaneous existence of the two kinds of results of sacrificial acts—one, the immediate result being in the course of being destroyed, while another, the second result, in the shape of the long-standing *apurva,* not being destroyed, but just coming into existence. But there still remains another difficulty. If the cause of something being apprehended consists either in the *samavā ya* (according to the Logician) or in the *identity* (according to the Bhāṭṭa) of that thing with another thing (the cognising Self)—which is connected (with the internal organ) by the so-called *saṃyoga*-relation—it will follow that the cognition which apprehends the cognition would at the same time directly apprehend all the other qualities—such as size, taste, etc.—which reside, through *samavāya* or *tādātmya,* in the substrate of right cognition (and it, of course, is evident that such is not the case]. To this it might be rejoined that the reason of this not actually happening is that the cognition which apprehends *pramiti* does not possess the capability of immediately cognizing either the attributes of the Self—such as extension and so on,—or the attributes of the jar, such as taste and so on. But even allowing this, we further must point out that as knowledge (*pramiti*) is in itself nothing but pure *light,* it cannot possibly be held to be the object of knowledge in the part of something else; while jars and the like no doubt are such objects. Nor may it be pleaded that the so-called *prākaṭya* is something produced in the object, (*e.g.*, a jar) by a special energy of the Self called *pramāṇa,* and hence may be known through another cognition, just as colour and the other qualities of the jar. For of what kind should that energy of the Self be—motion, (*parispanda*)? or change (*pariṇāma*)? The former is not possible since that which is omnipresent cannot move. And as regards the latter alternative, we point out that, just as the jar which is the result of a transformation of the clay has the clay for its substrate, so the *prākaṭya*—if the result of a transformation of the Self—would have the Self for its substrate (and not belong to the object). If you rejoin that, just as from that change of the hair which consists in its turning grey there results old age in the body, so the result *prākaṭya* may arise in the object in consequence of a change in the Self;—we ask, what do you understand by an object being the substrate of *prākaṭya.* Does it mean being conscious? or producing *prākaṭya* ('manifestedness' of the object)? or being the substrate of the energy, termed 'cognition,' which produces *prākaṭya*? The first alternative would mean that jars and the like objects are conscious (which is absurd). The second alternative would mean that the sense organs, the eyes and the rest, are conscious (which we know not to be the case). Nor can the third alternative be accepted. For you would in that case have to infer the Self's being the abode of cognitional activity, in the following way: 'The Self is the substrate of the action of knowing (*jñāna-kriyā*) because it is connected with the result produced by that action (*viz.,* the *prākaṭya* of the object); just as Devadatta is the substrate of the action of eating because he is connected with the result of that action, *viz.,* satiety.' But this inference would be invalid on account of the reason on which it rests being something non-established; for the Self is *not* connected with the result of the action of knowing.* But such connexion *is* proved by consciousness which declares 'the jar is perceived by me.'

Well, we rejoin, if you (the Prābhākara) accept this reasoning, then you yourself allow that consciousness contradicts your theory according to which the result of the act of knowing is in the object, not in the Self!** For these reasons we must reject the totally perverse theories of the Naiyāyikas and the Bhāṭṭas, and hold fast to the view that knowledge (*pramiti*) which is the result of the cognitional energy (*pramāṇa*) of the knowing subject (*pramātṛi*) is (not the object of another act of knowledge but) self-luminous.***

[*Page 56*] The Bauddha indeed maintains that one and the same conscious state (*saṃvedana*) is *pramāṇa, i.e.*, cognitional energy and result of that energy (*i.e.*, cognition, *pramiti*) as well. But this involves the absurdity of a thing operating upon itself (the *Saṃvedana* being the cognitional energy operating upon itself as the result of that energy). The knowing subject *i.e.*, the Self, does not indeed really engage in any energy; but we, figuratively, ascribe to the Self the *pramāṇa*, which in reality is nothing but the combination of four factors, *viz.*, Self, Internal organ, Sense-organ and Object. And since the invariable result of this combination is knowledge (*pramiti*), we cannot (as some do) accept either definite action towards appropriating an object, or active avoidance of an object, or indifference, as the result of the *pramāṇa*; for these three so-called results may be or may not be present.

Nor finally, the Prābhākara concludes, is there any proof for the theory of the Vedāntin according to which the *Self* is self-luminous. For

---

* On the third explanation of *prākṭyādhāratva* some inference will have to be formulated as to the cognitional energy (jñāna) of which the *prākatya* is the result, residing in the Self; but this inference, as given in the text, would not be valid since the proving reason (the connexion of the Self with the result of that energy, *i.e.*, with the *pramiti*) is one that cannot be used by the Prābhākaras according to whom that *pramiti* (= *prākatya*) is connected not with the Self, but the object.

** This sentence may also be taken as addressed to the Bhāṭṭa, and not to the Prābhākara: 'In putting forward this reason you admit that it is the *object alone, and not the Self*, that is the *result* of cognitional activity; and this would be contradictory to your theory, on which the Self is the *result* or *object* of the cognition of *I*.' ['For an exposition of the Bhāṭṭa view, see *Shloka-Vārttika*, Ātmavāda, Shl. 107, 126; and *Shastradīpikā*, pp. 98, 99].

*** The Prābhākara view is that the Self is perceptible, not indeed by itself, but as the agent of the cognitions of objects, which cognitions are self-luminous; while according to the Vedāntin, the Self is nothing more or less than the cognition itself, and hence is itself self-luminous. (For the Prābhākara view, see *Prakaraṇapañchikā*, Chaukhambha Sanskrit Series, Benares, pp. 152-53.)

as all empirical thought and speech can be accounted for on the view of the *cognitions* being self-luminous, rich view is admitted by both of us (the Vedāntins as well as the Prābhākaras)—it creates a needless complication to ascribe self-luminousness to the Self also. We thus must finally adhere the Prābhākara view; *i.e.*, we maintain that the Ego which in all judgments, such as 'I know the jar,' presents itself as the substrate of the self-luminous cognition of the object—thus being comparable to the wick which is the substrate of the self-luminous flame—is nothing more or less than the Self, and is *not*, as the Vedāntins maintain, a composite entity comprising an objective as well and as a non-objective factor.

XXVII

[But we must reject the Prābhākara's own theory. No distinction can be made between a Self forming the substrate of consciousness or knowledge, and consciousness or knowledge itself: the two are absolutely one, *i.e.*, the Self *is* nothing else but the universal 'light of intelligence or consciousness' (*chitprakāsha*). The Self is neither a substance nor a quality nor an action; it is mere consciousness, and becomes an *I* only when illusorily associated with the non-intelligent organ of Egoity.]

This position of the Prābhākara we Vedāntins now counter-argue as follows:On due consideration we arrive at the result that the Ego (the organ of Egoity; *ahaṅkāra*)) is of the nature of the Not-self; since the Self is of the nature of consciousness (knowledge; *anubhava*).

In order to prove this we address to you the following question—What is it that constitutes the 'light of intelligence' ('light of consciousness; *chitprakāsha*)?* Is it the Self (*ātman*) only; or the Self *and* knowledge (consciousness; *anubhava*); or knowledge (consciousness; *anubhava*) alone?

The first alternative implies that knowledge (*anubhava*) is of the nature of non-intelligent (*jaḍa*; material) light;** and two possibilities

* i.e., that 'light of consciousness' the existence of which nobody denies; all schools and sects alike admitting that there is consciousness or knowledge which 'illumines' 'makes shine forth' all objects of knowledge; just as physical light illumines material objects.

** For if the Self alone constitutes the 'light of intelligence' then *anubhava* cannot be *chitprakāsha*, but can be of the nature of physical light only.

then present themselves: knowledge either, like the eye and the other sense organs—although not itself shining forth—manifests all other things; or, like physical light, it manifests objects while itself shining forth independently of other light of the same kind (*i.e.*, other physical light). But the former alternative cannot be accepted; since the eye gives rise to knowledge different from itself; and knowledge does not do that. And on the second alternative knowledge would possess the characeteristic mark of 'light of intelligence,' *viz.*, flashing forth of consciousness (*sphuraṇa*) independent of any knowledge beside itself; and this would mean that 'knowledge' and 'light of intelligence,' are identical. Knowledge, the eye, and physical light indeed have this in common that they all manifest objects such as jars; but knowledge does this in virtue of its being opposed to the *non-knowledge* of objects, and thus being known as 'light of intelligence; light (in the ordinary sense) manifests objects only by being opposed to the darkness investing the objects, and is non-intelligent (physical) light; and lastly, the eye manifests them as being directly instrumental towards the immediate cognition of things, and is such that its own instrumental character is not known (necessarily).* The three thus are of different kinds. But, an objection is raised, it is a mistake to argue that knowledge does not depend upon anything else of the same kind, just as physical light does not depend on anything else of the same kind; for as a matter of fact physical light is illumined (manifested) by the eye which is of the same kind as physical light (*viz.*, non-intelligent, material)! Not so, we reply. For what, we ask, does the eye do with regard to light? Does it ward off darkness, or does it give rise to knowledge? Not certainly the former; for light is in itself free from all darkness. And the latter alternative can only mean that light is manifested by knowledge to which the eye gives rise and which is of a *different* kind from light. It, therefore, is an un-exceptionable statement that knowledge does not, any more than physical light, depend on anything else of the same kind; and we hence must hold it to be light of intelligence. Were it mere physical light, the whole world would remain merged in blindness. Nor may the antagonist (who holds that the *Self* only is light of intelligence) give to his theory the following turn—'That which really illumines the objects is consciousness in the form of the knowing subject (*pramātri-chaitanya*); but it does this by means of knowledge which itself is non-intelligent.' For if knowledge,

---

* In the case of other instruments of knowledge—*e.g.* words—it is necessary that the word should be actually known as denoting a certain meaning; in the case of the Eye, this is not necessary; as even though we do not actually know the Eye to be the organ of vision, we shall *see* the object that comes before our Eyes.

in itself non-intelligent, acts only as the cause of the consciousness of the Self entering into connexion with the objects, it really is no more than a modification of the (non-intelligent) internal organ, and the theory then in no way differs from that of the Vedāntins. Let it then be said that knowledge is the cause of the light of the Self also! This is altogether impossible; for the light of that the nature of which is intelligence, cannot depend on what is non-intelligent. Let it then be said that knowledge is that which illumines the objects only. This view will not commit us to the theory of the Vedāntins, for what we now maintain is only that non-intelligent knowledge gives rise to another knowledge (different from the former) which serves the end of manifesting the objects—this other knowledge however being something apart from the consciousness which constitutes the Self. This view, the rejoinder is, would lead us into an infinite regress; for that other knowledge itself again being of non-intelligent nature, would stand in need of a further act of knowledge, and so on without end.

We now advance to the second alternative proposed above; and this also we reject. The Self and knowledge cannot both be 'light of intelligence;' for from this view it would follow that each has a completely settled and finished existence, independently of the other. And if this were so, who or what then would apprehend the connexion of the two—Self and knowledge? You will perhaps try to get over this difficulty by putting the case as follows: 'the Self does not shine forth by itself, since it is of the nature of intelligence; just as the states of consciousness of another person do not shine forth. The Self therefore depends on knowledge for its own accomplishment (*i.e.*, the Self is realised as Self, as consciousness, only through an act of knowledge). But against this we point out that the same would follow with regard to knowledge also.* Let us then say that knowledge is self-luminous, because it is not hidden or obstructed by anything else. Then, we reply, the Self is in the same case. For the following inference would be valid: 'The Self shines forth by itself; for, while being of the nature of intelligence, it also is not hidden or obstructed; just as knowledge is.'

There remains the third alternative, according to which knowledge only (not the Self) is 'light of intelligence.' But against this we assert the Vedāntic view that the Self must necessarily be held to be 'light of intelligence,' since the Self and knowledge are one.

---

* If this reasoning were accepted it would follow that knowledge also as being of the nature of intelligence, does not shine forth, and hence cannot be established by itself.

The Logicians and the followers of Prābhākara indeed teach that knowledge is a quality (*guṇa*) of the Self. The Sāṅkhyas maintain, by implication, that it is a substance since it constitutes the very nature of the Self (which they class as a substance). The followers of Bhāṭṭa again hold that knowledge is an action (*karman*), for, they say, it is the result of an activity of the nature of *change*, and the activity and the result should be considered as one.

Against this last view we remark that, if knowledge is a *karman*, like the action of moving, it cannot be considered either as *light* or as a *result*.

As to knowledge being a *substance* (the Sānhkya view) we observe that, on that hypothesis it must either be of atomic size,—and this would imply that like the feeble glimmer of a tiny glowworm it lights up only a small part of a thing (which actually is not the case);—or, secondly, it might be of infinite extent, and in that case the Self which is of the nature of knowledge, would manifest itself everywhere (which also is not the case); and if (instead of saying that knowledge constitutes the nature of the Self) you were to say that the Self is the abode of knowledge, the very same difficulty would arise;—or, in the third place, knowledge would be of medium size; in that case it would (like all things that are neither of infinite nor atomic size) be made up of parts and depend on those parts; it hence could not depend on the Self. Let us then say that it depends on the Self in the sense in which the jar is said to depend on the ground on which it stands. On that view also, we rejoin, it must be admitted that the Self and knowledge are non-different, no less than are the lamp and its light; for our thought and speech regarding things cognized by us are strictly analogous to what we thing and say of things lit up by a lamp—'this is shown by the light of the lamp' 'this is known by me.' If there were a real distinction of Self and knowledge, the expression 'this is known by me' would have to be taken (while it is actually not so taken) in a secondary, metaphorical sense—as we take the phrase 'this thing is lit up by wood' (where the *wood* stands for the flame of the burning wood.)

[*Page 58*] Finally, as to knowledge being a *quality* of the Self—the Logician's view. A quality does not originate apart from the origination of the substance,—the brilliancy of the flame, *e.g.*, originates together with the flame; knowledge, therefore, being eternal and invariably present where the Self is, the Self and knowledge are virtually one. You may ask how the Self, whose very proof and existence depend on knowledge, can be one with it; but the fact is that we do not admit such dependence, for it would imply that the Self is a mere Not-self like jars and the like. The further objection may be raised that since the cognition of blue colour, the cognition of yellow colour and so on, evidently are different things, knowledge cannot be one with the Self (which of course is always the same). But to this we reply that we are not conscious of these so called different states of cognition as differing in themselves (quâ cognition);* and that there is no means of proof to establish such difference. Nor may you argue that those states of cognition are different because they originate and pass away; for origination and passing away themselves presuppose difference, and your reasoning thus moves in a circle. But we must admit the origination of the later state of consciousness, in order thus to establish a purport for the operation of the instruments bringing about the new state, such as the eye and so on; and then, in order to preclude the (impossible view of the) simultaneousness of two states of consciousness the passing away of the earlier state must likewise be admitted! By no means, we reply. The whole process may be accounted for by the origination and passing away of successive connexions of one and the same consciousness with different objects; and it therefore would be needlessly cumbersome to ascribe origination and passing away to consciousness also.

The Bauddhas indeed assume that, in the same way as many really separate flames, originating and passing away in succession, are apprehended as one continuous flame, simply because they are similar to each other; so the states of consciousness are in reality distinct, but this distinctness does not manifest itself without some special condition. But this theory is untenable. The case of the flames indeed may be such as described, for they are apprehended by something different from them; but it is impossible that a difference abiding in self-luminous consciousness itself should not manifest itself. Nor does it avail to appeal to the non-manifestation of the true nature of the self-luminous Brahman as a proving instance; for the concealment of Brahman by Nescience has been established by valid means of proof.

Consciousness thus is one only and without a beginning. That it has no beginning follows from its being free from antecedent non-existence. As is said in Sureshvara's Vārttika (on the *Bṛihadāraṇyaka Upaniṣad* Ānandāshrama Series, Poona, Vol. II, p. 498, shloka 338.)

'Inasmuch as all effects, that are found to have antecedent non-existence, are objects of Consciousness, this Consciousness itself can have no antecedent non-existence.'

Self-luminous consciousness thus being eternal, there is nothing irrational in the theory which identifies it with the Self. A distinction

* The form of cognition always is the same; the contents only vary.

between the two may however be allowed insofar as we use the term *anubhava* (consciousness, knowledge) to denote the Self in relation to objects; while we speak of the 'Self' simply, when not wishing to emphasize that relation. In an analogous way we speak of a number of trees as a *wood*, when our mind dwells on the fact of their standing close to each other; while we speak of them as *trees* when not intending to bring out that special relation. Having thus established our point, how, we ask, can the Prābhākara assert that the Self manifests itself as the mere substrate of consciousness? and how should he prove that the non-intelligent *ahaṅkāra* is identical with the Self?

XXVIII

[We cannot allow the contention of the Prābhākara that '*I*-consciousness' is a permanent characteristic of the Self; for such consciousness is absent in deep dreamless sleep during which, as all admit, the Self persists. When a man, on waking from dreamless sleep, reflects '*I* slept well, *I* was not conscious of anything,' he transfers the *I*-character which belongs to all waking cognition to the state of deep sleep in which the Self, freed for the time of all shackles of Egoity was abiding in its own blissful nature and associated only with general non-particularized Nescience, not with any of its special modifications.]

But, the Prābhākara rejoins, when I think or say 'I see the jar,' it is evidently the *I* which is referred to as the seeing subject; and the seeing subject is neither more nor less than the Self !

By no means, we reply. If this were so, the Self would present itself in the state of deep sleep also in the form of the *Ego* (*i.e.*, there would be Ego-consciousness in deep sleep also). But this as we know is not the case. The 'I' therefore is not the Self, for it does not present itself in deep sleep (in which the Self undoubtedly persists).

[*Page 59*] "Let us then view the matter as follows. The *I* although present in deep sleep does not shine forth at the time because there is no consciousness of objects." But this view also we cannot accept. For, we ask, is there in deep sleep absence of pure consciousness? or absence of the affection of consciousness of objects? The former alternative is impossible, since consciousness is permanent and eternal. And the second alternative also is excluded, since the consciousness of Self does not depend on affection by objects. But, our opponent rejoins, it is that aspect of the Self which consists in its being a seeing (cognizing) subject, that constitutes the Ego, and the consciousness of that aspect depends on the affection by objects. In reply to this we ask the following question: what have we to understand by this 'aspect of being a seeing subject'? Is the seeing subject that which illumines (constitutes as objects of consciousness) the things seen? or that which is other than the objects seen? or pure consciousness (*chit*)? On the first and second definitions alike, the quality of being a seeing subject is defined by means of the objects seen, the quality therefore is something extrinsic or adventitious and hence cannot belong to the Self; the *Ego* therefore cannot be the Self. And on the third definition the Ego would be independent of objects, and hence there would be no reason why it should not present itself in deep sleep also. But there *is* consciousness of the Ego in deep sleep also! Were this so, we rejoin, the man who wakes from deep sleep would remember his *Ego* of deep sleep no less than his Ego of the previous day. It is not, we admit, an absolute rule that whatever has been experienced is remembered; but as in the case in question the Self is remembered, why should there not be remembrance of the Ego also, which, as you say, is nothing but pure consciousness? We can account for this: That cognition on the part of eternal consciousness of which the Ego is the object is not transitory (but permanent) and hence no mental impression (*saṁskāra*) of it is formed; it is owing to this that remembrance does not arise. For the same reason then, we rejoin, the Ego of the preceding day should not be remembered; while as a matter of fact it *is* remembered. On our view, on the other hand, the special Ego-consciousness which took place on the preceding day is *not* permanent; hence a mental impression of it is formed, and this later on gives rise to remembrance.

But all the same, the opponent resumes, we must admit that the man who wakes from sleep *does* remember the ego of deep sleep; for as a matter of fact he thinks '*I* enjoyed a pleasant sleep.' You now talk such random stuff, we rejoin, that even the wretched Naiyāyika may put you to shame; as follows:If a man thinks 'I enjoyed a pleasant sleep,' there is no direct reference whatever to the Self of deep sleep, or any pleasure enjoyed by it: what actually takes place is an inference, on the part of the man risen from sleep, that the Self of which he, now in the waking state, is conscious, was at the time of deep sleep characterized by absence of pain—such absence of pain being metaphorically called 'pleasure,'—'I, when wrapt in deep sleep, was free from all pain, because no pain connected with that state is remembered by me; *like a jar*.' Implied (secondary or metaphorical) meanings are indeed ordinarily assumed with regard to words only, not with regard to perception, inference and so on; all the same, the primary sense of the word *pleasure* being impossible in the case under discussion, *absence of pain* only can be admitted. Nor is it possible to *assume* the existence of pleasure in the primary sense, merely on the basis of the subsequent reflexion. For if pleasure had actually been experienced in sleep, the remembrance of it would present itself in connection with some particular thing, as *e.g.*, food or drink. And even if this latter difficulty were got over by assuming that the mental impression of the particular object is not resuscitated; yet the reflexion on previous absence of consciousness—which expreses itself in the form 'I enjoyed a pleasant sleep, I was not conscious of anything'—is distinctly opposed to previous consciousness of pleasure, and strengthens our view as to mere absence of pain. But does not the lightness of movement, the placid expression of the countenance and so on, which we observe in a person just risen from sleep, justify the inference that he had during sleep been enjoying positive pleasure?

Not so, we reply. In the moment immediately succeeding the time of direct consciousness, remembrance would be expected to take place; there is no room here for inference. Nor must it be argued that as we observe lightness of limb etc., on the part of persons just risen from sleep, in different degrees, we must assume, as their antecedent, pleasure of corresponding different degrees; since the mere absence of pain is always of one and the same kind. For even in the absence of different degrees of previous pleasure the subsequent differences can be accounted for on the ground of different degrees of rest enjoyed during sleep by the sense-organs and the rest, the activity of which gives rise to pain.

"Very well; but we are not particularly interested in the views of the Naiyāyikas. We rather want to hear how you, the Vedāntin, settle the question!" Listen then, with due attention, to my exposition.

The one fundamental Reality, *Bliss*—whose essential nature is constituted by self-luminous witnessing Consciousness—although indeed ever shining forth, yet, in the waking state and in the dreaming state, does not shine with full brightness, since then it is agitated by illusive ideas such as 'I am a man'—a condition comparable to that of the flame of a lamp which is shaken by a strong breeze. In deep dreamless sleep on the other hand, where all erroneous cognition has passed away, it shines forth with undimmed brightness. Obscuring Nescience indeed conceals the Brahman-aspect (the 'Bliss'—aspect) of Reality, but it does not conceal its aspect as witnessing Consciousness, by which Nescience itself is illumined. Were it otherwise, Nescience itself would be without a witness and hence not known. When therefore the sleeper wakes from sleep, he reflects on three things—the Bliss experienced in deep sleep, the Self, and positive Nescience; and his thought takes the form 'I slept beautifully, I was not conscious of anything.'

But, an objection is raised, in deep sleep the consciousness of these three things cannot be due to modifications of the internal organ, which, as you yourself hold, do not take place in sleep. And if, on the other hand, there were immediate experience (experience not depending on the internal organ) of these things by primal Consciousness, such experience—being something non-transitory, permanent—could not leave beind an impression, and hence no subsequent reflection on it could take place.

The case is otherwise, we reply. In deep sleep Nescience itself illusorily unfolds itself in three modifications which apprehend those three objects: the presentations to consciousness, determined by these modifications, after having mediated the experience of the three objects, pass away at the time of waking; and why then should the impression which they leave behind not produce remembrance? But on this view of the matter it is the Self determined by Nescience which experiences, and the Self determined by the internal organ which remembers; and hence there is no continuity of consciousness!

This objection also is unfounded, we reply. For we hold that at the time of waking also, it is none other but the Self qualified by Nescience which remembers. The function of the internal organ is to bring about the connexion of the thing remembered with ordinary thought as expressing itself in language. Nor can it be said that the expressions 'pleasant' and 'I was not conscious' (in the phrases meant to express the thought of the waking person) imply a reflexion on previous absence of pain and absence of consciousness. For although these two negations *exist* in sleep, the sleeper does not cognize them; since their counter-entities—pain and knowledge—are not at the time remembered.

But how then does the waking person apprehend that absence of pain and cognition which is characteristic of deep sleep, but of which, in sleep, there is no consciousness? By so-called presumptive reasoning (*arthāpatti*), we reply. The waking person remembers, in the manner detailed above, the untroubled bliss of deep sleep, and then immediately infers, as necessarily connected therewith, the absence of what is contrary to bliss, *i.e.*, pain. And in the same way, the remembrance of positive Nescience (which invested him in deep sleep) compels him to assume the absence of what is opposed to Nescience, *i.e.*, knowledge or consciousness.

[*Page 61*]—But, a further objection is raised, positive Nescience does *not* conflict with knowledge; for in the waking state the two co-exist. Not so, we reply. Although Nescience as a whole does not conflict with the cognitions of the empirical world, there is a conflict between those cognitions and Nescience as transmuted into particular forms. Nescience transmuted into the cognition of a jar is opposed to the cognition of a piece of cloth and other things. Were it not so, the entire world with all its objects would present itself to consciousness at the time when the jar is cognized. Hence we conclude that Nescience which has assumed the form of deep sleep is in opposition to all special cognitions. The presumptive reasoning detailed above therefore is well founded.

But, an objection is raised, why have recourse to such presumptive reasoning, while the following simple inference offers itself: 'There was no cognition in the state of deep sleep, since none is remembered'? Not so, we reply. Adopting this style of reasoning you might conclude that there were no herbs by the side of the road on which you walked because you fail to remember them. But how then is it that at noon we argue as follows: 'There was no elephant within this house early this morning; for we do not remember any such thing'? As a matter of fact, we rejoin, nobody argues in that way. What actually takes place is that having early in the morning perceived the things which fill the space within the house, heaps of grain and the like, and remembering this at noon we know, as an item necessarily implied therein, that no elephant was inside the house. The absence of pain and of cognition in the state of deep sleep is, therefore, known by presumptive reasoning, while the presence of positive Nescience, of bliss and of the Self, is remembered. This is our view of the question.

But what does this conclusion tell us as to the Ego?—That in deep sleep there is no consciousness of the Ego; and that the person who has risen from sleep does not reflect upon the Ego. But how then do you account for that Ego-consciousness which evidently finds its expression in the 'I' in 'I slept well?' As follows, we reply. In deep sleep the organ of egoity was resolved in general Nescience; at the moment of waking it again forms itself; what at that time is reflected upon really is the Self; but the Ego then is thought and spoken of as implying the Self, to the end of rendering empirical thought and speech more definite; this indeed being the only end of the *ahankāra*. As a matter of fact, the Self is never viewed as represented by any other modifications of the internal organ (but by the *ahaṅkāra* modification). This is set forth in the *Naiṣkarmyasiddhi* (Bombay Sanskrit Series, pp. 80-81) as follows:

'The Self is *implied* (by secondary or indirect signification) by the *I-modification* (of the internal organ), and not by any other modification; for the reason that this modification is something specially inward, extremely subtle, and specially subserving the intuition of the Self.'

'The Self is also *denoted* (by direct signification) by the *I-consciousness* (or the word 'I'); for the reason that consciousness must be regarded either as inseparable from the Self, or absolutely non-existent; no other alternative is possible.'

[*Page 62*] The conclusion then is that this, in itself non-sentient, *ahaṅkāra,* although in the waking and dreaming states presenting itself as the Self, does not constitute the nature of the Self, since it is non-existent in deep sleep (when yet the Self exists). This indeed all versed in Scripture and *Smṛiti* will have to admit. Thus Scripture (Chh. Up. VII. 25) after having—in the clause 'it is below, above, behind, before' etc.,—declared that *Brahman*, there called 'plenitude' (*bhūman*) is the Self of all, continues—'Now then the teaching as to the *I* (*ahaṅkāra*)'—and declares that the *I* also is the Self of all ('*I* am below, above' etc.,); and finally—in the clause—'Now then the teaching as to the Self (the Self is below' etc.)—refers to the Self as something different from the *I*.

But, it is objected, in the same way as the declaration of both the individual soul and of *Brahman* being the Self of all, is meant to prove the identity of the two, thus the scriptural passage quoted above may also be taken as meant to prove that the *I* is identical with the Self. Not so, we reply. The cases are not parallel. Since the individual soul and *Brahman* are, previously, naturally conceived as being different entities, it is appropriate that a declaration made with regard to them (*viz.*, that each of them is the Self of all) should be understood as meant to prove their identity; for two different things cannot be the Self of all. If, on the other hand, the *I* which previously is naturally understood to be one with the Self, is referred to in the sacred text as something separate, we are justified in concluding that this is done for the purpose of establishing its *difference* from the Self. Nor must you object to this, that on this interpretation of the text the declaration as to the *I* being the Self of all has no sense; for it really has the purpose of intimating that the transcendent (*parokṣa*) Brahman is identical with the *I* of which we are immediately conscious. But then the meaning is neither more nor less than that the *I* is the Self, and this brings you back to the same position from which you wished to escape,—your case being like that of the man who started very early in order to escape the payment of toll at the river-crossing—(which was not levied before sunrise), but reached the crossing when the sun had risen already. Not so, we reply. For the text finally sets aside the *I* (by mentioning the Self), and thereby teaches that Brahman only is the Self in the real sense. Moreover another scriptural text—'the *I*-maker (*Ahan-kāra*) and what is made *I* (*Ahan-kartavyam,*' Prashna Up., IV. 8)—distinctly mentions the *Ahankāra* as included in the group comprising the sense-organs and sense-objects. And *Smṛiti* (Bha. Gi, XIII. 5) mentions the *Ahankāra* among other things that belong to the world of 'effects'—'the great elements, the *Ahankāra,*' etc.

XXIX

[The *Ahankāra* of the Vedāntins—which essentially differs from the *manas* of the *Naiyāyikas*—is a especial modification of the so-called internal organ; which itself is one of the products of Universal Nescience. It is the Ahankāra which through its various functions or energies creates all individual experience; it of course being understood that this experience is *conscious* experience only owing to the fact that the Ahankāra is irradiated by Universal Intelligence. Universal Intelligence in itself has no specific cognitions or experiences of any kind—all these belong to the Ahankāra only; but as the Self is associated with the Ahankāra, the experiences of the latter are mistakenly ascribed to the former: the *I* is confounded with the *Self.* In reality the latter is no more touched by the doings and sufferings of the Ahankāra than the crystal by the reflexion, in it, of the red flower. For these two cases a valid analogy may be claimed; for ordinary reflection (for which some attempt to assign natural, physical, explanations) must be held to be something purely illusory, unreal—'a thing of Māya.'—While the Self can never be the *object* of knowledge, the *I* can be known; for if we abstract from the subjective element in it (*i.e.,* the reflexion in it of Universal Intelligence), it is of essentially objective character, a thing which exists *for* Intelligence.]

Well then, what really is this so-called *Ahankāra*? What is its material cause? What its instrumental cause? What its essential nature? Through what means of knowledge is it known? What are its effects? Why does it not exist in deep sleep? Listen to our explanation. The material cause of the organ of egoity is beginningless, inexplicable Nescience. Its instrumental cause is the circumstance of Nescience being ruled in all its operations by the Highest Lord. Its essential nature is constituted by the power of cognition and the power of action combined. The source through which it is known is ever unchanging consciousness. Its effects are action and enjoyment. It does not exist in deep sleep, because deep sleep is nothing else than the resolution of the organ of Egoity into universal Nescience. The vital breath (*prāṇa*)—whose nature is power of action—no doubt persists in deep sleep also, but this does not conflict with the *Ahaṅkāra,* which is different from the vital breath, then ceasing to exist. And if we should view the two as non-different, we may assume that the *Ahaṅkāra* ceases to exist in deep sleep, all but that element of it which constitutes the vital breath. If however, we accept the *Dṛiṣṭi-sṛiṣṭi*-theory, *then for the man in deep sleep everything may be held to cease to exist, in the ordinary sense of the word.

[*Page 63*] The theory held by the Sāṅkhyas on this matter is that what constitutes the material cause of the world is not Nescience ruled and controlled by the Highest Lord, but the Pradhāna which is a non-intelligent and fully real principle, not depending on any other principle; of this Pradhāna the so-called *Mahat* and the organ of Egoity are the first products. But this view is untenable. Were things as the Sāṅkhyas represent them, the organ of Egoity and all that depends on it, all action, all enjoyment and so on, would present themselves to consciousness in a purely objective form '*This* is a doer,' '*This* is an enjoyer' and not as something superimposed upon the Self; so that the (actual forms of consciousness, '*I* am a doer,' '*I* am an enjoyer,' would never arise. For the theory of superimposition of this kind being due to inexplicable Nescience is not accepted by the Sāṅkhyas; and all other theories concerning this problem have been refuted by us (so as not to be open to the Sāṅkhyas).

The theory of the Naiyāyikas on this matter is as follows: There is a peculiar organ, called *manas,* of atomic size, which is the instrumental cause of pleasure, pain, desire, cognition and so on. If no such organ existed, the merely occasional (not permanent) cognition which is observed to take place when the Self, the sense-organs and the objects are in contact, could not be accounted for. But we cannot allow what the Vedāntins maintain, *viz.,* that there exists a so-called internal organ which is different from the *manas* described, is of medium size, undergoes

* This is the name given to the theory on which a thing is regarded as existing only so long as it is perceived; the whole world therefore ceases to exist for the person who lies in deep sleep and does not perceive anything.

the changes of pleasure, pain and so on, and from a special modification of which the *ahankāra* arises. The Vedāntins illustrate the functions of this *ahankāra* by certain comparisons: As a lump of iron when heated superimposes upon the fire (which glows within the iron) its own form and extension—so that the fire is spoken of as big or small or globular, etc.; and as by the mirror the face of a person, although one only, is split up so as to appear in a double form, *viz.*, as thing reflected and as reflexion; and as the water in a pail superimposes upon the moon reflected in it all its own motions; so the *ahankāra* superimposes upon the Self all its own functions—action, enjoying and the rest; splits up the one Self so that it appears as Brahman and as individual soul; and superimposes upon the latter its own activities, such as going to another world and the like. Nor must it be said that this internal organ is nothing else but the so-called *buddhi* (organ of thought), for there is no *buddhi* apart from cognition, and cognition is nothing but a quality of the Self. The internal organ, imagined by the Vedāntins, therefore, has no existence.

This theory also is unfounded, we reply. For from more than one scriptural text (cp. *e.g.*, 'by the quality of *buddhi*,' Shvet. Up., V.8) it is well known that there *is* an internal organ which undergoes changes, has for its essential properties the powers of cognition and action, builds up for the Self the whole empirical world, and is variously designated as *manas, buddhi*, etc. Were there no such organ, no world would arise for the Self which in itself is altogether unrelated. But as there *is* such an organ, through it an unreal world is superimposed upon the Self, just as unreal red colour is superimposed by the China rose on the crystal placed near it.

There indeed are some who refuse to admit the appositeness of this last parallel instance, on the ground, that the red colour of the crystal, is not unreal. But, we ask those opponents, how do *you* then explain the phenomenon? Do you hold that the visual rays of the beholder proceed towards the crystal, are reflected by it, and then proceed towards the red flower? or does the colour of the flower, being reflected in the crystal, appear as if belonging to the latter? or does the light of the flower, analogous to the light proceeding from certain gems such as rubies, permeate the crystal, so that the latter itself appears as red? or is that which appears as red the light of the flower only which permeates the crystal? or does the light of the flower produce in the crystal a new redness? On the first alternative the flower also (no less than its red colour) would present itself to the eye and hence be perceived. And if it were held that owing to some defect of a part of the eye there is no contact between eye and flower, then the red colour also should not be perceived; for there would be absence of the *Saṃyukta-samavāya* relation,—*i.e.*, the colour would not be perceived since that in which it inheres, (*viz.*, the flower) would not be in contact with the eye. The second alternative is inadmissible, since we never observe a reflexion of mere colour apart from the substance to which the colour belongs. As to the third alternative, the use of the phrase 'as it were' implies that you yourself admit the connexion of crystal and red colour to be an *unreal* one. On the fourth alternative the white colour of the crystal also should be perceived; there being no cause for its non-perception. It cannot be argued that the whiteness of the crystal is driven out by the radiance of the flower, the colour of which is opposed to that of the flower; for if this were so, the crystal no longer having *any* colour would cease to be an object of visual perception. Nor again can it be said that the whiteness is (not entirely driven out but) obstructed (lessened); for if this were so the obstruction would extend to the crystal itself. Substances are not visible apart from colour; were it so, we should see the air also (which has no colour). And on the fifth alternative, if the radiance of the flower were the *instrumental cause* of the production of red colour in the crystal, that colour would persist even on the withdrawal of the flower's radiance. Let us then view the radiance of the flower as the *material cause* of the redness of the crystal. This also, we reply, may not be; since we do not perceive in a flower a radiance analogous to that of a gem; and thus this view becomes open to the objections urged against the previous alternative. We thus are led to the conclusion that the redness of the crystal cannot be viewed as anything else but an unreal (illusory) appearance caused (in the instrumental sense) by the flower. And analogous to this superimposition is the superimposition, due to the organ of Egoity, of action, enjoyment, and so on, on the Self.

But, our opponent asks, which of the two following alternatives do you mean to maintain—are certain characteristics belonging to the *ahaṅkāra,* such as being an agent etc., falsely superimposed upon the Self? or is a second unreal quality of being an agent and so on produced in the Self itself? On the former alternative the redness of the crystal—which you adduce as an analogous instance—would *not* be analogous (since you said above that an unreal redness is produced in the crystal itself). And on the latter alternative the organ of Egoity would be a real agent, and the Self an unreal one: there thus would be two agents! Not so, we reply. Our former alternative is un-exceptionable. For we set forth the analogous instance only in order to prove that the characteristic of being an agent, while not really belonging to the Self, yet *appears* to belong to it. This view is by no means identical with the so-called *Anyathākhyāti* theory. For what *we* maintain is that the organ of Egoity together with its attribute of being an agent, is merely superimposed upon the Self and hence unreal. According to the *Anyathākhyāti* theory, on the other hand, the thing superimposed, *e.g.*, the silver that appears in the shell, is something real. Nor in fact is there any real objection to the second alternative. For as the Self and the *ahaṅkāra* are really one, the result of there being two agents does not follow. But, it is objected, the *ahaṅkāra* cannot be the cause of anything evil, such as being an agent, because in such texts as 'the knot of the heart is torn away, &c.,' [Muṇḍaka Up. 2.2.8] it is the 'knot of the heart' that is spoken of as that cause. This is not right we reply. For what is figuratively spoken of as the 'knot' in that passage, is only the *ahaṅkāra* along with its substrate, the Self, possessing as such, the mixed character of 'intelligence' and 'non-intelligence' (the Self as the substratum, being the *chit* or intelligent factor, and the *ahaṅkāra* by itself the *jaḍa* or non-intelligent factor).

But, another objection is raised, if the *ahaṅkāra* were something superimposed merely, there would be no consciousness of it. We maintain this on the ground of the following inference: The self is not conscious of what is superimposed on it; because the Self is a (mere) substrate; as crystal is (with regard to the red colour superimposed on it, of which it is not conscious). Not so, we reply. The reason in your inference has proving power only with the special condition added that the substrate be something non-intelligent. But the Self is intelligent. But as the Self is destitute of such cognitional energy as has for its object the thing superimposed, it is virtually non-intelligent. By no means, we reply. For as the presentation to consciousness of the thing superimposed is due to the immediate connexion of the thing with consciousness, it does not depend on cognitional energy. But then you cannot hold that the *ahaṅkāra* contains an objective element; for it presents itself to consciousness without the meditation of cognitional energy, like the witnessing consciousness itself! You are wrong again, we reply. In witnessing consciousness, there is absent the characteristic mark of objectivity, *viz.*, being the *object of consciousness;* with regard to the *ahaṅkāra*, on the other hand, this characteristic feature is proved by immediate experience.

The *Prābhākaras* and others indeed, ignorant as they are of the mysteries of Philosophy, find—in agreement with vulgar thought—the characteristic mark of a thing's objectivity in its being the object (*i.e.*, that which is acted upon; *karman*) of the activity of cognition, and thus are led to the idle and confused doctrine that the *I* which does not possess that mark, is the Self. The *ahaṅkāra* also is the object of such cognition as consists in modifications of the internal organ—for were this not the case, the *ahaṅkāra* of the previous day could not be remembered [its actually being remembered being due to the impression left behind by the modification of the internal organ]; but as this cognition is a part of the *ahaṅkāra* and hence not really different from it, the fact of the *ahaṅkāra* being an *object* of cognition is not so evident as the body, the sense-organs and the rest being objects. But the fact is evident to all men of deeper insight! All the same, we reply, the characteristic feature of being the object of cognitional energy on the part of the internal organ does not subsist in Nescience, which is set aside by that energy. Hence the only true characteristic feature of objectivity is 'being the object of consciousness.' But how then do you account for the fact that although (as you hold) the characteristic mark of objectivity belongs to the organ of Egoity no less than to the body, the sense-organs and the rest, ordinary thought and speech attribute it to the latter things only, and not to the organ of Egoity? Because, we rejoin, ordinary people have not the true insight. An ant-hill, a stone, a tree—all these things equally consist of the element *earth*; yet people devoid of discriminative insight think and speak of the ant-hill only as made of earth, not of the stone or tree. Those on the contrary, who possess the requisite insight, view the intelligent element in the *ahaṅkāra* as subjective, and the non-intelligent element as objective. But although competent persons thus define the *ahaṅkāra* carrying within itself the reflexion of universal Intelligence, as being partly of the nature of Self and partly of that of Not-Self, ordinary men, confounding these two elements, are conscious of this composite entity simply as the *I*.

XXX

> [The reflection of Universal Consciousness in the Ahaṅkāra constitutes the so-called Jīva (individual soul). Nor can it be argued that the Jīva, if a reflexion, must be something different from Universal Consciousness (Brahman); for so-called 'reflected images' in genral are *not* really different from the things to which they belong; they only *appear* to be so, owing to Māyā.]

But, if the individual Self is a reflection of universal consciousness in the organ of Egoity, it must be something different from universal consciousness; just as the reflection of the face in the mirror is something different from the face. That the head on the shoulders of the man and its reflected image are really different, follows from the fact that we perceive the two as facing each other. Not so, we reply. The recognition of identity which finds its expression in the judgment 'This is my face' negatives the perception of difference. Nor may you retort that it rather is the recognition of identity which is negatived by the perception of difference. For if there were difference, there would be no reflexion. To explain: What do you understand by the *counter-object (pratibimba*, reflected image)? Is it an impression stamped upon the mirror by the face? Or do you mean that the constituent parts of the mirror transform themselves into the counter-object, under the influence of the object's proximity? The former alternative is inadmissible since the face in the mirror is smaller than the real face. And when, in a big mirror, the reflected face also is perceived as big, it yet cannot be an impression stamped on the mirror; since the real face and the mirror are not in contact. Nor can the second alternative be accepted; for from it, it would follow that the reflection persists even when its cause, *i.e.*, the face in proximity to it, is removed. But as a matter of fact it does not persist; and when the person reflected looks at the mirror sideways, or when another person looks at it straight, the reflected image is not perceived. Nor must you plead against this that in some cases an effect vanishes as soon as the operative cause ceases to act; that, *e.g.*, a mat which has been unrolled by the action of the hand is seen to roll itself up again as soon as the cause of the unrolling, *i.e.*, contact of the mat with the hand is removed. For in this latter case the effect does not cease because the cause is removed, but because, through the impression made on the mat by its having remained rolled up for a long time, an effect is produced which is contrary to the effect produced by the unrolling hand. In the case under discussion, on the other hand, the thing may remain close to the mirror for ever so long, but as soon as it is removed, the reflexion also vanishes—which shows that the thing does not produce a change in the substance of the mirror. And should you attempt to prove your case by another instance, *viz.*, that of the lotus-flower, the expansion of which after having lasted for a considerable time ceases as soon as the operative cause, *i.e.*, the sun-light, is withdrawn,—we must contradict you here also. What actually takes place is that the expansion of the flower ceases when, owing to the operation of certain earthy and watery constituent parts of the lotus which were the causes of the original closed, budlike, condition of the flower, that budlike condition is restored at night-fall, and counteracts the expansion. Were it otherwise, the expansion would cease at night in the case of faded flowers also, which no longer possess the constituents referred to. If certain parts of the mirror really transformed themselves into a face, what should be the cause of the subsequent restitution of the original blank surface? Apart from the activity of an artificer, those parts truly have no capability of producing any effect. For an analogous reason the particles of the mirror-surface cannot be held to transform themselves into a face merely owing to the influence of the proximity of the real face. Truly, if this could happen, any one wishing to have the portrait of a face on a mirror would only have to bring the face to be delineated near the mirror, and there the portrait would be, without the need of any artist! And should you say that the work of an artificer may be needed for imparting to the material of the mirror some other form, and not for the mere production of the reflected image and the subsequent return of the surface to its previous state,—we rejoin that thus also the change of the mirror into the form of the reflected image cannot be rendered plausible. For we fail to perceive in the image that relation of raised and depressed parts which characterizes the real face: in the image the nose does not project, the eyes do not lie deep, and so on; the hand passing over the mirror feels an even surface only. And should you say that the smooth surface of the mirror interposes itself between the hand and the face (produced in the mirror),—we reply that in that case the face should not be visible at all. Our conclusion, therefore, is that there exists no second face in the mirror, since the causes required for the production of such a face are absent; just as the head of a hare is without horns,—because the causes of the production of horns are absent.

[*Page 67*] But, if the reflected image is unreal like the silver illusorily appearing on the shell, you cannot say (as you did say above) that it is one with the thing reflected; and the reason for such oneness which you there set forth, *viz.*, recognition, is too wide, since such recognition may take place in the case of shell-silver also, 'this is my silver.' The latter instance, we rejoin, is of a different nature. Since the cognition of silver is erroneous—as proved by the subsequent sublative judgment 'this is not silver'—the recognition also of the silver as *my* silver, must be held to be erroneous. In the case of the mirror, on the other hand, there is no judgment sublating the face itself; we do not say 'this is not a face,' but only 'there is no face *there* (*i.e.* in the mirror); the negation thus applying only to the connexion of the face with a definite place. The recognition 'this is my face' thus is in no way erroneous. Nor must you object that in the given case there can be no recognition by perception, since nobody knows the parts of his own face by perception. For perception of the whole is possible on the basis of perception of some parts, as *e.g.*, in the case of a jar; and a man actually *does* see some parts of his own face—*e.g.*, the tip of the nose. That when the mirror is removed the reflected image also vanishes, does not sublate the image; the same conclusion would otherwise hold good with regard to the mirror itself. But the enunciation 'thou art that' does completely sublate the individual soul—which in this case holds the place of the reflected image; for in its form, *i.e.*, the co-ordination of the members, that enunciation is of exactly the same kind as the judgment 'That (thing mistaken by me for a) post is (in reality) a man (where *the post* is completely sublated by the cognition of the *man*). And if the transmigrating individual soul did not pass away completely, there would be no Release.

Not so, we reply. Co-ordination may express *oneness* also, as *e.g.*, it does in the judgment 'this person is that Devadatta (whom I saw before).' And Release is effected through the sublation of that part only of the individual Self which is, in its nature, opposed to Release. If the entire individual Self were annihilated, Release truly would not be something beneficial to man.

Some indeed are of opinion that there is no counter-object in the mirror at all, but that the visual rays being repelled by the surface of the mirror turn back to the eye and apprehend (not a *counter object* but) the object, *i.e.*, the real face itself as non-separated from the mirror. This view, however, is obviously refuted by the clear perception of the counter-object as facing the object. But how, the opponent asks, can one and the same material thing, *viz.*, the face, at the same time abide, in its totality, in two different places?

Because, we reply, its abiding in the mirror is the work of *Māyā*! To *Māyā*, truly, nothing is impossible: in dreams it presents to us things of the strangest kind—such as the dreamer cutting off his own head.

But how then is it, on your view of the nature of reflected images, with the following case? You hold that the reflexion of a tree in a pool of water, where the tree appears with its top downward, is one with the reflected tree on the bank; the tree on the bank, therefore, is the substrate, and on this there are superimposed by *Māyā* characteristics of the reflected tree, *viz.*, being in the water, having its top below, and so on. But in this case there is no true cause of superimposition, since the substrate (the real tree on the bank) is perceived in its totality. How then can this be a case of superimposition? Why, we rejoin, should there be no *adhyāsa* in this case? Is it because there is nothing to conceal the tree; or because there is no defect; or because there is no material cause; or because the true nature of the substrate is known at the time and such knowledge is opposed to *adhyāsa*?—The first reason is not valid; for as that which conceals consciousness (*i.e.*, Nescience) is the substrate of all *adhyāsa*, there is no occasion here for a separate factor concealing a non-intelligent thing.—This remark at once disposes of the third reason also.—The second reason is invalid, since in cases where the error is due to the presence of a certain limiting adjunct (which, in the instance under discussion, is constituted by the water) it is just that adjunct which constitutes the required *defect*. Nor is the fourth reason valid; for the knowledge of the true nature of the substrate is opposed to such error only as does not depend on the presence of the limiting adjunct. The error, then, of the Self being an agent—which does depend on a limiting adjunct (*viz.*, the *ahaṅkāra*) is terminated not through the cognition of the true nature of the Self, but through the removal of the limiting adjunct, *i.e.*, the *ahaṅkāra*! Well, the matter lies as follows: *Real* (in the empirical sense) limiting adjuncts, such as mirrors and the like, and the erroneous conceptions due to them are not indeed terminated by true cognition; but limiting adjuncts such as the *ahaṅkāra* which are products of Nescience and are of the nature of error *not* due to an adjunct, are terminated through the cognition of Truth; and this implies that the agency of the Self also comes to an end through the cognition of Truth.*

But how, on this your view, does the cognition of truth take place? Is not the following reasoning valid—the individual Self does not know its oneness with the universal Self; since it is a mere reflexion; just like the reflexion of the face in the mirror? Not so, we reply. That a thing is a mere reflexion does not constitute a reason for its not cognizing; we are only justified in saying that, that which is a mere reflexion and at the same time of non-intelligent nature, cannot cognize.

XXXI

> [The individual soul—*jīva*—is a *reflexion* of Brahman, the conditioning adjunct (*upādhi*) which gives rise to the reflexion being in this case the internal organ; just as it is the mirror which, acting as an *upādhi*, gives rise to the reflexion of the face. More particularly, however, it is in the state of dream only that the internal organ, by itself, constitutes the *upādhi*; in the waking state the entire body constitutes a

* The mirror is called '*pāramārthika upādhi*' (real adjunct), because it is as real as the reflected substance. The *ahaṅkāra*, on the other hand, has not the same degree of reality as the 'Self' that is reflected in it.

further *upādhi*; and in deep sleep—when the internal organ ceases to exist—it is general Nescience which is in connexion with the *jīva*.]

Against the Materialist who holds that intelligence (or consciousness) belongs to the body (and who on that account might contest the non-intelligent character of the reflected image) the non-intelligence of the reflected image may easily be established, on the ground that intelligence on the part of the reflected image is obstructed by the admittedly non-intelligent character of the mirror. If the image were intelligent it would move by itself, independently of movement on the part of the body reflected. The case of the individual Self is different; for although it likewise is a mere reflection, its intelligent nature is, as immediate consciousness witnesses, *not* obstructed by the non-intelligent nature of its limiting adjunct (the *ahaṅkāra*). Although according to ordinary thought it is Devadatta—who is not a reflexion—that is the substrate of that knowledge of truth which puts an end to error, yet what determines his being a substrate of the kind is not his being reflected, but rather his being the substrate of error. And that the individual soul *is* the substrate of error, is due to the circumstance that Nescience although, properly speaking, residing in pure consciousness (not in the *jīva*) yet has a *leaning towards* the individual soul and hence produces error in it.

But if Brahman does not cognize the identity of the individual soul with itself, it is not omniscient; and if it does cognize it, it must view the error abiding in the individual soul, as abiding within itself! This, we reply, does not follow. As a matter of fact, Devadatta although realizing the oneness of his face and its reflexion in the mirror does not ascribe to his own face the small size and the dimness of the reflected image. Nor is there absence of proof for the individual soul's being a reflexion; for this is amply vouched for by Scripture, Smṛiti and the Sūtras. Scripture says 'It (the universal Self), is the counter-form to every form' (Kaṭha Up. v. 9); and Smṛiti— "He is seen as one and as many, like the moon reflected in water; and the Sūtras—'For this reason comparisons such as that to the image of the sun (in water and the like) (Ve. Sū. iii 2-18).' Nor must it be urged, that Brahman as being without definite form is, on that account, incapable of being reflected. For we see that the ether, although devoid of definite form, is, together with all the clouds, stars and the rest, of which it is the substrate, reflected in water. It cannot be urged that in this case what is the substrate of the reflexion of clouds and the rest is only the ether (*i.e.*, space) within the water. For we see a vast expanse of ether in water which is knee deep only. But should we not rather say that, like the ether limited or particularized by a jar, the individual Self is limited or particularized by its limiting adjunct, but is not a reflexion! On this hypothesis, we reply, if Brahman were held to be present within the limiting adjunct also that determines the *jīva*, consciousness would exist within the jar in a double form; while we do not observe that a double ether exists within the jar. If, on the other hand, Brahman were not present there, it would cease to be omnipresent and all-ruling.—Let us then say that omnipresence and universal rulership belong not to Brahman but to consciousness (*chit*) which is common to the individual Self and to Brahman. This may not be, we reply; for the text 'He who rules the Self from within'—which occurs in a section treating of Brahman distinctly declares that it is Brahman only which abides within the soul as ruler. All those texts therefore which speak of the ether within the jar must be understood as setting forth or exemplifying only the *non-relatedness* of the *jīva*, not its *jīva*-character. On the reflexion-theory, on the other hand, no fault can be found with Brahman as well as the individual soul abiding within the *ahaṅkāra*. For in water there is present at the same time the real ether—knee deep as the water is—and the reflected universal ether. We therefore define the individual Self as a reflexion of Brahman, due to the organ of Egoity acting as a limiting adjunct (*upādhi*).

We have above said that Nescience is the limiting adjunct which particularizes the individual soul: we now have to set forth a further distinction. The individual soul is, in the state of deep dreamless sleep, particularized by Nescience in general. Next, in order to account for the limited degree of clearness with which the world presents itself to a dreaming person, we assume that the soul in that state has the internal organ for its limiting adjunct. And in the waking state, finally, where the world presents itself with full clearness and distinctness, the entire gross body constitutes the limiting adjunct of the soul. Nor does this difference of adjuncts imply a difference of souls: it is the very same soul which, particularized by the antecedent adjuncts, is particularized by the following ones also.

XXXII

[Although a reflexion, the individual soul is not unreal: in itself it is real, for it is Consciousness; it is unreal only quâ reflexion. It is in this latter aspect that it undergoes Bondage and Release. Universal Consciousness becomes *I*-consciousness by its association, as described, with the organ of Egoity.]

A further question here arises. Does this particularization of the soul abide in error (*bhrama*), or in consciousness? On the former view it could not subsist in the states of deep sleep and swoon, in which error does not exist. And from this it would follow that Nescience and its effects—among them the states of deep sleep and swoon—do not *lean towards* the individual soul. On the latter view the particularization of the *jīva* would either be an effect, and hence absent in deep sleep and swoon: so that we should again be met by the difficulty just stated. Or it would not be an effect, and then it would not be dependent on Nescience. To this we make the following reply. In the waking and dreaming states the particularization of the individual soul is effected by the gross and subtle bodies, and it is of the nature of error and hence the effect of Nescience. In the states of deep sleep and swoon, on the other hand, the particularization of the soul although having Consciousness for its substrate and being without a beginning yet must be viewed as dependent on Nescience in the same way as the connexion of Self and Nescience is. Although the particularization does not abide in Nescience—while the connexion does so abide—it yet abides in Consciousness inasmuch as qualified by Nescience, and hence it is not irrational to view it as dependent on Nescience; just as we say that the distinction of face and reflected image which really abides in the face as qualified by the mirror depends on the mirror,—so, in the case in question, the distinction depends upon an inexplicable 'saṁskāra' (impression), which does not necessarily arise from error. Thus then it is quite reasonable to hold that the Self, though essentially *pure consciousness* entirely *subjective* in its character, is yet reflected in the *ahaṅkāra* superimposed upon itself;—the particularization of the *jīva* (necessary for the reflexion) being due to Nescience, no less than the connexion of Self and Nescience. But an objection is raised, you hold reflexions to be unreal and hence the individual soul cannot be a reflexion! You misconceive our view, we rejoin. We do not hold either the face which is the 'reality' of the reflexion, or consciousness, to be unreal: what we do hold to be unreal is the face's attribute of being reflected, and the false notion of difference on which that attribute rests. That the recognition of the reflected image (expressing itself as 'this is my face'), and the enunciation 'Thou art that,' prove the reflexion (whether of the face in the mirror or of the self in the *ahaṅkāra*) to have its self (its reality) in the real reflected thing, we have already stated. Although the attribute of being reflected is false, yet the substrate of the attribute, *i.e.,* the individual soul, does undergo bondage and attain release. Bondage and release thus on the one hand are not impossible, nor on the other hand do they extend to the 'reflected thing' *i.e.*, Brahman.

But the opponent objects, if the adhyāsa of difference of the thing and its reflceted image depends on the *ahaṅkāra* and other limiting adjuncts, how is the superimposition of the *ahaṅkāra* itself (on the universal self)—for which there is no limiting adjunct—to accomplish itself? Just as the superimposition of the snake on the rope, we reply. But in the latter case, although there be no independent thing to act as the limiting adjunct, there at any rate is the image of previously seen snakes, impressed on the mind of the mistaken person, to supply that adjunct! Why then, in the case under discussion, should not the mental impression of the *ahaṅkāra* constitute the required limiting adjunct? For there is no rule that only such mental impressions as are due to sources of true knowledge should function as limiting adjuncts, and not such also as are due to error.—We sum up the result of the preceding enquiry in the following words. The self—although in reality nothing else but pure Consciousness and of an altogether non-objective character—, insofar as reflected in the organ of Egoity superimposed upon it (the Self), becomes capable of relating itself to that sphere of thought and speech which is connoted by the word *I*, and thus presenting itself to consciousness as fused with the organ of Egoity—which is superimposed upon the Self in the *I*-consciousness—itself is thought and spoken of, in a derived or metaphorical sense, as the object of this '*I*-consciousness'. It is in this way that the superimposition of the 'I' on the Self shows itself to be possible.

XXXIII

[But, the Bauddha objects, the superimposition of the organ of Egoity with all the distinction it implies, on Consciousness which is essentially free from distinctions, is an impossible assumption. Nor will it avail to say that distinctions belong to *Consciousness* insofar as it is *knowing subject* (pramātṛi)—a condition itself to be accounted for as due to similar previous conditions due to previous Ahaṅkāras. For no philosophical school is able to give a satisfactory account of the meaning of *knowing subject* (pramātṛi) and the correlate notions (*pramāṇa* and *pramiti*).]

[*Page 70*]—But, an objection is raised, it after all is not possible that on Consciousness which presents itself as free from all distinctions (*nirvikalpaka*) there should be superimposed the organ of Egoity which is affected with distinctions. For such Adhyāsa is nowhere observed. Nor again can it be said that such Adhyāsa *is* possible since Consciousness after all does present certain distinctions as *e.g.*, being the subject of knowledge (*pramātṛi*). For that Consciousness should appear as a knowing subject, itself presupposes the presence of the organ of Egoity. Nor will it help you out of this difficulty to say that Consciousness presents distinctions owing to the impressions left behind by previous 'states of being a knowing subj-ct' due to a series of previous Ahaṅkāras. For the fact is that none of the philosophical schools are capable of giving a satisfactory account of what is to be understood by the *knowing subject* (*pramātṛi*), *the means of true knowledge* (*pramāṇa*) and so on. We will show this in detail.

First as concerns the Vedāntins and Sāṅkhyas. According to them, is the *knowing subject* constituted by the organ of Egoity, or by the Self? The former cannot be, since the organ of Egoity is of non-intelligent nature. Nor also the latter; for *being a knowing subject* means being the subject of changes consisting in the activity called *pramāṇa i.e.* true cognition; and how can such changes be attributed to the Self which is essentially non-changing? And if Consciousness illumined objects without being a knowing subject, all objects would present themselves to it at once—for Consciousness is omnipresent; and hence that distinction of states of consciousness which corresponds to difference of *karman* could not establish itself.

Next as concerns the Naiyāyikas. According to them knowledge is something that is originated in the infinitely extended Self. What then, we ask, is the substrate of such knowledge—is it the Self in its whole extent? or that part of the Self which is particularized by the body? The former alternative is inadmissible; for it would imply that—as there is no other determining factor—all things would present themselves to Consciousness at once. But there *is* a determining factor *viz.*, merit and demerit! Not so, we reply. Merit and demerit may be supposed to act as determining factors with regard to objects of experience that give rise to pleasure or pain, but truly not with regard to quite indifferent objects, such as grass, herbs and the like.* Let us then assume that the required determination takes place

* It may be assumed that merit and demerit are the causes of such special experiences of the soul as possess a retributive character, but not of altogether indifferent states of Consciousness as, *e.g.* the perception of such surrounding objects as grass, trees and the like.

according to the rule that whatever thing *gives rise* to a cognition that thing alone is illumined by it (is its object)! Not so, we reply. This theory would imply that the eye and the other sense-organs are known through the cognitions to which they give rise (which of course is not the case).

Let us then say that through any cognition that thing is known which gives rise to the cognition and at the same time is its object (*viṣaya*). This theory also we cannot accept; for so far we have not defined what an *object* is. And even if we accepted the ordinary definition, we cannot acknowledge it as a binding rule that knowledge—whether viewed as a quality or an action—apprehends only those objects which give rise to it. The light of a lamp—which is a quality of the lamp—illumines the jar, although the latter does not give rise to the light. And similarly the action (motion) of an arrow or a similar thing produces an effect on any things with which the substrate of the action (*i.e.* the arrow) comes into contact, even if those things were not aimed at (and hence did not cause the action). Let it then be said that, since the Self which is the substrate of cognition is without parts it is not in contact with things, and that this is the reason why all things are not presented to Consciousness at once. In that case, we rejoin, nothing whatever would appear to Consciousness; for knowledge—whether being a quality or an action—cannot pass outside its substrate and enter into connexion with other things. And if it apprehended what it is not in contact with, there would be no limitation to its scope (and then would apprehend anything and everything). On the latter alternative view—knowledge having for its substrate that part of the Self only which is particularized by the body—that part either would be defined by the essential nature of the Self—whence it would follow that the Self consists of parts;—or else it would be defined by the limiting adjunct (the body). If, in that case, knowledge apprehended only what is in connexion with that place (*i.e.*, the place of the body), things external to the body—such as jars and the like—would not be presented to Consciousness. And if, on the other hand, it also apprehended what is in connexion with that part of the Self that is external to the body, all things would be simultaneously presented to Consciousness. But, it is objected, even on those things which are not in contact with it, the action of knowledge can produce an effect only within strict limits; in the same way as a magical rite, even though operative upon people a thousand miles away will strike dead only that person at whom it is aimed. The analogy does not hold good, we reply; for we are obliged to infer some determining factor which is in connexion with both the person striking dead and the person struck—whether it be some inferior deity, or the Lord, or the magical rite itself,—the inference being in the form—'The magical rite produces an effect on something with which it is in connexion; for it is an action, like the action of an arrow.' Let us then conceive the case as follows: The internal organ (*manas*) is conjoined with the Self which is the substrate of knowledge; with the *manas* there is conjoined the sense-organ; and with the sense-organ the object. It is this chain of conjunctions which determines the actual origination of knowledge. This explanation also, the opponent replies, we cannot accept. For that entire chain of conjunctions spends itself, before cognition begins to exist, in the origination of cognition. If, even after cognition has come into existence, the object were presented to consciousness by means of that chain of conjunctions, the whole world would be presented to consciousness; for the object is connected with other things, these again with others and so on, the connexions in the end extending to all things whatever. In a similar way we might set forth the difficulties connected with the view of the Self being either of atomic size or of the same size as the body. The conclusion from all this is that no system is capable of giving a satisfactory account of the process of cognition, the cognising subject and so on.

XXXIV

[This objection is met by showing that on the Vedānta theory an intelligible and coherent account of empirical cognition and the distinctions implied in it can be given. In any individual act of cognition the internal organ exhibits itself in various aspects and functions; and according to its several relations to these, Consciousness comes to be viewed and spoken of as being either *pramātṛ*, *i.e.*, subject of knowledge, or *pramāṇa* (means of knowledge) or *pramiti* (knowledge).

To this we Vedāntins make the following reply: You are right with regard to other systems; but on the Vedānta theory the processes and entities in question admit of being accounted for.—Positive Nescience, hiding the omnipresent intelligent Self, illusorily unfolds itself (*vivarttate*) in the form of this manifold world. That particular illusory product of Nescience which abides within the body and is termed *internal organ,* on being stimulated by merit or demerit passes out of the body by way of the eye or some other sense-organ, and completely penetrating some object appropriate to its special nature—as *e.g.*, a jar—assumes the form of that object; just as in our ordinary experience the water of a tank, passing out of it by means of an opening in the embankment, flows through several canals into the fields requiring irrigation and assumes the several forms of those fields, whether square or triangular or circular. The internal organ does not however move like water; if it did so it would be incapable of reaching in a moment the most distant objects, such as the moon, the *nakṣatras* and the pole star; but, being capacitated for this by its fiery nature, transforms itself into a long thread of light. Like a ray of light it is also capable of suddenly contracting itself. That it is capable of undergoing changes of form is due to its consisting of parts; like milk (which thereby is enabled to turn into curds). Thus, changing its form in a suitable way the internal organ on the one hand completely penetrates the body to which it belongs *and* the object, and on the other hand, lengthening itself out, extends through the space between the two. That part of it which is limited by the body is called organ of Egoity (*ahaṅkāra*), and agent (*kartṛ*). That part of it which stretches itself out between the body and the thing (*e.g.*, the jar) is termed *vṛitti* (modification; function) or action (*kriyā*). And that part finally which penetrates the thing and constitutes it an object of knowledge is called 'that which serves for manifestation' (*abhivyakti-yogya*). As the internal organ, made up of these three parts, is of an exceedingly pure and transparent nature, Consciousness is manifested through it. Consciousness thus manifested indeed is one only, but is, according to the three several parts of the internal organ which manifest it, denoted by three different terms. That part of Consciousness which is particularized by the *agent*-part of the internal organ is called 'knowing subject' (*pramātṛ*); that part which is particularized by the *action*-part is called 'means of knowledge' (*pramāṇa*); and the part particularized by that part of the internal organ which serves for the manifestation of the object is called '(right) knowledge' (*pramiti*). In this way the 'knowing subject,' 'the means of knowledge' and 'knowledge' are clearly distinguished. In all these three, however, the form of the internal organ is the common factor; and as this form consists only in the relation subsisting between the knowing subject and the object known, it becomes possible for people to make use of such expressions as 'this is known by me'— wherein all three appear as qualifying one another (this mutual qualification being made possible by the fact that the three have a factor common to them all.) As the manifested factor (*i.e.*, Consciousness) and the manifesting factor (*i.e.*, the internal organ), are, through *adhyāsa*, erroneously identified, there is no objection to the view that in ordinary thought and speech, the attributes of either are erroneously imputed to the other.

But, if by what you call the 'manifestation of Consciousness' by the internal organ there be meant the destruction of what conceals Consciousness, it would follow that the mere cognition of a jar effects Release; if, on the other hand, there be meant by it some change in the Self itself, the Self then would be subject to change! Not so, we reply. What is meant by the 'manifestation' of consciousness is only the *suppression* (for the time being, and not entire *destruction*) of what conceals Consciousness. Nor is there any force in the objection made above that, as the organ of Egoity is non-intelligent and the Self not liable to change, there can be no such thing as a 'knowing subject.' For we have shown just now that the 'knowing subject' is nothing else but the *ahaṅkāra*, liable to change, insofar as qualified by the manifestation of Consciousness.

Nor is there any force in the objection that as Consciousness is present everywhere, there can be no distinction of states of consciousness corresponding to difference of *karman*. For, we ask, what do you understand by the absence of such distinction? Do you mean that the consciousness of all men is one and that hence the pleasures and pains experienced by one man must be experienced by all? Or, do you mean that the consciousness of any individual man is present everywhere, so that Devadatta when conscious of a jar must at the same time be conscious of the entire world? The former alternative does not touch us. For we certainly do not maintain that Consciousness by itself is the cause of the perception of objects;—this cannot be, since Consciousness is obscured by Nescience. What we maintain rather is that Consciousness is the cause of perception issofar as it is manifested by the internal organ. Now there is a different internal organ for each man; how then can you say that our view implies a confusion of the experiences of all men? Nor does the second alternative touch us. For the internal organ of any individual man, being bounded by its limitations, cannot connect itself at the same moment with the entire world; it, therefore, is impossible that it should, through Consciousness which it manifests, perceive all things at once. But may not even a limited thing undergo a certain change so as to become all-pervading, like a solar ray? By no means, we reply. For as for each individual object of Perception the causal apparatus on which the change of the internal organ depends—comprising Merit and Demerit, the several sense-organs and so on—necessarily is a different one, the change also would have to be a different one for each object (and hence there can be no change which would enable the internal organ to perceive all things at once). At the same time we admit that a man who through the assiduous practice of Yoga creates for himself the causal apparatus required for such a change of the internal organ as capacitates it to pervade all space, is able to perceive the totality of things at the same moment.

XXXV

[To this theory it may be objected that the existence of an internal organ is a mere assumption, which can neither be proved, nor is capable to account for the fact of several individual experiences.]

But, a further question is asked, what is the determining motive for assuming the internal organ as the limiting adjunct of Consciousness? is it the need to account for the fact that Consciousness which is of an essentially non-related nature and hence incapable of being affected by objects, actually *is* so affected? or, such affection being presupposed, the need to account for Consciousness *illumining* objects? In neither case the assumption would seem to accomplish what it is meant for. For, as regards the former alternative, just because Consciousness is essentially non-related, it cannot be affected by objects even when the internal organ is present as a limiting adjunct. And as regards the latter alternative, the limiting adjunct is not required for the purpose of illumining objects, since such illumination is due exclusively to their connexion with Consciousness. As the hypothesis of the internal organ thus serves no possible purpose it must be given up; and how then shall we ward off the conclusion that Consciousness, omnipresent and hence connected with all objects whatsoever, illumines them all at the same time?

[*Page 73*] The Vedāntin will perhaps attempt to meet this conclusion by establishing the following alternative: "The 'simultaneous consciousness of all objects' that you urge against us—do you view this consciousness as belonging to the consciousness of the individual soul which is a mere reflexion, or to the Brahman-consciousness which is the *thing* reflected? The former cannot be, since the *jīvā*-consciousness is something limited. If you mean the latter, your objection loses its force; for that view is just what we accept; and even though the individual soul and Brahman are really *one*, yet the *limited* consciousness of the one remains quite distinct from the *universal* consciousness of the other; just as the darkness of the image reflected (in a stained mirror) is entirely distinct from the brightness of the object reflected."

But this reasoning is unsound; because all consciousness of objects being the consciousness of Brahman, the individual soul could not have even limited consciousness; just as it has no universal consciousness; for the simple reason that universal consciousness can have no connection with the individual soul which is always limited by the organ of Egoity.

"But as the internal organ which is the limiting adjunct of the individual soul is, through the eyes and the other sense-organs, in connexion with the objects, the soul may in this way cognise objects!" Not so, the opponent replies. For if the soul were to cognise all such things as are in contact with the internal organ, it would also permanently cognise Brahman itself which, as being omnipresent, is in contact with (all things and hence with) the internal organ also. Perhaps you will now advance the following view: "Having Nescience for its limiting adjunct the individual soul,—even though all-pervading (as being one with Brahman)—is yet unable to illumine the entire world; for as it is concealed by Nescience it does itself not shine forth, as appears from the Consciousness 'I am not-knowing.' Nescience itself may be limited; but this constitutes no reason why it should not obscure Consciousness although present everywhere; for we observe that even a finger if held close to the eye may conceal big objects, such as the sun. We, therefore, hold that whatever the obscuring effect of Nescience is overpowered by the *affection* of the internal organ, there consciousness is manifested, and then illumines something, but not all things." But this view also has no foundation; for clearly the internal organ, which is a mere product of Nescience, cannot overpower Nescience, its own material cause. The conclusion is that the Vedantin is unable to account in any way for the distinction of different states of Consciousness, on the part of different individual souls.

XXXVI

[But to this the reply is that without the assumption of internal organs actual individual cognition, in its positive aspects as well as its limitations, could not be accounted for. It is this assumption only which makes it intelligible how there should be the endless illusory play of limited finite minds with limited spheres of objects of cognition. This could not be explained on the mere assumption of a general principle of Nescience. Nor is this view of cognition liable to being confounded with the theory of the Bauddha Idealist (the Vijñānavādin); for according to us (Vedāntins) cognition (or consciousness) is one only, absolutely homogeneous and unchanging and eternal; an element of difference is introduced into it by its objects only, *i.e.*, the innumerous special modifications of that great magic show of Māyā or Nescience which, though existing *for* Consciousness only, is not of its essence. The Vijñānavādin on the other hand holds that there exist numberless series of individual acts of cognition—or states of consciousness—each of which is momentary and has its own distinctive character: the distinction of these cognitions belongs to them *essentially*, and is *not* due to the difference of objects; for objects of thought, in any sense, do not exist.]

To this reasoning we, Vedāntins, make the following reply: The consciousness of the individual soul, although on account of its *non-related* character it is not affected elsewhere, is affected through the internal organ, since such is its nature. In an analogous way, generic character (*jāti*), as *e.g.*, of cows, although present everywhere (as being eternal) is affected (so as to manifest itself) only in certain individual bodies characterized by dewlaps and so on; not in any other place. If to this analogy it be objected that *jāti* ('*gotva*') even though all-pervading exists in certain individuals only, we refer you to the light of a lamp as furnishing a fully analogous instance. The light of a lamp, although penetrating alike places where there is colour, taste, smell, sound etc., manifests colour only, nothing else. In the same way, we assume, the limiting adjunct constituted by the internal organ serves the purpose of bringing about the affection of Consciousness by objects. Nor is the light of Consciousness capable of illumining objects, apart from such affection; for like the light of a lamp, it illumines only what is in actual contact with it. Brahman indeed—as being the material cause of all—illumines the entire world as belonging to its Self and non-different from itself, even without the affection due to a limiting adjunct. The individual soul, on the other hand, is incapable of doing this, since it is not the material cause of the world. Nor must it be thought that as the individual soul in itself has no illumining power, it is incapable—as a jar would be—of acquiring illumining power through connexion with something else; for we observe that while mere fire has no power to burn grass and the like; it acquires that power when pervading a lump of iron. Hence even on the supposition of the individual soul being nothing else but pure witnessing Consciousness, essentially unrelated and not concealed by Nescience, the distinction of different states of consciousness may be explained as due to the internal organ. If, on the other hand, the individual soul is conceived as a reflexion of pure Consciousness in the internal organ, it of course is something limited, and the distinction referred to will explain itself all the more easily. The cognition of objects at bottom no doubt belongs to Brahma-consciousness; but since that Brahma-consciousness is not manifested in the modification of the internal organ, which is the limiting adjunct of the individual soul and which pervades the object,—it may without contradiction, be viewed as *Jīva*-consciousness also. Brahman again no doubt is connected with the internal organ (for it is connected with all things), but there is no modification of that organ which has the form of Brahman; and this explains why the individual soul does not at all times cognize Brahman. For it is not the mere internal organ as such which manifests a thing, but the change of the organ into the form of the thing. Otherwise merit and demerit etc. also—which abide in the internal organ—would manifest themselves to consciousness. The individual soul itself also is manifested not in the mere internal organ, but in that organ when undergoing a certain *Ego*-modification which has the form of the soul. In deep sleep where that Ego-modification does not take place, there is no consciousness of the individual Self. It thus appears that also on the view of the individual soul being a reflexion of pure Consciousness in the internal organ, the fact of there being many distinct states of individual conscious experience, in accordance with the many distinct *karmans*, presents no theoretical difficulties.

If, again, the individual soul is viewed as omnipresent Consciousness having Nescience for its adjunct, then also the distinction in question (*viz.*, of many different states of individual experience) can be accounted for on the ground of the internal organ *concealing* the *concealing* factor (*i.e.* Nescience). For it is by no means impossible that an effect should conceal its material cause; we observe *e.g.*, that such products as scorpions and plants conceal *their* material causes *i.e.*, cowdung and earth; that is to say, we do not recognise in the body of the scorpion the dung from which it has sprung, nor in the plant the earth out of which it is formed. We thus arrive at a conclusion which disposes completely of the objection raised above (p. 70). The Vedānta system *does* supply us with the means to account for the current distinctions of *subject of knowledge, means of knowledge* and so on; we, therefore, are justified in holding that an element of distinction is introduced into Consciousness by the impressions left behind by previous states of 'knowing subject,' due to previous *ahaṅkāras*; and that hence, the superimposition on such Consciousness of an *ahaṅkāra*, containing within itself elements of distinction, is something possible.

Nor may it be urged against this view that, as on it all objects of knowledge are mere illusory products (*vivartta*) of, and have no existence apart from, Consciousness, the theory of the *Vedāntin* thus becomes identical with that of the *Vijñānavādin*. For if doctrines were declared to be identical on account of some partial agreement, a general confusion of all doctrines would be the result. In the case under discussion there certainly is no complete agreement. The *Vijñānavādin* holds that there are many momentary cognitions (*vijñāna*) and that the (so-called) objects are non-different from the cognitions. We, on the other hand, who hold the true doctrine, maintain that there is only one eternal cognition (Consciousness) upon which there are superimposed (through *avidyā*) objects possessing separate causal powers, and that there is nothing to sublate the permanency of those objects. This Consciousness we hold to be without a second (one only), because it is everywhere recognised (as one and the same). The appearance of difference implied in the several cognitions of a jar, a piece of cloth and so on, depends on the objects; it does not belong to the essential nature of cognition. From this non-duality of consciousness there at once follows its eternity. Nor is it true that cognition and its objects are non-different; the truth rather is that they are of an absolutely different nature, consciousness having the characteristics of *inwardness* and *continuity,* objects those of *outwardness* and *discontinuity.*

The separate causal efficiency of objects is proved by immediate experience; and their permanence follows from the fact of recognition. Hence although the organ of Egoity and the rest (*i.e.*, the entire objective world) are merely superimposed upon Consciousness, (and hence not *real* in the true sense) the *Vedānta*-theory can by no means be confounded with the theory of the *Vijñānavādin.*

XXXVII

[Nor can we allow the Vijñānavādin's argument that the so-called consciousness of real objects of thought may be resolved into a mere succession of several momentary cognitions or ideas. For what we actually are conscious of is not a series of discrete momentary cognitions, but cognitions which extend over some time, during which they remain identically the same; identity is immediately *recognized* by us.]

[*Page 75*] At this point, however, the *Vijñānavādin* comes forward and sets up the following plea for his own theory:

'As blue colour and the idea of it are necessarily experienced together, the two are identical. If the blue colour were something different from consciousness, it would not present itself to consciousness at all. If it presented itself to consciousness (although different from it) why should not all things present themselves in one act of consciousness? In neither case do we discern a determining connexion of blue colour and the idea of it.'

Should you say that it is just the fact of the thing's producing the idea which constitutes the necessary connexion for which we ask,—we deny this for the reason that from this it would follow that the sense-organ also is an object, since the organ also produces the idea. We hence hold the object and the idea to be identical. "But the judgment 'I know this thing' implies immediate consciousness of the knowing subject, the object known and the act of cognition as three entities essentially different, although related to one another!" I cannot admit this, the *Vijñānavādin* rejoins, since merely momentary existences cannot be related. If the knowing subject and the object of knowledge were of a permanent nature, they might be connected by the act of knowledge which results from the desire of knowledge; but how can there be a connexion between two momentary entities? We, therefore, must represent to ourselves the process as follows: At first there arise in succession three different cognitions, the *I*-cognition, the *this*-cognition, and the cognition '(I) know,'—each cognition having its own specific character. After this there originates from that third cognition, which is coloured as it were by the after-effect (*vāsanā*) of the first and second cognitions, a new cognition, similar to the third cognition and weighted with the characters of the three preceding cognitions. This being so, it must be admitted that what has the character of an object is nothing else but a momentary cognition. Otherwise (*i.e.*, if there were an independent external object), since no satisfactory definition of the connexion between idea and thing can be given, there could be no consciousness whatever of an object of knowledge. Nor can the momentary nature of cognitions be contested. For just as the cognition of blue colour implies the cognition of the difference of blue colour from yellow and other colours,—so, we conclude, the cognition, which presents itself to consciousness as *present,* implies the exclusion of any connection of that cognition with either the past or the future. The momentariness of cognition thus is proved by immediate knowledge (*pratyakṣa*).

This position we Vedāntins counter-argue as follows: Cognition is not momentary, for (when engaged in some special cognition) we are not conscious of any difference, in successive moments, in the nature of the cognition. Nor do we allow that this absence of consciousness of difference is due to the extremely close resemblance (of the successive momentary cognitions). For we put the following alternative: Is the difference of cognitions (which you maintain) an attribute of each cognition and to be known through a further cognition? or does it constitute the essential nature of the cognition itself, so as to be cognized by this very cognition? On the former alternative, if the two cognitions pertaining to the object, were not themselves cognised by a third cognition, the difference between them would not be apprehended; and if they were cognised by a third cognition, the cognition of difference (between the two) would apprehend all the three factors—(1) the object, (2) the two cognitions and (3) the difference between the cognitions,—with which trinity it would also have to be identical or non-different. On the latter alternative, your contention, that the difference which constitutes the essential nature of the cognitions does not present itself to consciousness because the several cognitions are so very similar, really comes to this that the cognition itself is not apprehended by consciousness; from which there follows a universal blindness of the world (*i.e.,* absence of all consciousness). Nor can we allow you to plead that the difference of the cognitions is assumed in order to account for their similarity; for this alleged similarity is not established by any of the valid means of knowledge and is flatly contradicted by the consciousness of the oneness of cognition. Against this you will perhaps argue as follows: 'Since the appearance of oneness is erroneous, it does not contradict the similarity maintained by us; but as the erroneous appearance of the oneness of different cognitions cannot be accounted for but on the ground of similarity, we are compelled to assume the latter. But this is clear reasoning in a circle. You at first prove the erroneousness of the appearance of oneness of the cognitions on the ground of their being separate but similar, and then you proceed to prove the latter fact by the former. You will possibly attempt to retaliate by charging us with the same logical mistake—'You prove the validity of the consciousness of the oneness of the cognitions, on the ground of their similarity not being established by any means of knowledge, and being contradicted by some; and at the same time you prove the latter fact by the former!' But there you are mistaken. For we hold that the recognition which assures us of the oneness of cognition constitutes an independent means of true knowledge.

XXXVIII

[The Vijñānavādin attempts to upset this argument by denying that a non-contradictory conception of so-called Recognition can be formed. But against this we maintain that Recognition may validly be conceived as perceptive cognition with which there combines an impression left behind by a previous perception. On such recognition there also rests the incontestable consciousness of personal identity; for of the Self, inasmuch as determined by an ahaṅkāra, there may be a mental impression and hence remembrance and recognition. This view also disposes of the Prābhākara theory according to which there is no direct recognition of a permanent identical Self; the latter being proved indirectly only by the fact of the recognition of permanent objects of thought.]

Here our adversary raises an objection against the use we make of Recognition (*pratyabhijñā*). "What," he asks, "do you understand by Recognition? Do you define it as immediate perceptive knowledge (*pratyakṣa*) having for its object the relation of one thing to two points of time, *viz.*, a past one and the present one? This definition we reject; for perceptive knowledge apprehends present things only. 'But recognition *is* of the nature of Perception; for it is originated by what is the cause of the valid cognition of a present thing—such cause being conjoined with the impression left by a previous perception!' This definition also does not satisfy us; for it does not meet the case of the recognition of the Self which expresses itself in the form 'I *now* am the same person I was *then*.' For your (the Vedāntin's) Self is eternal and self-illumined, and hence there can neither be an impression of it, nor can knowledge be originated in it. Nor again can Recognition be defined as neither more nor less than the cognition of a thing's essential nature. For such cognition, like the light of a lamp, illumines only what is present here and now, and hence does not imply reflexion on what is earlier and later (reflexion of which kind after all is implied in Recognition). On our (the Vijñānavadin's) view, the judgment 'I (am) *that* one (*i.e.* the same person I formerly was)'consists of two cognitions each of which has its own specific character, and is not a 'recognition.' As *Recognition* thus does not admit of a satisfactory definition, you may not use it as a means to prove the oneness of cognition."

To this we Vedāntins make the following reply: Although knowledge cannot indeed be originated in the pure Self, and there can be no impression of it, yet both these things are possible with regard to the Self qualified by the internal organ; and of this Self, therefore, there can be recognition as defined by us. Nor must you object to this on the ground that, if the Self qualified by the internal organ is the object of recognition, and at the same time the recognising subject also, there arises the contradiction of one and the same thing being object of action and agent. For, the followers of all philosophical schools are agreed that the Self is agent and object of action, insofar as it is the object of certain inferential reasonings as to its difference from the body and similar things. Against this the following objection will perhaps be raised: In inferential reasoning the so-called 'object' (*viṣaya*) is not an *object of action (karmaṇ)*, since when we infer something past or distant or the like, the object (*viṣaya*) not being present cannot give rise to cognition. On the other hand, even what is not present may be an object (*viṣaya*), for cognition has that character. In inference, therefore, the Self is (*not a karmaṇ* but) agent (*kartṛ*) only; in perceptive knowledge, on the other hand, the object of which gives rise to cognition, it is *object of action* (*karmaṇ*) also. Hence the contradiction animadverted on above (of the Self being at once *karmaṇ* and *kartṛ*) is not removed (since the instance of *anumāna* is not analogous). Your objection, we reply, is invalid, for you overlook the following point. In recognition of the Self, the Self insofar as qualified by the internal organ is the recognising agent, and the Self insofar as qualified by earlier and later time is the object recognised: it is this difference of conditioning adjuncts which renders it possible for the Self to be at the same time agent and object of action.

But, a final objection is raised,—why take all this trouble to prove the validity of Recognition? Let us rather say that there is no such thing as recognition! Impossible, we rejoin. For, recognition expressing itself in the form 'I now am the same person I formerly was' is vouched for by immediate consciousness. And as all men are agreed as to this, it cannot be a case of error. The contention of the Bauddha, that in the judgment 'I (am) that' we have to do with two separate cognitions each of which has its own character, cannot be upheld. For were this so, we should have to conclude that also in the judgment 'cognition is momentary' we have to do with two cognitions, and in that case the theory of the momentariness of cognition (which is the Bauddha's great mainstay) could clearly not be established. And if to this the reply were given that in the view of those who hold that cognitions only exist, all attributes, including momentariness, are unreal, we ask—what then prevents you from admitting also *permanency* and similar attributes as unreal? This would at any rate be in accordance with such immediate deliverances of consciousness as 'I am now the same person as I formerly was.'

We next turn to the view of the nature of recognition, held by the followers of Prabhākara. In their opinion the permanent Self is established, not by the fact of its being the object of recognition expressing itself in the form 'I am the same I was'; but by the fact of its being the substrate of recognitive cognitions such as 'this is that jar (I perceived previously).' This view we must reject. For that which is distinguished by connexion with earlier and later time cannot be the substrate of a recognitive act which is a momentary function only, and hence the permanency of the Self cannot be proved from Recognition.

To this the Prābhākara makes the following reply: "A previous cognition of a jar or the like object, when remembered at the present moment in the form 'I then had such and such a cognition' establishes as the substrate of that cognition a Self existing at the time of the cognition; and, again, the act a remembrance proves the existence of a present Self as the substrate of that act. It is in this way that the existence of a permanent Self is established, and there is no need of the hypothesis—not resting on any valid means of knowledge—of a recognition—'I am the same person I was'—which has the Self for its object." This, we rejoin, is unsound reasoning. The remembrance and the original perception, being two several acts of cognition, no doubt prove the existence of a Self at those two points of time; but there is nothing to prove the connexion with both those times of one and the same Self. "But it is just that double cognition which proves that connexion also!"

But then in the same way in the case of the jar also the permanence of the object will be established by the two several cognitions and an additional recognition will not be required! The recognition will serve the purpose of strengthening the proof of the object's permanence! Let us then return to the question under discussion (*viz.*, whether there is a direct recognition of the Self or not). Do those two cognitions on which you insist, prove the connexion of the Self with two points of time directly, or by giving rise to recognition? On the former alternative, either cognition by itself cannot prove that connexion, since either by itself cannot have for its substrate the Self as related to two points of time. Nor can the two in combination prove that connexion; for a past perception and a present remembrance cannot be simultaneous. And the second alternative implies that you also accept the recognition 'I am the same person I was' as having for its object the permanent Self. Nor must you say that the Self is at no time the object of cognition, and hence cannot be the object of recognition, for in the judgment 'there took place such and such a cognition of mine,' the Self is the object of the cognition of remembrance. In the remembrance the Self, insofar as connected with the time when the remembrance originates, indeed is presented only as the substrate of the cognitional activity, not as its object; but at the same time the Self which was the substrate of, and contemporaneous with, the remembered cognition, becomes the object of the present cognitional activity. But should we not rather say that the remembrance constitutes as its object the original cognition only, and that this remembered cognition suggests to consciousness the Self which was its substrate, as substrate only? Not so, we reply. For at the time of remembrance the original cognition is not present, and therefore incapable of establishing its substrate. Only such states of consciousness as are self-illumined prove their substrate, and not such as are the object of remembrance and hence illumined by something outside themselves. Otherwise it would follow that also merit and the rest which are established by something else have the power of proving the Self which is their substrate. It therefore must be admitted that the Self of past time *is* the object of remembrance. And this then justifies us in holding that also the recognitive judgment 'I am the same I formerly was' has the Self for its object. Hence the *Prā bhākaras* also have to reject the doctrine of the momentariness of the conscious Self, on the ground of that recognition of which the Self is the object.

XXXIX

[Nor is there any force in the arguments by which the Bauddha endeavours to prove the momentariness of all that *is*, *i.e.*, on the Vijñānavāda view of all cognition. Particularly he fails to effect this on the ground that *being* means *having causal power*; for he is quite unable to give a satisfactory account of the 'causal power' of momentary states of cognition.]

Well, the Bauddha resumes, let us then prove the momentariness of jars and the like (*i.e.*, things generally called *external*) in the following way. 'The penultimate and all preceding moments of the existence of the jar are invariably accompanied by the destruction of that jar which will exist in the next following moment (*i.e.*, each moment of the jar's existence implies the non-existence of the jar of the next following moment), for they all are moments of the existence of the jar; just as the last moment is (which is avowedly followed by the jar's destruction).' But this inference is invalid, since it may be met by the equally specious, following inference. 'The moment of the jar's destruction implies the existence of the jar; for it is a moment of time, just as those other moments of time, in which the jar is acknowledged to exist.' And if to this latter inference you object that the conclusion contradicts the actual consciousness of the jar's non-existence (consequent on destruction), we reply that your inference as to the momentariness of the jar equally contradicts an indubitable fact of experience, *viz.*, the recognition 'the jar of the present moment is the same jar I perceived in previous moments.'

Well, the Bauddha resumes, we then set forth the following inference: 'whatever has being (all existent things; *bhāvāḥ*) is momentary; for it possesses causal power. (The underlying *vyāpti* being 'whatever possesses causal power is momentary'); while absence of causal power implies non-being as exemplified by the 'hare's horn' (which is a non-entity).

Nor may this be met by the counter-assertion that the capability of producing effects which are preceded by causal activity belongs only to permanent things other than the conjunction of efficient causes, and not to momentary existences. For, we ask, does your permanent thing produce one effect only; or several effects simultaneously; or several effects in succession? On the two former alternatives the permanency of the thing lapses; for an effect originating once only can be due to a momentary cause only. And the third alternative is inadmissible; for a thing capable of producing effects is not capable of delay (*i.e.*, no reason can be assigned why the effects which a thing is at all capable of producing should not be produced all at once. The characteristic feature of existences thus is that they produce all their effects in one moment.

To this we Vedāntins make the following reply: Your reasoning is invalid, since you are unable to give a satisfactory account of causal efficiency. For in what sense can cognitions (*saṃvid*; states of consciousness) be causally active? Does this mean that a state of consciousness originates a cognition, the object of which is the originating state of consciousness? or that it originates another momentary existence (cognition)? And in the former case, does the cognition produced belong to its own series (*i.e.*, the series constituting the person to which the originating cognition belongs)? or to the series constituting some other person? or to the series of the All-knowing one? The first alternative is inadmissible; since states of consciousness are self-illumined (and hence require no cognition outside themselves to illumines them).

"Let us then accept the second alternative. For a state of consciousness of Devadatta may, although self-illumined, be the object of, and hence that which produces, a state of consciousness of Yajñadatta." This also is untenable, we reply. For the consciousness of Devadatta cannot be the object of, and hence produce, *perceptive* cognition on the part of Yajñadatta; for the reason that we never observe that the state of mind of one person is an object of perception on the part of another person. Nor again can Devadatta's consciousness be the object of, and hence produce, *inferential* cognition on the part of Yajñadatta; for you admit that perceptive cognition only is produced by its object. "The third alternative then will hold good. For the perceptive (intuitive) cognition of the all-knowing Lord constitutes as its objects the states of consciousness of all men, and hence is produced by them." By no means, we reply. For if this were the case, the consciousness of the Lord would be perturbed by the troubled thoughts of the creatures involved in the *saṃsāra*. For in your view the cognition and the object of cognition are one.

"But may we not say that the consciousness of the Lord although troubled in this way does not suffer from these troubles, for the reason that they are sublated by the knowledge of truth?"

Not so, we reply. A cognition cannot sublate its own trouble; for the latter cannot in one and the same moment be brought about and also sublated. Nor can a further cognition refer itself to the trouble and sublate it; for the trouble of a previous cognition is not the object of a subsequent one. And if it were that, the subsequent cognition would be perturbed just as the previous one; and how then could it sublate the trouble? Nor finally can the conscious element of the cognition, separating itself from the element of trouble, be the object of—and thus produce—a cognition on the part of the Lord. For if this were so, the Lord would not be aware of the trouble of the creatures, and how then could He impart the instruction required by them?

Nor can we accept the second of the above alternatives, *viz.*, that momentary existences have causal efficiency insofor as originating other momentary existences. For from this it would, on your theory, follow that the last 'moment' (momentary existence) has no being. To explain. You hold that there arise in constant succession cognitions perturbed by the false imaginations of permanency, of the distinction of substance and quality and the like, by desire and other defects, and by objects—each cognition being originated by impressions having the character of former cognitions of the same kind. The true conception 'All this is momentary' puts an end to the imagination of Permanency. The conception 'everything is *svalakṣaṇa*' destroys the imagination of substances, qualities and the rest. Through the conception 'all this is pain' the troubles caused by desire and other imperfections, by action, by pleasure and pain, pass away. And finally the conception 'all is void' dispels the trouble due to objects. Those four true conceptions, antagonistic to all impressions left by previous cognitions, thus having gradually allayed thee four-fold trouble, there originates from the penultimate state of consciousness, which is the last state in which the true conceptions preponderate—one further state of consciousness which is free from all trouble. This state, being the last link of the chain that constitutes the *saṃsāra,* is called 'the last moment.' Now, since this last moment does not originate any effect of its own, it follows (on the view of the *Vijñānavādin*) that it has no being; and from this there follows, by a retrogressive extension of the same reasoning, the non-being of all the preceding 'moments.' But that last moment being an object of cognition on the part of the Lord produces cognition in him (and hence does possess causal efficiency)!

From this it would follow, we reply, that the 'last moment' (of consciousness on the part of the individual being) and the cognition on the part of the Lord, being both of them absolutely pure, (free from all perturbation) would be of the same nature, and hence be constituents of one and the same chain;—for the relation of cause and effect between two things of the same nature is just what constitutes the characteristic mark of one chain. And as thus the chain would not be broken, there would be no release. Let it then be assumed that it is just this entering (of the last link of the chain of individual consciousness) into the chain of the All-knowing one that constitutes Release! On this supposition also, we reply, it would be difficult to explain in what way that last moment should be the object of the Lord's cognition, and hence it cannot be shown to possess causal efficiency. For two states of consciousness can stand in the relation of object (*viṣaya*) and that *for* which the object is (*viṣayin*), only if they are different; but in the present case no difference exists. One state of consciousness (quâ consciousness), does not differ from another state of consciousness; difference between the two could be established only by denying the character of consciousness to that other state. Nor can the former state be said to differ from the latter quâ non-consciousness; for that would imply that a state of consciousness is a state of non-consciousness (which is absurd). It, therefore, cannot be proved that the 'last moment' possesses causal efficiency, inasmuch as producing a cognition on the part of the All-knowing one; and hence that last moment has no *being* (in the sense allowed by the Bauddha). Again, if we were to *assume* that the last moment produces an effect, the question would arise whether the causal efficiency thus manifested establishes the *being* of its cause (*i.e.*, the last moment), or the *idea* of it. The former cannot be accepted, since the cause exists before the effect: otherwise it could not be a cause. If the latter were the case, the effect would bring about the idea of the cause only when itself manifested by its cause; and similarly the idea of the cause also, being an effect, would manifest the idea of its own cause, and so on; there thus would be a *regressus ad infinitum.* And should you say that a state of consciousness manifests itself and that hence no such *regressus* takes place, you give up the position that causal efficiency is the cause of the idea of a thing having *being* (as under your last hypothesis the idea would not have causal efficiency). If, in order to avoid this, the idea were to be regarded as its own effect and cause, this would involve an objectionable self-dependence (*atmāshraya*). The conclusion from all this is that 'being' (*Sattva*) does not consist in possessing causal energy, but is a certain specific attribute not further to be explained. Hence there is no reason why a permanent thing which after having in one moment produced an effect is at rest (*i.e.*, does not produce effects) in the subsequent moments should not possess *being*. We now turn to the assertion, above made by the *Vijñānavādin,* that a permanent thing cannot produce several effects in succession, since that which is at all capable of producing effects cannot delay doing so. This also is quite unfounded. It is in full accordance with reason that a thing capable of producing certain effects should produce them in succession only, such succession being regulated by the succession in which the different auxiliary factors co-operating towards the production of the effect combine with the causal thing. For that this actually takes place is a matter of common experience.

Against that our view the following objection will possibly be raised. As after all it is irrational to view a thing capable of producing certain effects as standing in need of co-operating factors, let us assume that all things are in themselves destitute of causal power and give rise to the required causal apparatus by their mutual relations, and that the causal apparatus thus produced is what produces the effect. But this theory also is untenable. For if the several things possess the capability of producing the causal apparatus, their mutual relations are not required; and if they do not possess that capability and hence do not produce the apparatus, their mutual relations will remain fruitless; so in either case we can do nothing with those mutual relations. Let us then say that nothing ever depends on co-operating factors (for producing an effect). This, we reply, is in conflict with experience. Nor can such experience be held to be erroneous, since there is nothing to refute it. You no doubt have declared that the need of co-operating factors cannot rationally be assumed either for that which in itself has causal power or for that which has no such power; but such need may be assumed in the case of the *mere thing*, conceived as devoid alike of causal power and its absence. For this is what you also will have to accept: for instance, when you are faced by the following difficulty—'if the effect has *being* (real existence), you, implicitly, abandon your fundamental theory; if on the other hand, it has no real being, it becomes impossible satisfactorily to account for the connexion of special causes with special effects, and this would imply that anything may spring from anything'—you will have to put aside all connexion or non-connexion (of cause and effect) with being or non-being and simply define a cause as that which has regular previous existence, and an effect as that which has regular subsequent existence. And if, accepting these definitions, you point out that positive and negative experiences determine what actually has regular previous existence and hence is a cause, and what has regular subsequent existence and hence is an effect—we point out that just in the same way positive and negative experiences determine that certain auxiliary factors, co-operating with the causal thing, have regular previous existence. And this conclusively proves that there is the need (for the causal thing in the narrower sense) of co-operative factors.—A further question is in what special way these auxiliary factors affect the causal thing by their action.

On this question a certain school propounds the following view. In the case of the causal thing termed *seed* certain co-operative factors, such as earth, water, etc.,—the co-operation of which is proved by positive and negative experience—produce *in the seed* a certain condition termed *turgescence, (uchchhūnatā)* and it is thereby that the seed acquires causal power with regard to its effect, *i.e.,* the sprout; were it otherwise, earth, water and so on, would not be helpful and hence not required by the seed. But this also is an untenable view. For the question arises, is the seed capable of giving rise to that special condition of itself, or is it not so capable? If it is not capable, it will not give rise to that condition even when a thousand co-operative factors are at hand, and consequently it will not be capable of producing the sprout. If, on the other hand, it *is* so capable, we ask—is it capable of giving rise to the condition called 'turgescence' only after having passed through another (intermediate) state due to the co-operating factors; or (directly) without having gone through an intermediate state? In the former case that intermediate state will again presuppose another intermediate state, and that again another and so on, in *infinitum*. And in the latter case, why then, possessing causal power as it does (according to the assumption), should it not give rise to the sprout directly, without any intervening condition? But, the opponent says, the origination of the sprout presupposes the origination of the condition called 'turgescence; while the origination of this latter condition is effected by the mere presence of the co-operating factors; for this is what is actually observed. If this were so, we reply, the cause, capable of producing certain effects, would require co-operative factors which do not produce any helpful effect upon it; and this is a conclusion that contradicts your original position. This last view, held by a certain school cannot therefore be established.

Well, the advocate of general momentariness now resumes, just from this it follows that our view must be accepted. For we hold not that the co-operating factors have a helpful action on the cause itself; but that the effect springing from the momentary original cause demands co-operating causes, since an effect is brought about by many causes. So much indeed we hold in common with you who maintain the existence of permanent causes. But on your view it is difficult to escape from the conclusion that the effects should originate immediately, as soon as the cause exists; for there is nothing to determine successive production of the effects. Nor may you say that there *is* something to account for such successive production of effects; *viz.*, the successive connexion and non-connexion of the causal thing with auxiliary factors. For this 'connexion' also must persist so long as the correlates of that connexion exist (and hence the contingency of the immediate origination of effects remains). Nor may you say that what determines the connexion is a further connexion; for this leads us into an infinite regress. Nor may you urge against us that, 'on the view of universal momentariness also the effect cannot be conceived as originating in the moment of the existence of the cause, since that would imply the simultaneousness of cause and effect (and thus contradict the very nature of cause and effect); and that, if we should maintain that the two are not simultaneous but that the effect exists at *another* moment, there would be nothing to determine that moment'. For there *is* such a determining circumstance: the moment of the existence of the effect is the moment which immediately succeeds the moment of the cause. All which proves the doctrine of general momentariness to be the only sound one.

But this we, Vedāntins, finally re-argue as follows: In all cases the relation of cause and effect is to be ascertained on the basis of invariable concomitance. Let us take a special instance. Does, in your opinion, the invariable concomitance of cause and effect exist between individual fire-moments and smoke-moments, or between the two entire respective series? The former cannot be, since mere momentary existences cannot persist during the time required by the two cognitions of positive and negative concomitance (through which the *Vyāpti* is established). And on the latter alternative it would follow that smoke would originate also from fire in the condition of glowing coals; for fire in that state also is a member of the 'fire series,' just as fire in other conditions is. Nor is it open to you to argue that in this latter case the non-production of smoke is accounted for by the absence of wood; for wood also exists at the time,—*viz.*, in its own series. Nor may it be said that there is, in the given case, no connexion between the wood and the fire (and hence no smoke); for as the two series are permanent, such connexion must necessarily be admitted. Nor again can it be said that the connexion is not permanent (eternal), since it depends on another previous connexion; for this would lead us into an infinite regress. But from this latter difficulty we escape by accepting the view (generally allowed) that we need not go beyond three or four steps backward (in the series of previous connexions accounting for the present connexion!)* Well, we reply, if you admit this the difficulty of an infinite regress may be avoided with equal ease by those who accept the view of the cause being something permanent, and the objections raised on that ground against the latter view thus falls to the ground. But, our opponent resumes, the upholder of the permanence of causes may perhaps smooth over the difficulties of his theory by the assumption of the helpful action of co-operating factors; but it is just this assumption to which we object! Not so we reply. Positive and negative experiences fully prove that the relation between smoke—the effect—and wood—the co-operative factor—is that of a thing helped and a thing helpful; and that relation; therefore, must necessarily be admitted. And that positive and negative experiences prove the relation of thing helped and thing helpful is observed in the case of the original cause and its effect, *viz.*, fire and

---

* The supposition being that which is established by three or four links of the retrogressive causal chain is sufficiently established for all purposes. Compare *Shlokavārtika*, Sū 2, Shloka 61.

smoke. The need of co-operative factors exercising a helpful influence on the cause thus has to be equally admitted on both views. On the theory of the momentariness of causes the one fire is held to produce, owing to difference of co-operative factors and of place, several simultaneous effects—in its own place it produces another fire, (*i.e.*, the next momentary fire of that series of momentary existences which we term *fire*); in the space above it produces smoke, and in the space below it produces ashes, and in the beholder's mind it produces the idea of fire. On the theory of the permanence of causes, again, one and the same cause produces several effects, in dependence on difference of time and of co-operative factors. What then are the grounds for denying that there may be production of effects, by one cause, in succession? Nor must it be imagined that the two theories thus virtually come to the same (and hence are equally valid). For we have already demolished the former theory at the conclusion of the section on *Pratikarmavyavasthā* (pp. 73-74).—The final conclusion to be drawn from all this is that setting aside the utterly perverse theory of those who hold cognition to be momentary we must hold fast the absolutely unexceptionable Vedānta view according to which all objects of cognition are mere unreal superimpositions on the one eternal and unchanging Consciousness.

XL

[It is objected to the Vedāntic view that if consciousness illumines all things superimposed upon itself, there would be equal immediate presentation of things perceived and things inferred, there being nothing to differentiate the two. But the reply to this is that there *is* a differentiating circumstance inasmuch perceived things, and not inferred ones, are in contact with the organs of perception and thus directly act on the internal organ. The objection that consciousness which is free of all distinctions cannot have superimposed upon itself things marked by distinctions is disposed of by the observation that a manifold world is superimposed upon a consciousness affected by the impressions left by previous states marked by distinction. That, at bottom, non-differenced Consciousness is the ultimate substrate of general avidyā rests on its *āparokṣya,* the directly presentative character.]

But—an objection to the Vedānta theory is raised on a new ground—this Vedānta view also after all is untenable. For if non-changing consciousness immediately illumines all things superimposed upon itself we are driven to the conclusion that there is immediate presentation also of things inferred (no less than of things directly perceived). If, on the other hand, consciousness be held not to give rise to immediate presentation of things inferred, it will follow that also things directly perceived—such as jars and the like—are not immediately presented. For there is nothing to determine a distinction between the two cases. Against this it must not be said that it is the sense-organ which, in the case of perception, determines immediate presentation. For if it be the external sense-organs that possess that power, it will follow that pleasure, pain and the like (which do not depend on the activity of the external organs, but on that of the internal organ) are not immediately presented. And if, on the other hand, it be the internal organ that has such power, it will needs follow that also things inferred are immediately presented.

This objection, we reply, is unfounded. For there *is* something to determine the distinction you refer to, *viz.*, the instrumental and manifesting power of objects immediately perceived. For jars and similar things are the objects (*karman*) of that modification of the internal organ which, passing out by way of the eye or some other sense-organ, completely pervades the thing; the thing thus effects the modification of the internal organ; when the thing is absent that modification does not take place. And Again, after that modification has been produced by the thing, consciousness is manifested; the thing thus possesses manifesting power. There thus is a special reason why things perceived should be immediately presented to consciousness. In the case, on the other hand, of things inferred the two attributes—of possessing effective and manifesting power—are not necessarily present; for things inferred frequently are either past or future and things of these two kinds cannot be the substrates of *present* attributes. But, it is objected, when we infer, *e.g.*, that there has been rain, rain is present to the mind as something that is past, and it hence may be the substrate of those two present attributes! Not so, we reply. Do you mean that, at the time when the inference is made, rain is present, or that the attribute of being past is present? On the former alternative rain would at the same time be past and present; which is a contradiction. Nor is the second alternative admissible. For being past means to be connected with past time which is different from present time: while, therefore, the present time is connected with a jar or the like (when this is perceived) and so defines the thing perceived, this is not the case with regard to the attribute of being past; we can only say that the present time determines (helps in the conception of) that attribute in the same way as the jar determines the non-existence of the jar. The attribute of being past, therefore, is not present in the same sense as the jar—which is now perceived— is present. But, our opponent objects, if that attribute did not admit of being viewed as present in the full sense of the word, we should have to say that it is an absolute non-entity like the horn of a man; we, therefore, must conclude after all that it is simply present! Even thus, we retort, rain as qualified by that attribute does not possess those efficient and manifesting powers which belong to rain actually present. Devadatta when dead cannot produce a jar, and a lamp which has gone out cannot manifest that jar.

But, our opponent asks, if things inferred do not possess the efficient and manifesting power of things perceived, how is it that the ideas of them which are produced by the inference have the form of the respective objects? Our reply is that the inferential mark (*liṅga*), the word and so on, owing to the strength of certain connections,—*viz.*, that of *avinābhāva, i.e.*, invariable connexion between the *liṅga* and the thing inferred; and that of *shakti* ('power') between the word and the thing denoted by it—impart to the idea the form of the thing. Nor must it be said that as we allow to things inferred, past or present, the attribute of being objects (*viṣaya*), so we must also allow to them the attributes of having effective and manifesting power; and that as in Perception so in Inference also it is only through this relation of their being objects that a definite form is imparted to the ideas. For the 'being an object' of a thing inferred is not some positive attribute which could be used to establish the above conclusion; but means only the cessation of that condition in which the thing inferred was previously to the mental act of inference. Nor must it be imagined that this very condition can be used as a proving instance; for it is no more than the antecedent non-existence of the said termination (*i.e.*, it is something entirely negative). It, therefore, is impossible to establish for things inferred, whether past or future, a positive grammatical case character (*kārakatva*). But if things inferred do not stand in the *karmaṇ*-relation (*i.e.* are not objects of action), how then can we put them in connexion with transitive (*sakarmaka*) verbs—as we actually do when we say that the person who infers past rain 'knows the rain? By a kind of metaphor, we reply. Inference has a result in the same way as 'sakarmaka' perceptive cognition has; and on account of that result we speak of it as if it were itself 'sakarmaka.' If we allowed to Inference an object (*karman*) in the primary sense, we could not avoid allowing to it also immediate presentation, as we do to Perception. When, therefore, the inference is concerned with a thing that (is not past or future but) exists at the present time—as *e.g.* a fire burning now—, that thing also, because sharing the general nature of being a thing inferred, must be viewed as not holding the position of a *karmaṇ*; for otherwise we should have to acknowledge that it is presented immediately. In the case of Perception on the other hand where invariable connexion (*avinābhāva*) and other connexions do not operate, we must hold the thing to be a true object (*karmaṇ*), so as to account for the form of the thing imparting itself to the cognition. And there in fact is no difficulty of attributing that position to the thing perceived, since that thing is necessarily one existing at the time. The conclusion, therefore, is that although all things are at all times equal insofar as being merely superimposed on non-changing Consciousness, the quality of being immediately presented belongs to the objects of Perception only; for they only possess efficient case character and manifesting power.

Nor again is there room for the doubt whether it be possible that on Consciousness which in itself is free from all distinction there should be superimposed things marked by distinctions. For— as we have shown in the section treating of the distinctions of consciousness corresponding to *karmaṇ*,—what constitutes the substrate of the *adhyāsa* of Egoity and so on, is (not consciousness absolutely devoid of distinction but) Consciousness as differentiated by the impressions left behind by previous states in which the Self was (not pure consciousness but) an individual personal knowing subject (*pramātṛ*). But, our opponent resumes, after all you will have to admit that fundamental Nescience—which is the material cause of the entire phenomenal world including impressions, etc.—is superimposed on pure distinctionless Consciousness. For all other things which impart to Consciousness the character of being something marked by distinction depend for their very existence on this primary *adhyāsa* of Nescience. And then we are again confronted by the difficulty that something free from all distinction cannot be a substrate; since experience shows that that only which is marked by distinction is a substrate. How then can that (Consciousness) which is without distinction be superimposed upon by Nescience? This argument does not affect our 'position, we reply. For all that is necessary for Consciousness being the substrate is that there should be an immediate perception of it; and it is of no consequence whether or not it be qualified by distinctions;—and that it is immediately perceived is to be inferred from the fact of its never being non-perceived. Nor can we allow the objection that the Self is something continuously inferred, and hence not something of which we have an immediate presentation. For this latter view is refuted by the fact that it is in conflict with the immediate consciousness which every one has of his 'I,' as has been explained in the Section on the *Ahaṅkāra*. "But may it not be held that the I-consciousness also really rests on inference, but is erroneously considered as an immediate presentation for the reason that owing to the ease resulting from constant repetition the inference arises with extreme rapidity, without the constant concomitance (*vyāpṭi*) and the other constituents of the inferential process entering into consciousness." By no means, we reply, if this were so, Ḍevadaṭṭa cognizing a jar would not be conscious of the relation which expresses itself in the form this jar is cognized by *me*.' He would apprehend that relation no more in the case of a jar cognised by himself than he apprehends it with regard to a jar cognized by another person. For as, on the view we oppose, both these relations would be objects of continuous inference, there would be no difference between them. "But there *is* a difference," our opponent rejoins, "inasmuch as at the time when a person himself cognizes something, his Self is the abode of the cognition!" This will not avail you, we reply. For if the Self is not immediately apprehended, we have no right to say that it is apprehended as the abode of the cognition. Nor also can it be said that its being the substrate of cognition is inferred from the connection of the Self with the fruit of cognition (*i.e.*, the ultimate acceptance or rejection of the jar, as resulting from its cognition); for at the time of the cognition, there is no possibility of any such connection (the *fruit* appearing *after* the cognition). We hence must hold to the conclusion that the Self is not known through Inference, but is immediately presented, owing to its self-luminousness.

[*Page* 85] There indeed are some to contest this 'self-illuminedness' of the Self (which by us has been advanced as the cause of the Self's *āparokṣya*). But to them we address the following question: What then, according to you, does constitute the cause of the immediately presentative character of the Self? Is it that the Self is the abode of Consciousness? or that there is a general connexion between Self and Consciousness? or that the Self is an adventitious concomitant (*Upāḍhi*) of Consciousness? or that the Self is the object (*Viṣaya*) of Consciousness? The first alternative we dispose of by the following syllogistic argument—It is not on account of its being the abode of consciousness that the Self is immediately presented; for it is so presented without being the object (*karman*) of consciousness; just as states of consciousness are. Nor is the second alternative admissible; for it would be unduly wide (*viz.* to argue that whatever is in some way connected with consciousness is immediately presented). As to the third alternative, we ask what is meant by the Self being an adventitious concomitant (*Upāḍhi*) of consciousness? It cannot, in the first place, mean that the Self is the abode of Consciousness; for this would imply that an object (*viṣaya*) which is not the abode of consciousness, is *not* immediately presented (while as a matter of fact it is so presented). Nor, in the second place, can it mean that the Self is *either* the abode *or* the object (*viṣaya*) of consciousness; for so far we have no sufficient definition of *object*. Should you say that by *object* of consciousness you understand that which naturally enters into all those activities and conceptions (*vyavahāra*) which depend on Consciousness; we point out that on this definition the *Self* would itself be an *object*. If, next, you should say that to be an *Upāḍhi* of Consciousness means being that which defines (*vyāvarṭayaṭi*) Consciousness, while not being its abode; we reply that this definition is too wide, inasmuch as it would comprise sight also (and the other sense organs). And if, next, you should say that to be the *Upāḍhi* of Consciousness means being that which naturally enters into all the activities and conceptions which depend on consciousness, while not being the abode of Consciousness; we point out that this definition would include also the connexion (*sambanḍha*) between Self and Consciousness. But a connexion according to you, can not be *viṣaya*; for this would imply that it is something immediately presented, in contradiction of your theory that the *Samavāya* relation (which, in the case under discussion, would be the *Śambandha*) is (not immediately presented, but) the object of a continuous inference.

Regarding the fourth alternative, finally, (which implies the Self's being a *viṣaya* of Consciousness) we make the following remarks: That state of Consciousness of which the Self is the object, could not, in the first place, engross a time different from the time which is engrossed by that state of Consciousness of which the jar is the object; for if this were so, the connexion of the two objects of consciousness—which finds its expression in the thought 'this *jar* is recognized *by me*'—could not be realized. Nor, in the second place, can the two states of consciousness be assumed to engross the same time; for two Cognitions through which contrary objects are apprehended cannot originate at one and the same time; no more than a person can at one and the same time engage in two opposite acts of motion bringing him up to one object placed in front of him and to another placed behind him. Nor may you contend that, while indeed it is not possible to make, at one and the same time, two muscular efforts tending in different directions, it *is* possible that two different changes (transformations; *pariṇāma*) should take place at the same time. For (this could only mean that different changes may take place, at one and the same time, in different parts of a thing; while) that which is not made up of parts (the Self *e.g.*) cannot undergo two *partial* changes. Nor, on the other hand, can a thing undergo at the same time two different changes affecting it in its entirety. For experience shows that changes which affect a thing in its entirety—as, *e.g.*, the bodily changes connected with childhood on the one, and old age on the other hand, which affect the whole body—are in no case contemporaneous.

There thus remains, as the only possible one, the view that the immediate presentation of the Self is due to its being 'self-illumined.'

Nor may it be objected (*viz.*, to the conclusion that the Self may be the substrate of an *adhyāsa,* for the reason that owing to its self-illuminedness, it is *aparokṣa*—immediately presented) that we in no case observe an *adhyāsa* due to the mere fact of the immediate presentation of the substrate, unless at the same time that which is superimposed on that substrate be apprehended by the same sense-organ as the thing superimposed. For, as a matter of fact, we have, by means of the eye, immediate presentative knowledge of dark blue colour as superimposed upon Ether, (which is not perceived either by the eye or (any other sense but) of which latter we have immediate knowledge either through witnessing consciousness *sākṣin*) or the internal organ by itself (without the help of the eye or any sense-organ); so that, in this case the two are not apprehended *by the same sense-organ*). We of course decline to accept the view of the Bauddhas and the followers of the Bhaṭṭa, according to whom Ether is something perceived by the eye; for from this it would follow that it possesses colour and tangibility. The presence and absence of visual perception (as actually observed to be factors required for the cognition or non-cognition of Ether respectively), are accounted for thereby that the eye has for its object that absence of solid bodies which urges us to infer the existence of Ether (Space).*

There are some Vedāntins, however, who, in accordance with certain general principles of theirs, hold space to be something (not directly presented but) continuously inferred; and as against these, the citing of the instance of Ether, by our opponent, would be quite effective; inasmuch as, according to that view, there would be nothing to show that it is possible to have immediate presentative knowledge even without the

* Visual perception does not give us a direct presentation of Ether; but its operation is required to present to us that absence of solid space-filling objects which leads us to cognise Ether (empty space).

superimposed being apprehended by the same sense-organ. And, to ward off a final objection, we point out that as the Self is not the material cause of the *aḍhyāsa*—which cause rather is constituted by Nescience and its effects,—and as the *aḍhyāsa* is put an end to by true knowledge, the Self though no doubt the substrate of the *aḍhyāsa*, is in no way affected by the good or evil qualities of the thing superimposed.

The final conclusion then is that, since all objections to the Vedānta theory admit of being refuted with ease, the superimposition on the Self of the Not-self must be acknowledged as something that *may* take place.

XLI

[It having been shown so far that Aḍhyāsa can be satisfactorily defined and is something possible, it remains to show that it is *actual*. And this actual existence of Aḍhyāsa is proved by Perception, Inference, Presumption and Authoritative Tradition].

[*Page 86*] "But," our opponent resumes, "although so far you have shown that the superimposition on the Self of the Not-self, in the first place, is something of which a satisfactory definition may be given, and, in the second place, is not an impossibility, yet such superimposition cannot be established as something actual without a valid means of proof (*pramāṇa*); for in all cases things to be known depend for their proof upon means of proof." Well, we reply, in the case under consideration, there is no lack of means of proof; in fact, Perception, Inference, Presumption and Authoritative Tradition combine to supply the proof required. *First* as to Perception (intuitive knowledge). It is a matter of immediate, intuitive, experience that all animated beings superimpose upon a material aggregate,—consisting of a body distinguished by certain generic characteristics, of sense-organs and the rest,—identity with their non-material, intellectual or spiritual, Selfs,—which erroneous identification expresses itself in intuitive judgments such as 'I am a man,' 'I am a God,' 'I am a beast,' and on the basis of such erroneous identification carry on empirical life with its distinction of knowing subjects, objects of knowledge, and so on. Although in cases where the Sense-organ has suffered derangement it does not enter into the means of proof leading to such cognitions,—and hence there is no possibility of the ordinary causal apparatus for Perception being operative—, yet there is nothing at any time to prevent that kind of intuitive knowledge which depends purely upon the *Sākṣin*. For it is a recognised Vedānta principle that where there is intuitive cognition (immediate presentation), even in the absence of the ordinary apparatus of perceptive cognition, such cognition is due to 'witnessing' consciousness. *Secondly* as to Inference. Inference in the present case operates in the following form: the waking and dreaming states of Devadaṭṭa imply all the distinctions—*viz.*, of knowing subjects, objects of knowledge, and so forth—on the basis of which practical life is carried on, and these in their turn presuppose the *adhyāsa* 'I am a man;'—for they occupy times different from the times when the same Devadaṭṭa is in the state of dreamless sleep or swoon; what does not thus differ is not such (*i.e.*, does not imply those distinctions, etc.); *e.g.* the state of deep sleep. *Arthāpatti*, Presumption, next, operates in the present case as follows: 'Ordinary thought and action, with their distinction of knowing subjects, etc., are not possible without the *adhyāsa* of identity of Self and body; for where, as in the state of dreamless sleep, such *adhyāsa* is absent, there is no consciousness of the empirical world.'* Authoritative Tradition, finally, (as proving *adhyāsa*) is represented by scriptural texts such as 'A Brāhmaṇa should offer sacrifices.'**

"But," an opponent objects, "empirical existence with all its distinctions presupposes no more than that there should be some kind of relation between Self and body, not that they should be identified through *adhyāsa*." What kind of relation then, we ask in reply, do you assume in the case? Do you mean that the Self is to be conceived as the master (Lord) of the body? In that case the empirical world with all its distinctions might as well be founded on the body of a servant.'*** "Let us then say that the

---

* In reality the two proofs, Inference and Presumption, as put forward above are one and the same; there is however a difference in the form or verbal statement; and this justifies our putting them forward as distinct proofs. Some such sameness is to be found in the case of all Presumption, which, on that acount, is regarded by the Naiyāyika as only a form of Inference.

** The text cited means that the Brāhmaṇa should perform sacrifices, which means that he should acquire the results of such offerings. These results come to the man only in future lives, when the body which equipped the man who offered the sacrifices has ceased to exist; and the names 'Brāhmaṇa' and the like refer to the body; hence the text cited implies the identification of the Self with the Body.

*** If the relation between Self and body on which empirical existence rests, is not that of (wrongly imagined) identity, but no more than the relation between a ruling Self and a subservient body, we might as well say that the world is due to the relation between the Self of one person and the body of another person who is his slave.

connection of Self and body consists therein that the latter complies with, and acts according to, the wishes of the former. This definition will not be liable to the objection raised against the previous one; for the body of a servant complies with and carries out the Master's *verbal* commands only." Not so, we reply. Do you understand by such 'compliance' the potentiality of compliance only? If so, your definition breaks down; for such potentiality exists in the state of deep sleep also, and hence there should exist in that state also the distinction of knowing subject, objects of knowledge, etc. (while as a matter of fact the empirical world with all its distinctions does not exist for him who lies in dreamless sleep). Or do you, in the second place, mean 'actual compliance' with the wishes of the Self?—This also will not do; for when a man is in a state of intense mental perturbation, we observe that his body does *not* comply with his wishes, and then, according to you, no empirical world would exist for that man! (which, of course, is not the fact). "But," our Opponent resumes, "it after all is a matter of immediate experience, that the body's complying with the wishes of the Self is the basis of all practical life!" Do you mean to say, we ask in return, that this is so invariably, or only occasionally? You cannot uphold the former alternative; for we observe that in the case of evil smells and the like a man is a cognising agent, although the body does not at the time comply with his wishes (inasmuch as it conveys to him the bad smell, contrary to his wishes). Nor is the latter alternative tenable. For as all wishing itself has *aḍhyāsa* for its root, it is nothing else but *aḍhyāsa* that is the root of all empirical thought and action. Apart from the *aḍhyāsa* of its identity with the internal organ, the Self, which in itself is of an absolutely unchanging nature, is incapable of the change called *desire*.

Nor, in the next place, can either conjunction (*Saṁyoga*) or intimate relation (*Saṁavāya*) between the Self and the Not-self constitute the *relation* which is the cause of empirical existence; for these two relations would persist in deep sleep also, and hence the empirical world should continue to exist for the sleeper also (which as we know is not the case). Other definitions which might be given of the relation of Self and body are equally invalid. Should it, *e.g.*, be said that the relation is that between Enjoyer (experiencing subject) and object of enjoyment; or that the body is that which is originated through the actions of the Self; or that the body is the abode of the organs of the Self, and so forth;—we point out that none of these relations could constitute the ultimate cause of the *vyavahāra*; because enjoyment and the rest are themselves rooted in *aḍhyāsa*. Moreover all these relations exist not only between a person's Self and his own body, but likewise between that Self and the bodies of slaves or servants (which are objects of enjoyment and so on for the master, so that all these definitions evidently are too wide). "Let us then," the Opponent resumes, "with a view to exclude servants and the like, say that the relation of Self and body consists therein that the latter is the immediate (non-mediated) object of enjoyment to the former." This again, we rejoin, would mean either that the body is the potential object of enjoyment, and such it is in deep sleep also (where the empirical world does *not* exist); or else it would mean that the body is the object of actual enjoyment on the part of the Self; and then, considering that the (omnipresent) Self is in immediate contact with all bodies, places and times equally, a further fundamental connexion would be required to determine which bodies and which times and places are to be the objects of actual enjoyment (experience). (But no such connexion can be assigned).

The conclusion from all this is that nothing else but the *aḍhyāsa* of identity of Self and Not-self can be accepted as the cause of all empirical existence, thought, and action.

And if with regard to this view it should be finally asked what is the cause determining the connexion of the *aḍhyāsa* with a special body (*i.e.*, the cause of the Self erroneously identifying itself with this or that body); we reply that this cause consists in a special subtle body. The connexion of the Self with special subtle bodies is without a beginning (exists from all eternity); hence the question as to a further connexion does not arise.

XLII

> [But if these means of proof are rooted in *Aḍhyāsa*, what validity can they claim?—They are perfectly valid, the Vedāntin replies, within the empirical sphere; not beyond it. The Vedānta texts on the other hand though at bottom also mere things of *Aḍhyāsa*—since they are other than Brahman—yet have the power of conveying a knowledge of Brahman, the Real; just as an unsubstantial dream-vision may portend something real as, *e.g.*, good luck for the dreamer].

Our opponent may here urge a new objection—"If, he says, "all empirical being and doing rests on the *aḍhyāsa* of identity of Self and body, Perception and the other means of knowledge lose their authoritative character, since their cause (*viz.*, the *aḍhyāsa*) is a 'defect'." But this objection also has no force. That the means of knowledge other than the Veḍānṭa texts have no power to enlighten us with regard to the ultimate reality, is an admitted fact; but this does not deprive those other means of knowledge of their authoritative character within the empirical sphere. For within this latter sphere there is nothing to sublate them: that at bottom they are mere things of *aḍhyāsa* is admitted only an account of their being sublated in the sphere of final release. Nor may you say that there is a contradiction between their being on the one hand mere things of *aḍhyāsa* and on the other hand, constituents of non-contested or correct empirical existence. For there are valid proofs for both these characteristics. The proofs of the former characteristic have been already set forth by us at length; the latter is proved by immediate experience. Should you rejoin that the incontestability or correctness of empirical existence cannot be ascertained,—we reply that 'witnessing' consciousness bears testimony to a *prima facie* incontestability of empirical existence as ascertained through Perception and the other means of knowledge; its *absolute* incontestability is not maintained by us. The Veḍānṭa texts, on the other hand, have for their object that which is absolutely irrefutable, and hence are held to be authoritative means for cognizing fundamental truth. That what in itself is unreal (as the Veḍānta texts are, being something distinct from Brahman, the only Reality) yet may serve to intimate what is not liable to refutation, is illustrated by the fact that certain dream-visions, *e.g.*, of a beautiful woman, although in themselves unreal, yet portend *real* good luck.

"But," our opponent resumes, "you reason as follows—'Perception and the other sources of knowledge are valid within the empirical sphere because they have for their objects things possessing causal efficiency within that sphere;' and this implies that the authoritativeness of those sources of knowledge rests on something outside themselves." Well, we reply, you are in no better case: For you have to argue as follows: 'Perception and the rest are valid means of knowledge because they have real things for their objects.' And, should you rejoin that the reality of the objects is established by that very cognition of which they are the objects and not by any further cognition, and that hence the authority of Perception and the rest requires no extrinsic proof;—we reply that we may make a perfectly analogous claim—*viz.*, that it is nothing else than just the cognition of objects which proves their capability to be causally effective within the empirical sphere.

XLIII

[But, if, as the Vedāntin maintains, Aḍhyāsa is the substantial cause of the Cognition of Brahman, that Cognition cannot be but false!—I admit, the Vedāntin replies, that the Cognition *quā* Cognition is unreal; all the same its object, *i.e.*, Brahman, is real. Nescience is a defect only insofar as it gives rise to the appearance of a manifold world other than Brahman; but it is not a defect insofar as it leads through the Cognition of the phenomenal world to the Cognition of the under-lying reality.]

"But,"—our opponent raises a fresh objection—"if *aḍhyāsa* is the substantial cause of the cognition of Brahman (as of all other cognitions), it follows that this cognition is as false as the cognitions of the empirical world?" This objection has no force as against us, we reply. For we ourselves hold that the cognition in itself (*quâ* cognition) is false.* It is the falsity of the object then that has to be proved; and the determining condition for this is, in the case of the cognition of the empirical world, that this cognition apprehends what is perishable. "But the cognition of Brahman also must be regarded as apprehending what is perishable; for it is produced by a defective cause, just as the cognition of the snake in the rope (in which case the cognition apprehends what is perishable)." Not so, we reply. The reason upon which your inference rest (*i.e.,* the defectiveness of the cause) is not established in the case under discussion; for the cognition of Brahman is *not* produced by a defect analogous to those imperfections of vision which give rise to the erroneous perception of a snake. "But," the opponent replies, "the defect is there, *viz.:* that very Nescience which is the material cause of the cognition of Brahman." The case is otherwise, we reply. Nescience no doubt constitutes a defect in Consciousness insofar as, impeding the presentation of Non-duality, it gives rise to the presentation of Duality; but on the other hand, it constitutes an 'excellence' (the contrary of a defect), insofar as constituting the material cause of, and thus rendering possible, the cognition of Brahman. "But it implies a contradiction to view one and the same thing as being a defect and an excellence at the same time." You are mistaken, we reply. For those defects of vision also (which cause the erroneous

* The *cognition of* Brahman lies within the sphere of the unreal, but the object of that cognition is real. This cognition thus essentially differs from the cognition of the empirical world, the *object of which* is false.

cognition of a snake, etc.) indeed are defects insofar as they are antagonistic to the cognition of Truth (*e.g.*, the rope); but at the same time they are excellences insofar as enabling one to infer, on the basis of them, the mischief (in the shape of past misdeeds) to which they are due. The fact is that in the case of all instruments of right knowledge, that which causes want of validity in any case is some adventitious defect, such as a morbid affection of the eye, which counteracts the normal operation of the instrument of knowledge concerned. In ordinary experience we observe that affections such as hunger and thirst, although antagonistic as it were to the normal condition of the body, are not considered as defects; and that is simply because they are *natural*; Nescience on the other hand is not only natural but also positively advantageous (insofar as it leads us to the cognition of the Real), and hence can all the less be viewed as a 'defect.' The conclusion then is that Perception and the rest, although things of *aḍhyāsa*, are not devoid of validity, and *aḍhyāsa* thus is rightly held to be the material cause of all *vyavahāra*.

XLIV

[Aḍhyāsa is the substantial, not only the instrumental, cause of Cognition; for although cognition ultimately rests on a knowing subject which in itself is free from Aḍhyāsa , yet actual cognition does not come about without Aḍhyāsa].

Against this view the following counter-view will possibly be maintained—"The *aḍhyāsa* under discussion is the instrumental (*not* the material) cause of empirical existence with its distinction of knowing subjects and so forth; for it is an *aḍhyāsa,* just as the *aḍhyāsa* of silver on the shell." But this also is untenable; because the fact of this *aḍhyāsa* (of silver on the shell) not being the basis of empirical existence, vitiates your reasoning: as a matter of fact, we find that, even in the absence of the *aḍhyāsa* of silver, we find such empirical existence being carried on as implies the Self being regarded as the knowing subject, &c.; and this shows that the *aḍhyāsa* of silver is not the basis of empirical existence; what does form the basis of empirical existence is the *aḍhyāsa* of Body and Self; because we find that during deep sleep, when there is no such *aḍhyāsa*, there is no empirical existence.*

* The reading *'na taḍashrayaḥ.'* gives no sense: that there is no *vyavahāra* when there is no *aḍhyāsa* should be a reason for regarding the one as the basis of the other; hence the correct reading appears to be '*hi taḍashrayaḥ.*'

Another counter-view is set forth: "Empirical existence rests on the knowing subject; and to be 'a knowing subject' results from the intelligent nature of the Self, without any *aḍhyāsa*." But this also cannot be upheld. For as the Self, which is essentially free from all relation and all activity cannot without *aḍhyāsa* give rise to actual personal cognition, the condition of any one being a personal knowing subject,—which implies the character of being an instrument or agent,—is something not possible (without *aḍhyāsa*). We are thus again led back to the conclusion that empirical existence with its distinctions of knowing subjects and so on has *aḍhyāsa* for its material cause.

XLV

> [This holds good with regard to all cognition, even that part of that cognition of a man (not of the ordinary kind, but, possessing discriminative knowledge, which refers to actions, such as sacrifices, which are based on the Veda. For although the scriptural passages determining such action point to a Self other than the (gross) body, that Self is not the absolutely non-related Self of the Vedānta texts, but a Self on which an internal organ is 'superimposed.']

[*Page 89*] "This may be true," our opponent resumes, "with regard to the empirical existence of those who do not possess discriminative knowledge; but not of those who do possess such knowledge!" But this also we decline to admit. The *ordinary* thoughts and activities of such men even as possess discriminative knowledge do not essentially differ from those of animals; and hence must be viewed as due to *aḍhyāsa*. Animals also are observed to act and intelligize in a way that points to their identifying their 'I' with their body, and this proceeding is of the nature of *aḍhyāsa*; for it implies the cognition of the oneness of two things the difference of which fails to be apprehended; just as in the case of the cognition of the oneness of shell and silver. And even men possessing discriminative knowledge, as long as they keep within the sphere of everyday thought and action, do not apprehend the difference of Self and body, and thus do not essentially rise above the level of animals; like animals they form judgments with regard to things beneficial to the body, such as food and drink, and things harmful, such as blows—'This thing is beneficial to *me,*' 'That thing is harmful to *me,*' thus identifying the body and the Self;—and frame their action and abstention from action accordingly; which would not be possible if they realized the difference of body and Self. Nor may this argument of ours be met by the counter-assertion that even common people do realize the distinction of Self and body,—this being proved by the fact that even ignorant women and Shūḍras engage in acts, such as bathing in the Gangā, which are meant to benefit the Self in future forms of existence (while they in no way benefit the body). The insight into the distinction of body and Self is, in the case of those people, acquired only on the basis of traditional teaching current among cultivated men; were it otherwise, Scripture would not make it its aim to impart knowledge of the Self. We hence maintain that the everyday thoughts and actions of such persons even as do possess discriminative knowledge are founded on *aḍhyāsa.*

"But," a further point is raised, "in the case of men possessing discriminative knowledge that part at any rate of their thought and action which is determined by Scripture does not rest on *aḍhyāsa*; for they apply themselves to the active duties enjoined by the Vedas only after having gained from the instruction of competent persons the knowledge of a Self which is related to a future world also."

As against this view, says the opponent of the Purvapakṣin, a preliminary question here requires to be settled: What class of Scriptural injunctions is it that should induce us to assume a Self distinct from the body and related to a future world? (*A*) Is it those injunctions which intimate that special results are connected with special actions—as *e.g.* 'A man desirous of increase of cattle should make the *Chiṭrā*-offering,' or 'He who is desirous of the heavenly world should offer the *Jyotiṣtoma* sacrifice?' (*B*) Or is it injunctions of permanent obligation, as *e.g.* 'A man should offer the *Agnihoṭra* as long as he lives'? (*C*) Or is it that group of injunctions which refer to special occasions—as *e.g.* 'A man whose house has been destroyed by fire should offer a sacrifice'? (*D*) Or is it, finally, the injunctions of expiatory ceremonies?—(*A*) On the first alternative the further question arises—(*a*) whether it is results such as the acquisition of cattle that are impossible without the assumption of a Self distinct from the body; (*b*) or results such as obtaining the heavenly world. (*a*) Not certainly the former; for cattle and such things can clearly be gained in this life. Nor must it be thought that if the results of offerings of the *Chiṭrā* type are obtained within this life, there would be no difference between these offerings and those the results of which are found to be realized immediately, such as, *e.g.* the *Kārīrī*-oblation (which is performed for bringing rain); for the difference is that, as human life comprises different periods—youth, old age, etc.—the results of the *Chiṭrā* offering are not bound to any definite point or period of time; while in the case of the *Kārīrī*— which is an offering enjoined on the occasion of grain drying on the stalk owing to want of rain—the result must be obtained immediately. (*b*) Not is the latter alternative admissible; for—

'They tell us, on the strength of valid means of knowledge, that heaven and hell are to be found nowhere but here on earth:—Heaven is whatever delights the mind; hell whatever is of a contrary nature';—

—and according to this view—which implies that such delight also as is due to the possession of cattle and the like may be denoted by the term 'heaven'—the results of the *Jyōṭishṭoma* may be realised here on earth; and the delights resulting from this latter sacrifice cannot be identical with that resulting from the *Chiṭrā*-offering; as this latter is laid down for those people who desire cattle only [so that the above-quoted verse must refer to both kinds of delight]. And even if 'Heaven' were held to denote (not ordinary delights but) *Supreme* delight, such delight also may be realized on earth,—*viz.*, through the attainment of supreme rulership and the like. And should it be objected to this that the sacred books understand by 'Heaven' a definite locality on Mount Meru (not 'delightful' things in general), we reply that Heaven in this sense also may be reached by man in his present bodily existence; *viz.*, by those who by means of magical formulas and drugs, etc., have acquired extraordinary powers. If persons of that kind do not actually attain to 'Heaven,' we must assume that their magical practices were somehow defective; just as the eventual failure of rain compels us to conclude that the *Kārīrī* offering was defective in some respect. (*B*) (*C*) The second and third of the above alternatives can likewise not be accepted. For in the opinion of the Guru (Prabhākara) acts of permanent obligation and acts meant to meet special occasions have no results whatever; [they are performed solely with a view to meeting the obligations imposed by the Shāsṭra]; while in the view of the Bhaṭṭa (Kumārila) their results can be realized in this life only. (*D*) Nor finally will the fourth alternative help us. For expiatory ceremonies have for their only result the warding off of evil. Should you object that crimes such as the murder of a Brāhmaṇa, unless atoned for by certain expiatory ceremonies, are punished by 'Hell,' and that hence there must be a Self, other than the body, which goes to Hell;—we point out that 'Hell' no less than 'Heaven' may mean something that is experienced in this life. And if to this you object that according to Scripture evil-doers have to undergo their punishment in new lives, in the bodies of dogs, pigs and the like; we reply that Scripture may mean nothing more than that evil men are punished by having to undergo sufferings equal to those of vile brutes. The conclusion from all this, the Opponent of the Purvapaksha in sums up, is that there are no scriptural injunctions of any kind which justify the conclusion that there is a Self different from, and surviving, the body (upon which supposition the scriptural actions of the learned would be based).

"All this is not so," the Pūrvapakṣin replies. "As fully explained in the section of the 'Divinities' (Ved. Sūtras I-iii-26-37), authoritative *manṭras* and *arṭhavāḍa* passages alike intimate that there are certain results of actions, 'Heaven' among them, which must be experienced in special places, at special times and in special embodiments; and this proves that there *is* a Self other than the body. You may not object that this latter tenet, although proved in the 'Divinity' section of the Vedānta, is not held by Jaimini. For although Jaimini, in his *Sūṭras,* does not explicitly set forth the theory of there being a Self distinct from the body,—and this for the reason that for the discussion of Vedic injunctions that theory is not required—; yet the *Sūṭras.imply* that theory; inasmuch as they set forth the authoritative character—consisting in independence of all extrinsic support—of the entire Veda, whether dealing with things to be accomplished (actions, such as sacrifices and the like), or with things accomplished (permanently existing things, facts, such as the Self). I such were not Jaimini's view, how could the author of the Great Commentary on the Sutras (Shabara) have discussed the existence of a Self other than the body, on the very basis of the authoritativeness of *manṭras* and *arṭhavāḍas*? Nor may it be objected that in the 'Divinity' Section of the Pūrva-Mīmāmsā (IX-i-6-10), both the author of the *Sūṭras* and the author of the Commentary disprove the authoritative character of the *Manṭras* and *Arṭhavāḍas*. For what they there aim at disproving is not the authoritative character of *Manṭras,* in general, but only of what, in the *Manṭras*, is contrary to reason. The argument is that if on the basis of *Manṭras,* such as 'Indra is great, he carries the thunder-bolt in his hand,' divinities were held to have definite bodily shape, they would help the sacrifice by presenting themselves bodily at it; just as the priests do; and this is contrary to experience: the statement in the *Manṭras* has therefore to be set aside. Such *Manṭras* on the other hand as are not in conflict with reason are allowed to have authoritative force; and even such *Manṭras* whose mere indications are contained in *Arṭhavāḍa* passages, are referred to in the many places of the Mimāmsa-Sūtras as authoritative. The legitimate conclusion therefore is that intelligent men learn from *Mantras* and *Arthavādas* that there is a Self distinct from the body; and on the strength of this knowledge engage in actions prescribed by the Veda; and this proves that activity and thought of the latter kind does not rest upon *adhyāsa.*"

[*Page 91*] All this, we reply, does not shake our position. For we ask the following question: men engaging in dutiful action as prescribed by the Veda learn from *Mantra* and *Arthavāda* that there is a Self other than the body;—but of what special nature is that Self? Is it a Self absolutely one and non-related? or a Self that, after death, moves into another world? Not the former indeed; for that there is a Self of *that* kind can be learned from the *Vedānta* texts only. And as to the second alternative, we ask you whether the knowledge of a Self capable of moving into another world terminates all *adhyāsa*? or only the *adhyāsa* of the Self being identical with the gross body? The former is not possible; for as a Self free from all *adhyāsa* and hence infinite in extent (omnipresent) could not move into another world, it must be allowed that (even when the identification of Self and gross body comes to an end), the *adhyāsa* owing to which the Self identifies itself with the internal organ, persists. And the second alternative also we cannot accept; since an *adhyāsa* of an immediately intuitive kind (and such is the *adhyāsa* owing to which Self and gross body are identified) cannot be terminated by any non-intuitive knowledge (such as the knowledge acquired from *Mantras*, etc., that the Self survives the body and goes to another world). We thus arrive at the conclusion that in the case of men with insight also even that part of their thought and action which refers to actions enjoined in the Veda, rests upon *Adhyāsa*.

XLVI

[The theory of the 'superimposition' of the Not-Self on the Self is illustrated by the facts of ordinary experience—a man looks upon persons and objects near and dear to himself as identical or one with himself. Other things, not equally near and dear, he yet views as *his*. On these undoubted facts we base the generalization that, through Adhyāsa, the fundamentally non-related Self erroneously relates itself to the entire phenomenal world—the internal organ (mind), the sense-organ, the gross body, the external world. The primary and fundamental identification is that of the Self with the so-called internal organ or mind, owing to which the universal non-personal Self becomes a limited personal Self—the Self becomes an I: On this fundamental erroneous identification the entire series of further identifications builds itself up in succession. The internal organ is something of which the Self is immediately conscious; and we therefore reject the theories of the Naiyāyika and others who hold that our knowledge of the internal organ is acquired by indirect means. Nor, of course, do we admit the view that internal states such as desire, feeling, etc., belong to the Self; the absolutely changeless Self merely witnesses the changes going on in the internal organ. That it views them as its own, is the great error to free us from which is the task of philosophy.]

"If, then, all thought and action rest on *aḍhyāsa,* we call on you to explain in detail which thing is superimposed on which, and how the whole *aḍhyāsa* of Self and Not-self has to be conceived!" Well, give your careful attention to the following account: On witnessing Consciousness (*sākṣi-chaiṭanyam*) there are superimposed in succession, the internal organ, the sense-organs, the body, and finally the things external to the body and their attributes—consciousness as qualified by each earlier *aḍhyāsa* constituting the substrate for each later *aḍhyāsa.* That the external things also are superimposed upon Consciousness there is no reason to doubt; for ordinary experience shows that a man thinks and speaks of himself as sound and entire or the reverse according as his wife, children, relations etc. are sound and entire or the reverse. "But," our opponent objects, "thought and speech of that kind are not to be understood in their primary (literal) sense, for they do not extend to all cases; when, *e.g.*, the wife of somebody's son dies, the father does not consider himself to have lost his own wife." Your reasoning is unsound, we reply. From the fact that the identification under discussion does not take place in some cases, it does not follow that where it does take place it is not to be taken in its full literal sense. It is quite true that in many a cases shells are not treated—either in thought or in action—as being silver; but from this it does not follow that when a shell actually presents itself to somebody's mind *as* silver, his thought and action connected with that silver are not fully serious (but of a merely secondary or metaphorical kind, as if the man were at the time conscious that the silver after all is not real). "Well," our opponent rejoins, "let us admit that the identification of shell and silver is, for the time, an identification in the full sense of the word; but a man's identifying himself with his body or with his son—where after all there is a clear consciousness of difference—can have a metaphorical meaning only; analogous to the meaning of the phrase, 'Ḍevaḍaṭṭa is a lion." The two cases, we reply, are not parallel: Ḍevaḍaṭṭa is not affected by the pleasures and pains experienced by lions: he who thinks and speaks of him as a lion, therefore, can have nothing else in mind than a metaphorical identification of the two; the father, on the other hand, experiences a state of consciousness which expresses itself as—'I am affected by the pleasures or pains of my son.'

"But why not hold that this peculiar state of consciousness is due to excess of paternal love rather than an *aḍhyāsa* of identity?" This is impossible, we reply; sine love itself rests on an *aḍhyāsa*. Were this not so, how could it be that after having entered towards the close of his life on the state of a houseless mendicant and attained to full discriminative insight, the man no longer feels the same love towards his children and their relations? *Real* love (not due to an erroneous identification of one's self with the beloved person) would not depart merely in consequence of discriminative knowledge; for it is a generally valid truth that knowledge puts an end to non-knowledge only. "But if the identification of a man's self with his son, &c., which directly is due to love, rests on an *aḍhyāsa* only, how is it that the author of the Veḍānṭa-Bhāṣya (under the Sūṭra 'an account of seeing,' Veḍ. Sū. I. 1.5) quotes the case of a king whose estimate of a well- beloved servant, who is constantly active in his master's interest, expresses itself in the form 'Bhaḍrasēna is my Self,' as an instance of merely metaphorical identification?"* In this case also, we reply, you over-look a difference. The king's affection for his servant is not really due to Bhaḍrasēna himself, but to all the excellent work that Bhaḍrasēna does in his master's service; this is proved by the fact that the king's love turns to hatred as soon as Bhaḍrasēna begins to do things harmful to his master. On the other hand, the love of a father for his son does not depend on any conditions; it does not depart when the son is unable to do anything for his father or even does him positive harm.

* How is it that this identification also is not treated by Shaṅkarāchārya as one of erroneous complete identification due to aḍhyāsa, but is admitted by him to be a metaphorical one only, the king being all the time fully conscious of not being one with his servant?

"But," our Opponent resumes, "at any rate, we may maintain that the love entertained towards such objects as fine clothes, ornaments and the like, does not rest on aḍhyāsa; for nobody identifies himself with things of that kind!" The aḍhyāsa of 'I,' 'we reply, no doubt is absent in those cases; but there is present the aḍhyāsa of 'mine.' That the aḍhyāsa of identity snould assume those two different forms, so that of some beloved objects we think as being *ourselves,* while others we only view as *ours*—explains itself from the greater or lesser degree of love we feel. The different degrees of which love is capable are noticed by Vishvarūpāchārya (Surēshvarācharya) when commenting on the text 'dearer than a son.':

'A son is dearer than wealth; one's own body is dearer than a son; the sense-organs are dearer than the gross body; dearer than the sense-organs is life; and dearer than life is the Self.'

In accordance herewith we observe that the aḍhyāsa of a person's connection with wealth—which is simply *dear*—expresses itself throughout in the form 'this is *mine.*' In the case of children—who are *dearer*— the aḍhyāsa *some times* assumes the form of oneness. With regard to the body—which is *dearest*—the aḍhyāsa is prevailingly one of identity. And the internal organ, finally,—which is something dearer than the body even—is invariably thought and spoken of as one with the Self. "But, if the conception of one's identity with a son rests on aḍhyāsa, how is it that in the Commentary, towards the end of the section dealing with the first four Sūtras, such identity is referred to as of a merely metaphorical character?" What that passage means to intimate, we reply, is no more than that children are not so invariably treated as identical with one's Self as one's body is; not that they are never viewed in that light. It otherwise would be hardly possible to account for the scriptural text 'Thou art my Self, called son' (*Bṛihaḍ. Upa.* 6-4-26) which refers to the identity of a father with his children as something familiar to all from ordinary experience. The conclusion thus is that a man really, though erroneously, identifies himself with external objects such as wife, children and so on.

However, we will assume that you do not fully agree with us as to this identification of a person with his children, &c. But on the other hand, you must admit that parents refer to themselves attributes belonging to their children. For when a baby son is 'honoured' by a gift of fine clothes, ornaments and the like, the father thinks '*I* am honoured.'—In the same way a man by pointing to his body and saying 'This is me' intimates that he identifies *himself* with his body. Such every-day expressions, again, as '*I* am lean,' '*I* am dark-complexioned,' clearly show that men commonly ascribe to *themselves* qualities belonging to the gross body. Similarly qualities of the sense-organs (or, in this context rather 'of the sensory powers') are constantly ascribed to the Self: men say '*I* am dumb,' '*I* am a fluent speaker,' '*I* am blind,' '*I* have eye-sight.' In these latter cases, it is not that to which these attributes belong—*viz.* the sensory powers,—which is superimposed upon the Self; for as those powers are not objects of direct knowledge, but of permanent inference only, they are incapable of direct *adhyāsa.* In the same way, finally, attributes of the internal organ are superimposed upon the Self: '*I* am desirous,' '*I* am angry,' and so on. Nor may you maintain that desire, anger and the like are attributes *not* of the internal organ, but of the Self itself; for they originate only when the internal organ is present. And against this it must not be urged that the Self may after all be the real material cause of desire, anger and the rest (all these belonging to the Self as real conditions of it), while the internal organ is no more than their instrumental cause,— and that this theory sufficiently accounts for the fact that all those affections arise only when the internal organ is present, and are absent in its absence. For the absence of the internal organ—if no more than a mere instrumental cause—would not explain why in the state of deep sleep desire and all such affections cease completely (their material cause, the Self being present all the while, some trace of them should certainly remain). "But can we not say that the absence of those affections explains itself from the absence of conjunction between the internal organ and the Self—which conjunction in this case constitutes the (third kind of cause which has to be present if an effect is to be produced, *viz.*, the) so-called non-inherent cause?" You may not, we reply; for as you represent the case you should at once conclude that the internal organ is the material cause of those affections, since this appears, from what you say, to be the principal factor in the causal agency bringing them into existence. "But, the instrumental cause also is the principal factor in the causal agency, since in the absence of that cause no effects are produced!" Not so, we reply. There are present other operative causes, *viz.*, the sense of sight and so on; and hence there is no need to assume that the internal organ is the principal cause. On the other hand, there exists in that case no other *material* cause, and it hence cannot be argued that there is no need of the assumption that the internal organ is the material cause required. If—as you argue—the Self were the material cause, our consciousness would co-ordinate the 'I' and the 'desire' in the form '*I* am desire;' while as a matter of fact our consciousness testifies to a connexion expressing itself as 'I am desirous' ('affected with desire'), analogous to such judgments as 'Ḍevadaṭṭa *has* a stick' (not '*is* a stick'). On the other hand, Scripture actually speaks of the internal organ and certain mental states in forms of co-ordination, as *e.g.* in the passage 'Desire is volition' (*Bṛi. Upa.* 1-5-3). We thus claim it as a well-settled conclusion that attributes of the internal organ are superimposed (erroneously attributed to) the Self; while that organ itself is, by aḍhyāsa erroneously identified with the Self which merely 'witnesses' it. Were this not so, we should not (as we actually do) *view* pure witnessing Consciousness as having the attribute of limited 'I-consciousness.'

"But," our opponent resumes, "the internal organ is not something of which witnessing Consciousness has an immediate, intuitive knowledge. The fact rather is that the existence of the internal organ is postulated for the reason that the successive origination of actual cognitions as it is observed to take place, when the Self, the sense-organs and objects are in contact, cannot be otherwise accounted for." Not so, we reply. The process *can* be accounted for otherwise; for we may assume that the Self, by itself, possesses the capacity of originating cognitions in succession. Nor may you argue that, as necessarily *some* factor determining the whole process must be assumed, we must assume the existence of the internal organ. For it is simpler to assume that the Self—the existence of which is something independently and absolutely certain—possesses the capacity of originating the actual succession of cognitions, than to postulate an altogether new entity endowed with that capacity. "Well," our opponent resumes, "we then prove the existence of the internal organ by the following inference: 'The succession under discussion (*i.e.* the successive origination of cognitions, in the presence of several objects) requires some common cause by which the successive order, due to the Agent, is effected; for the case is one of the class of successive production of effects on the part of the agent who finds himself in the presence of several objects; such as *e.g.* the successive order of the acts of cutting—on the part of Ḍēvaḍaṭṭa, to whom several things to be cut present themselves—which requires an axe as its common cause." The inference is not sound, we reply; for the reason put forward is not conclusive; as we find that there is an actual order of the successive conjunctions of the internal organ with the several senses (on which the actual order of succession of the several cognitions depends). For there is no common cause for the order of succession of the conjunctions of the internal organ with the sense-organs. "Well, let us say, that common cause is to be found in the unseen (retributive) principle." Then we meet you by another instance (of absence of a common cause determining the order of succession of a series of effects): in the order of succession of the series of momentary contacts, on the part of a fruit that drops from a tree, with the several points of space. "Here also there is a common cause," our opponent replies., "*viz*, the heaviness of the fruit." Very well, we reply; we then must point out that, as regards the matter under discussion, you have failed to assign the common cause for the actual order of succession of the contacts of some one particular sense-organ, such as the eye, with its several objects. You may not say that the unseen principle determines that order also; for what you are bound to prove in this case is the existence of a common cause other than that Unseen Principle! And for this same reason, the first objection that we put forward against your inference remains unshaken (as you sought to escape this by putting forward the Unseen Principle).

"Let us then," our Opponent resumes, "give a different form to our inferential argument: 'The origination of special qualities such as cognitions and the like, requires that in the substrate—in which that origination takes place—there should reside a non-inherent cause constituted by the conjunction of the substrate with another substance; for it is an origination of special qualities in a permanent substance—as *e.g.* the origination of red colour in an atom—which requires the contact of the atom with fire.' And in the case under discussion, that other entity (through conjunction with which there arise cognitions, etc., in the Self) is nothing else but the internal organ." This inference also, we rejoin, is not valid, for it establishes only what is established already; inasmuch as that non-inherent cause of cognitions (which you declare to be necessary, and to supply which you assume the existence of an internal organ) is already given in the conjunction of the Self with the body and the sense- organs. "But does not the fact of dream-cognitions prove the existence of the internal organ? (considering that in the state of dream the connexion between Self and sense-organs is suspended)." Not so, we reply; the connexion between the Self and the (gross) body which does *not* cease in the state of dream, constitutes a sufficient cause of the rise of dream-cognitions (so that, on that ground, the assumption of an internal organ is not justified). "Well then," our Opponent resumes, "(if these inferential arguments are not valid) let us assume that the internal organ is known through Perception (*pratyakṣa*)!" This also, we reply, is inadmissible. For the internal organ is either of atomic size,—in which case it is no more cognizable by the senses than other atoms;—or it is of infinite extension,—in that case its conjunction with the Self would have the consequence of the whole world presenting itself to consciousness at once;—and if it were of medium size, even then we could not allow that it is apprehended through the senses; for the simple reason that in the state of dream where the senses are admittedly non-operative, we yet are conscious of the presence of the internal organ (the Mind). We thus see that all attempts to prove the existence of the *manas* by the so-called recognised means of proof are unsuccessful. On the other hand, it can not be maintained that we have no consciousness at all of the existence of such an entity; for we actually experience states of consciousness expressing itself in the form—'my mind was somewhere else;' 'my mind was absent.' No other alternative remaining, we are thus driven to the conclusion that the internal organ is the object of direct cognition on the part of 'witnessing Consciousness.'

"But," a further objection is raised, "in the case of the Self and the Not-self there is mutual superimposition (*i.e.* if the two are identified in that way that either may be said to be identified with the other), then—both being superimposed equally— it will follow that *both* are false; and moreover if both are, equally, the substrate of the Superimposition, then both would appear to consciousness as equal, and not as different (one being known as the *imposed* and another *the imposed upon*)."

Not so, we reply: what proves the mutual Superimposition is the fact that one (the Self) is actually recognised as *intelligent* and the other (the Not-Self) as *non-intelligent,* the two thus being quite distinct from each other; for in all *Aḍhyāsa,* when one thing is known as superimposed upon another, this presupposes the fact that the two are actually known as entirely distinct. If there were Superimposition of only one of the two (and not of both upon both), then that would presuppose the recognition of the particular form of only one (not of both). Nor does our view imply the falseness of both (the Self and the Not-self). For as the intelligent principle (*chēṭana*) can not itself be superimposed upon the non-intelligent, the superimposition is of that kind only which is called *samsarga-aḍhyāsa.* Nor is the fact that both are known in their particular characters (and as distinct from each other) incompatible with both being the substrate (of the Superimposition); because the particular distinctive character is not cognised as belonging to the substrate; in fact what is actually cognised is that the Body is intelligent and the Self non-intelligent, there being only a reversal of the particular characters (which fact does not affect the characters of the substrate of the Superimposition).

Nor must it be said that, as the two present themselves with individual differences, the case cannot be one of superimposition; and the co-ordination in which their relation is expressed ('the Body is the Self' etc.) is to be explained in a secondary, metaphorical, sense. For as a matter of fact ordinary people do not transfer the idea of the Self to the internal organ and the rest in a merely metaphorical sense, but in its full primary meaning; and certainly no exception can be taken to what is a well-known fact.

[*Page 95*] "But," a new objection is raised, "the phrase 'and the rest' (see above) at any rate is not justified. For the pure Self is superimposed on the internal organ only; while as to the senses (which are meant to be included by the phrase 'and the rest') no more can be said than that they are connected with the internal organ which is qualified by that superimposition of the Self."

This is so, we reply. But all the same it is the Self, *not* the internal organ, which *appears* as determined by the sense-organs; and it is with reference to this *appearing* to Consciousness that the phrase 'and the rest' has been used. It is on account of this appearance—which is due to Consciousness being interwoven with the sense-organs and the gross body—that materialists and the like erroneously identify the Self with the senses, and the gross Body. Did no such appearance exist all people alike would identify the Self, not with the body but, with the internal organ only, on which the Self is directly superimposed.

We thus have fully shown that the mutual superimposition of Self and Not-self is something which can be satisfactorily defined; which presents no impossibility; which actually exists; and for the cognition of which there are valid means. We hence claim that this our *aḍhyāsa* theory is fully sound and cannot be controverted by anyone.

XLVII

[The removal of the *Aḍhyāsa* constitutes the purpose (aim; *prayojana*) of the *Vēḍānṭa-Shāsṭra*.]

Our opponent now raises a new difficulty. "You have," he says, "demonstrated the existence of *aḍhyāsa* in order to be able to formulate the following inference—'the *Veḍānṭa-Shāsṭra* has a possible object and purpose (aim); because it is antagonistic to bondage which is a thing of *aḍhyāsa*; just as waking consciousness is antagonistic to illusory dream-cognitions.' But now as to this purpose or aim (*prayojana*). Is it the cessation of all that is unprofitable or evil, such as action and enjoyment of any kind? Or is it the cessation of that which is the cause of all evil,—*viz.*, of the *aḍhyāsa* of nescience and all its effects?—It can not be the former; for as long as its cause persists, evil, although having been stopped for a time, originates afresh. Nor can it be the latter; for there can be no cessation of *aḍhyāsa* which is held to be beginningless. You may not say that such cessation must be allowed on the ground that Scripture teaches it; for it is contradicted by Perception. For we do not observe that when through Reasoning we have taught ourselves to discriminate between the Self and the body, the *aḍhāysa* of the identity of the two comes to an end."

To this we reply as follows: You yourself hold that the *beginningless antecedent non-existence* *which is the cause of the world, comes to an end. Why then should not the beginningless *aḍhyāsa* also come to an end? And if to exclude the analogous instance quoted by us, you should argue—'There can be no cessation of the *aḍhyāsa*; for it is a beginningless *positive* entity, just as the Self is;' we ask whether by a *positive entity* you understand something that is *real*, or merely something which differs in character from non-being. If the former, we point out that those who hold the *aḍhyāsa* to possess that kind of being which is called 'inexplicable' do not accept the reason in your argument as valid. And if the latter, we oppose to your argument the following of ours—'The *aḍhyāsa* is put an end to by knowledge because it is of the nature of non-knowledge (Nescience), just as the *aḍhyāsa* of silver on the shell.' You will perhaps say that this inference of ours is refuted by yours as set forth above. But this we deny; the fact is that our inference sublates yours. In the same way as a general rule is sublated by a special one, a general inference is sublated by a special one. "But," our opponent resumes, "by the cessation of a thing we understand a subsequent condition of its material cause; a jar *e.g.* is said to 'cease' when it comes to pieces—these pieces representing a different condition of the clay of which the jar was made. But the *aḍhyāsa* of Nescience has no material cause; hence there can be no cessation of it." We, our reply is, do not accept your definition. Cessation must rather be defined as a subsequent condition of the *abode* (*āshraya*) of that which ceases to exist. On your definition there could be no cessation of the original, beginningless, blackness and other qualities of atoms (which blackness *e.g.* does cease when that in which it abides is baked in fire). That recognition of the Self as distinct from the body which rests on mere argumentation is not indeed observed to put an end to the *aḍhyāsa*; but there is no reason to deny that when the true nature of

---

* The logician holds that antecedent non-existence is without beginning,—continuing to exist till the origination of the thing to which the non-existence pertains. Up to the time when the Jar is made we have its antecedent non-existence, which had no beginning in time. So with the entire world also.

Brahman has once been apprehended through sacred texts such as 'Thou art that,' all that is opposed to Brahman, *viz.*, Nescience and *aḍhyāsa* which is its effect, cease to be. For Nescience, which conceals Brahman, and its effects, are clearly opposed in nature to the knowledge of Brahman. The apprehension, on the other hand, of a Self distinct from the body is opposed to the view of the identity of the two, and therefore puts an end to that view only. It no doubt is a fact that the Self of the nature of Intelligence, which is presented in the 'I-consciousness,' is nothing else but Brahman but, it does not present itself *as* Brahman; and the 'I-consciousness' therefore does not constitute knowledge of Brahman. And for the reason that knowledge founded on argumentative reasoning (*yukṭi*)—although, in a way, having Brahman for its object—is not an authoritative source of knowledge (*pramāṇa*), or else for the reason—that it is not intuitive, it does not possess the power of putting an end to *aḍhyāsa* which is an object of intuitive cognition. There thus is no other means to put an end to *aḍhyāsa* than that intuitive apprehension of Brahman to which the *Veḍānṭa* texts give rise.

"But," a new objection is raised, "the purpose of the *Shāsṭra* is not merely to put an end to *aḍhyāsa*, but to help us to attain to blessedness!" True, we reply. But if it is declared that the object of the *Shāsṭra* is the oneness of Brahman and the individual soul, it will at once be understood that the attainment of bliss on the part of the individual soul falls within that object and is realized with it. For the text 'Bliss is Brahman' shows that what constitutes blessedness is nothing else but just Brahman. And that the attainment of bliss is the aim of man is of course proved by the fact that it is what man desires. There hence is no need of making a separate statement as to the attainment of bliss being the purpose of the *Shāsṭra*.

"Well then," our Opponent resumes, "the cessation of *aḍhyāsa* also should not be separately stated; for it is an object (*viṣaya*) of the *Shāsṭra* in the same way as the attainment of bliss!" Not so, we reply. Do you mean that cessation of *aḍhyāsa* is an object of the *Shāsṭra,* independently? or that it is contained within that object which is constituted by the soul's oneness with Brahman? The former alternative is inadmissible; since the *Shāsṭra* undoubtedly has to establish nothing else than the Soul's oneness with Brahman. Texts such as 'in the end there is the cessation of all Māyā (Shvē. 1-10), and 'the knot of the heart is broken' (Muṇd. 2-2-8) refer to the cessation of *aḍhyāsa* as something to be attained, only through the apprehension of the Soul's oneness with Brahman. Nor can the second alternative be accepted. For of those texts which establish the unity of Brahman and the Soul—'That art thou' and the rest—the object is not the cessation of *aḍhyāsa*. "But without the cessation of plurality (*saprapañchaṭva*) in Brahman, and of Nescience and its effects in the individual soul, the oneness which these texts declare is not capable of realization!" Well, we reply, this comes exactly to what we said above;—*viz.*, that the cessation of Nescience is effected through the cognition of oneness. Nor do we allow you to plead that, although the cessation of *aḍhyāsa* is merely implied in texts such as the *mahāvākya*, it is stated directly in texts such as 'it is not big, it is not small,' etc. For these latter texts set forth, not the cessation of bondage, which, in the state of Final Release, is accomplished through the intuitive realization of Brahman, but rather the fact that Brahman, which in itself is totally non-related, is also in all time essentially 'worldless' (*niṣprapañcha*). For only after having grasped this truth, can the individual soul later on realise the oneness of the Self and Brahman, on the basis of texts such as 'Thou art that;' for the term 'Brahman' is one the meaning of which cannot be apprehended on the basis of ordinary life and thought. Nor can it be said that the teaching as to Brahman's 'worldless' nature is contradicted by those means of knowledge which make us apprehend Brahman as associated with a multiple world. For the fact is that there are no such means. Perception and the rest no doubt have for their object the multiple phenomenal world; but on the other hand, they do not make us apprehend Brahman and, hence do not intimate any connexion of the two. And texts such as 'All this (world) is that Self' do not aim at teaching that Brahman is the Self of the phenomenal world—for this is already established by its being the material cause of all—; but connect themselves into a whole with those texts which set forth the 'worldless' nature of Brahman, in that way that they suggest matter to be *negatived* by those latter texts: this indeed is the meaning which they must have; how otherwise could they set forth the view that Brahman is associated with a world—a view which is in opposition to the supremely salutary view of Brahman being worldless, and hence is evil. That the absence of all relation to a multiple world is blissful, while connexion with such a world is an evil, is proved by the experiences of deep sleep and the waking state respectively, and moreover is vouched for by Scripture. Nor must it be thought that the true cognition that rests on a text teaching Brahman's worldlessness is sublated by the fact that such texts imply a reference to Brahman's association with a world as something known or settled; for a reference of this kind has no force; firstly because it is a mere reference (and as such has no power independently to establish truth), and secondly, because it merely subserves the cognition of Brahman as non-related to a world.

"But is it not an unmeaning procedure, on the part of Scripture, first, by means of certain texts, to establish the notion that Brahman is related to a world, and after that to negative that very view by other texts? Is it not a common, and well-founded, saying that better than washing off the mud from one's body is to keep at a good distance from it?"* The case lies as follows, we reply: The phenomenal world is *prima facie* suggested by those very texts which aim at setting forth the non-duality of Brahman, inasmuch as they imply that Brahman is the material cause of everything: if, then, there were no other texts to take up and deny the existence of the world, the non-duality of Brahman could not be established. The implied meaning of certain texts does not establish Brahman's connexion with a world as a final truth; it only suggests it *prima facie*; and when such implied meaning comes into conflict with a directly negativing text, it is the weaker of the two and has to give way. That a means of knowledge of a comparatively weaker kind should possess this *prima facie* establishing power until it is sublated by a stronger means, is in no way contrary to reason, and is illustrated by the cognition of silver in the shell and such other cognitions. Were it not so, there indeed would be no room for subsequent sublation or refutation; for in all cases that only admits of being sublated, by a stronger means of proof, which is established *prima facie*—not either that which is not so established or that which is *ab initio* proved by a valid means of knowledge. Nor must it be supposed that texts, such as 'All this indeed is Brahman,' which enjoin certain types of devout meditation, establish Brahman's connexion with a world as a final truth. For Brahman may be meditated upon (not in its true character only, but also) under merely superimposed aspects: those texts therefore may be understood as merely enjoining a meditation of that kind, and as ultimately sublated by those texts which intimate Brahman's absolute freedom from all relation as final truth. Nor, again may you object that there can be no superimposition (on Brahman or any substrate) of what is absolutely non-established. For Brahman's relation to a world *is* established by the texts speaking of the creation of the world—which, to the end that Brahman's non-duality may be firmly established, suggest that relation as something to be ultimately negatived. There thus is nothing irrational in the conclusion that Brahman is not related to a world.

"But," a new objection is raised, "how can a Brahman of that kind be the Self of the individual soul, which manifestly is related to a world in which it functions as an agent and so forth?" To this we reply as follows:

* A quotation from the *Mahābhārata*.

That the world with all it implies—agency and the rest—is related to the individual soul is, in the first place, not to be known through an inference and the subsequent means of proof; for the fact is one immediately cognised. Nor is it to be known through the eye or other sense-organs; for as the individual soul itself is not an object of the external senses, its attributes—such as being an agent—likewise are not. Nor is the fact to be known through the internal organ; since there is no proof whatever for this. The presence and absence of the internal organ may be explained to have their function (not therein that they make us know the connection of the individual soul with a world implying agency and such other characters, but) therein that they constitute the material cause of that world. Even on the supposition of the Self (and not the internal organ) constituting that material cause, it cannot, on the basis of its presence and absence, be shown that it is the internal organ which makes us know the individual soul's agency, &c., since that part of the argument which is based on the absence of the internal organ, is invalidated by a doubt. For the argument could have the following form only: where the internal organ is absent, there is no presentation to consciousness of one's being an agent, &c., as in the condition of deep dreamless sleep. But this argumentation is vitiated by a doubt, inasmuch as there is no means to decide whether this special non-presentation to consciousness in deep sleep results from the non-existence, at the time, of the internal organ itself, or from the fact that the soul itself, at the time, is *not* an agent, and so forth. And there is no reason to raise the objection that, in these circumstances, there would be no means to bring about the knowledge, of one's being an Agent, &c., for this knowledge is afforded by the witnessing Self.

[*Page 98*] The Bauddhas and the senile Prābhākaras assume that in the Self, the characters of the *Agent* and the *Enjoyer* and also Attachment and Aversion and Pleasure and Pain are self-illumined. But this is not right. For (a) if the said characters of the Agent and the rest are of the nature of 'substance,' then, rather than postulate the quality of 'illumination' in them, it would be much simpler to assume that they are rendered cognisable by the illumination of the Self itself; (b) if, on the other hand, the said characters are of the nature of 'quality,' then it is not possible for them to be possessed of the further quality of 'illumination'; as a quality cannot possess another quality. "But it is the very character of *Agent* &c., that constitute qualities in the shape of 'Illumination'." In that case it would not be possible for them to be produced in their own accidental substratum; just as the light of the Sun is not produced in any substratum. Nor will it be right to urge that, inasmuch as the characters of the *Agent* &c., in themselves, are not different from 'illumination,' they must be self-illumined. For their 'illumination' may be explained as being due to the light of the eternal Self.

"We grant that the characters of the Agent &c., are cognisable by the witnessing Self. Even so, they are *real.*"

Certainly not, we reply. The witnessing Self cognises right as well as wrong cognitions; and hence cognition by it cannot prove anything as to the object cognised being real or unreal. In fact, if all objects were regarded as real, that would go against the Shruti text, which declares the Self to be "free from attachment;" and further, such texts as '*Indro māyābhiḥ &c.,*' declare that all worldly characters are *unreal* [and the *character of Agent* is a 'worldly character'].

All this goes to prove that what the supplementary texts—such as 'not large' 'not small', 'It is not born, It does not die'—do is to point to the two entities denoted by the terms 'That' and 'Thou,' which are of the nature of pure Consciousness, and which, in reality, are entirely free from all phenomenal modifications,—the indication of these entities being necessary for the due comprehension of the Great Text ('That thou art'); and these texts do not describe the 'cessation of *aḍhyāsa.*' "This means that the desired unity is postulated by the Great Text, on the basis of what are denoted by the terms 'that' and 'thou', which are mentioned in the subsidiary texts, and which, by their very nature, are free from all phenomenal modifications; so that even though there is no indication (in these texts) of the cessation of *aḍhyāsa*, there is no incongruity; and under the circumstances, how could there be even an indirect implication (by the texts) of either 'cessation of Nescience' or its 'manifestation'?" Our answer to this is as follows: When there arises the recognition of truth, in regard to *Unity,* it does so, while at the same time, setting aside its contraries in the shape of Nescience and the *Aḍhyāsa* resulting therefrom, a fact which we find in the case of the recognition of the real truth in regard to the *shell* [which sets aside the Ignorance in regard to the shell as also the false notion of *silver* in regard to it]. "But in the case of the shell, what sets aside the *adhyāsa* (of silver) is the negative cognition 'this is not silver'. " It is not so; what the negative assertion refers to is the *real* silver (and not the *imposed* or *mistaken* silver), as we have already explained above, in the section on '*Akhyāṭivāḍa.*' What really happens in that case is that the negation of 'silver' strikes at the desire for activity (tending to the acquiring of the silver) on the part of the person who is seeking after *real* silver; and because it does this, it is figuratively regarded as destructive of the *Aḍhyāsa*. The direct cause of the removal of *Aḍhyāsa* consists in the *recognition of the Shell*; as we have already explained in the section dealing with '*Anirvachanīyakhyāṭi*,' while considering the question of the sublation (of cognitions). It will not be right to argue that—"What the *cognition of the Shell* does is only to make known the real character of the shell; it does nothing to remove the *aḍhyāsa*;"—because what is already implied in something that is accomplished does not require any further effort; for example, when the goldsmith is weighing gold in the balance, what his hand does is only to raise the balance; but there occurs the lowering of one pan, which is already implied by, and follows from, the raising of the balance, so that for that another operation of the hand is not needed; in all sciences it is well-known that things that necessarily follow from other things do not require a separate effort. "In a case where the sublation of a previous cognition is due to a verbal assertion,—*e.g.* when the cognition of 'silver,' in regard to the shell is sublated by the assertion 'this is not silver'—this assertion refers to the real silver; while the assertion 'this is shell' has no power to set aside the *aḍhyāsa* (of *silver*); so that in this case it may be that the recognition of the cessation of '*aḍhyāsa*' follows necessarily from the said sublation [and hence no special effort is needed for it in this case]; but in a case where the sublation is done by Perception, how can the recognition of the cessation of *Aḍhyāsa* be regarded as following necessarily from something else?" Our answer to this is as follows: In such a case, the absence *of the imposed (mistaken) silver*, being directly perceived, cannot be regarded as cognised by means of Non-apprehension; in fact neither the *imposed silver* nor its *absence* is capable of contact (with any sense-organ); for as for the mistaken silver, inasmuch as it exists only in the idea of the man, it can have no existence prior to that idea; and as such it could not come into contact with a sense-organ (before it is cognised); and, so long as the *imposed silver*, which is the counter-entity of its *absence*, is incapable of contact with a sense-organ, its *absence* or *negation* also can never be in contact with a sense-organ. So that, as in the case of sublation by verbal assertion, so also in that of sublation by Perception, the real character of the shell having been recognised by means of a sense-organ, the cessation of the mistake or *aḍhyāsa* follows as a matter of course. Analogously, when the identity of the Individual Self and Brahman has been recognised either by means of Verbal Assertion or by Direct Apprehension, the Cessation of Nescience and its products follows as a matter of course; so that this cessation does not fall within the scope of the subject-matter of the *Shāsṭra;* hence it is far more reasonable to regard it as the purpose, and not the subject-matter, of the Shāstra. And though the direct purpose of the Science of Reasoning consists in the removal of the doubts bearing upon the philosophy of *Vedānta*,—and the acquiring of the Knowledge of Brahman is the result of the *Vedānta* itself,—yet the *cessation of Adhyā sa*, being the result of that Knowledge, forms an object of men's desire; and hence it is only right to regard this *cessation of Adhyāsa* as the purpose of the *Shāstra.*

XLVIII

[The phrase 'acquiring of the Knowledge of Brahman' means the definite cognition of the nature of Brahman by means of the functioning of the Internal Organ, in accordance with Instruments of Right Cognition.]

The Opponent asks—"What do you mean by the 'acquiring' of the Knowledge of Brahman,—which you describe as the 'result' of the Vēdānta itself? In ordinary experience, what is 'acquired,'—as for instance, a Cow—is some such accomplished entity having a positive character of its own as has not been already attained; and never such as is either always attained—*e.g.* the man's own nature—or is one that has no positive character of its own, being an absolute non-entity,—*e.g.*, the 'man's horn.' As for 'knowledge,' while it exists, it always resides in the knower and illumines its object; and it is always conceived of as such; so that by its own character, and also by the way in which it is conceived of, it is something that is always *attained,* got at, (by the Agent); under the circumstances how can there be any *acquiring* of it (through the Vēdānta)?"

[*Page 100*] Our reply to this is as follows: *Knowledge* consists only in the functioning of the Internal Organ through an Instrument of Right Cognition; and when by means of this knowledge the true nature of a thing is definitely cognised, this is called the 'acquiring' of that Knowledge. In the case of such ordinary things as the Jar and the like, it so happens that as soon as the knowledge of these has come about, it at once, by its very coming into existence, brings about the definite cognition of its object; but the knowledge of Brahman does not lead to the definite cognition of its object in the same quick manner; and this for the reason that the object of this latter knowledge is obscured by absolute incapacity due to incomprehension and mis-apprehension. What is meant by 'incomprehension' is that the Mind is *incapable* of that concentration or one-pointedness which is essential for the comprehending of the identity of the Individual Self and Brahman; and what is meant by 'misapprehension' is the massive disposition towards mistaking the Body and such other things (to be the Self). "But as a matter of fact we have never found in experience that when a certain thing has been apprehended by means of such Instruments of Cognition as are conducive to direct perception, there is any absence,—due to the two deficiencies of the Mind,—of definite cognition by means of that perception." This is not right, we reply. When such things, as fresh pepper for instance, which have never been seen in the city of Benares, are brought over from remote countries to that city,— even though one actually sees them with his eyes, definite certainty in regard to them does not arise, on account of want of belief in the possibility of the presence of such a thing at that particular place. Similarly, even though the knowledge of Brahman may have been brought about by means of the scriptures, it remains obscured by reason of defects in the Mind, and it is only after it has been helped by deliberation that it leads to the definite comprehension of its object. "But as regards Deliberation, if this is a means of Cognition, then it must be regarded as an independent Instrument (and not merely as an auxiliary to Scriptures); while, if it is not a means of Cognition, it can serve no useful purpose (in the bringing about of any cognition); so that it is not possible for it to be regarded as an auxiliary to any Instrument of Cognition." This is not so, we reply. As a matter of fact, Deliberation *by itself* is not an Instrument of Cognition, and as such (by itself) it cannot bring about the definite comprehension of anything; yet this fact does not make it absolutely impossible for it to aid other Instruments of Cognition; for it takes the form of considering the probabilities and improbabilities pertaining to the exact nature of the Instruments of Cognition, their capacities and the objects of Cognition. It is for this reason that Logicians have declared that Deliberation or Cogitation serves as an aid to the Instruments of Cognition.

XLIX

[The Opponent raises objections against the utility of Deliberation. The utility of Deliberation, they argue, is incompatible with the intrinsic self-validity of Cognition].

"Well, if Instruments of Cognition stand in need of Deliberation, that goes against your doctrines. For in regard to cognitions, the *Sankhyas* hold the view that their *validity* as well as *invalidity* are both intrinsic;

according to the Logicians both are extrinsic; their *invalidity* alone is intrinsic, say the Bauddhas; and the Vēḍānṭins declare that it is the *validity* of Cognitions that is intrinsic.

Now, the view of the *Sankhyas* is not right; for what does it mean? Does it mean that both validity and invalidity belong to the same individual cognition? or that validity belongs to one and invalidity to another cognition? It cannot be the former; as that involves a self-contradiction. Nor can it be the latter; as there is nothing to determine which particular cognition is valid and which invalid; for the character of 'cognition' belongs equally to both; and according to one who regards Cognitions to be valid, no other determinant can be possible.

Nor again can both validity and invalidity be extrinsic (as held by the Logician); for in that case, at the moment that any particular Cognition appears, it would, for some time, remain devoid of both *validity* and *invalidity*; this certainly is not what is known to be the case in ordinary experience.

[*Page 102*] Now, it may be urged that (these two views having been excluded) the Bauddha view is the right one;—*viz.*, that invalidity is intrinsic, and validity extrinsic, in cognitions. But this also is not tenable. Does the *extrinsic* character belong to the *production* or to the *recognition* of the 'validity'? It cannot belong to its *production*; for cognition, produced by means of the Eye and such other causes, being momentary, it could never continue sufficiently long to allow of the extrinsic 'validity' being *produced* in it. 'But the Cognition having been brought about by the causes of the Cognition, after sometime *Validity* is produced in it by reason of a certain efficiency in the said causes;—this is what is meant by the *production* (of Validity) being *extrinsic*. If this were not possible, then how is it that *Validity* is concomitant with *efficiency* (of the Cause)?' This is not right; as the said notion of concomitance may be explained as being due to the absence of such defects as impede *validity*. It will not be right to urge against this explanation the objection that the concomitance (of Validity) being with the presence of *Efficiency*, if we attribute it to the *absence of defects*, it would be attributing it to something to which it does not belong (with which it is not co-existent). Because 'efficiency' is nothing more than 'absence of defects;' for instance, in the case of Sense-organs and such other things, we do not find any 'efficiency' apart from the 'absence of defects;' even if some sort of a positive efficiency were found, it would only be one that serves to remove a defect, and thus brings about the 'absence of that defect;' so that the said concomitance can, with every reason, be regarded as with the 'absence of defect' (and not with the efficiency). And as it is only after the cessation of defects (from its cause) that the *validity* of a cognition is accomplished, the concomitance of 'validity' with 'efficiency' must be through the 'absence of defects;' and not directly with the 'efficiency itself.' —Well then, in that case we may regard 'the absence of the obstructing defect' as the *cause* of 'Validity,' on the basis of the fact that it is with this 'absence' that 'Validity' is concomitant.—That also will not be right, we reply; for in that case it would not be possible to regard the *defect* as the *obstructor* (of Validity); as one thing can be reasonably regarded as the obstructor of another only when it is found that the former steps in and renders the production of the latter impossible, even though there is present a cause fully efficient to produce that thing; and certainly the *defect* cannot step in when there is 'absence of defect' [and this 'absence of defect' is a cause efficient to produce 'Validity']. From all this it follows that the *extrinsic* character of the 'Validity' cannot pertain to its *production*. As for the *recognition* of 'Validity,'—how could that also be *extrinsic*? The 'Validity' of a cognition consists in its being capable of apprehending its object (in its true form); and is this *capability* known from the cognition of its being produced by efficiency? or from finding that it agrees with (is compatible with) effective action (to which it gives rise)? The former alternative cannot be accepted; it would mean that even when the Jar may be known, unless it is known that the said cognition of the Jar has been brought about by an efficiency, it cannot be known that the cognition is *capable* of apprehending its object; so that there could arise no activity in regard to the Jar! 'But it may be that the required activity arises afterwards, when it does become known that the cognition has been brought about by an efficiency.' That cannot be; for just like the *cognition of the Jar*, the *cognition of that cognition being born of an efficiency* would be absolutely ineffective until there is a further cognition asserting the Validity of the latter cognition; and so on and on there would be *regressus ad infinitum*. This same reason would be equally applicable against the second alternative [that the Capability of the Cognition is known from finding it to be compatible with effective action]. The following explanation may be put forward— 'In the case of the cognitions of Eating, &c., being the means of *satisfaction* (of hunger), &c., we find that though their validity is recognised only when it is known that the said *Eating*, &c., do actually bring about an effective action in the form of the satisfying of hunger, &c., yet so far as the cognitions of the resulting *satisfaction*, &c., are concerned, their validity is recognised by itself (and not through the knowledge of any effective action); for the simple reason that there is no further effective action; so that there is no infinite regress at all.' But this is not right; because [the reasoning urged can be met by the following counter-reasoning]—the cognition in question of the means of satisfaction &c., must be regarded as valid by itself,—because it is cognition—just like the cognition of the result (satisfaction; which cognition is accepted to be self-valid);—specially as the contrary view is negatived by the undesirable interdependence that it involves; that is, the recognition of validity is dependent upon the cognition of the fact that the effective action of the man acting up to the cognition in question is in keeping with that cognition,—and the activity of the man in accordance with a particular cognition is possible only after he has been convinced of the validity of that cognition. 'But it is possible that, even before the validity (of the cognition) has been duly ascertained, the Agent has recourse to an action, for the very purpose of ascertaining that validity [as for instance, on perceiving silver, the man stoops to pick it up, just to make sure that what he has cognised as silver is really silver]; which shows that there need be no mutual interdependence.' This may be so in the case of *doubtful* cognitions; but how could there be any activity for the ascertainment of validity in the case of such ordinary and frequent cognitions as those of the Jar and such other well-known things,—in whose case there is no uncertainty at all? 'In the case of gold-testing we find that a certainty as to its being real gold comes about,—not merely by the first cognition of it, but—only after there come about four such cognitions (as that 'this is gold'), following upon the four actions of close examination, rubbing (on touch-stone), heating and cutting;—which shows that it cannot be denied that the validity is purely extrinsic.' This is not true; for in the case cited what the second and subsequent cognitions do is only to set aside such doubts as there may be in regard to (*i.e.*, obstructing) the validity of the first cognition; and they do not tend towards the ascertainment of that validity. From all this it follows that the validity of cognitions must be regarded as intrinsic or self-sufficient, in the sense that in its *production* as well as in its *recognition*, it is independent of any indicators other than what brings about the *cognition*;—while as regards the *invalidity* of cognitions, inasmuch as it is *produced* by defects in the cause of the cognition, and it is made known (indicated) by the subsequent sublation of the cognition,—it must be regarded as *extrinsic*. 'But the invalidity of Cognitions cannot be produced by anything outside the cognition itself; as *invalidity* is nothing more than *negation of validity*,—being just like the *prior negation of validity*.' This is not true; as the reason just forward is 'unknown,' not admitted by all parties; as a matter of fact the name 'invalidity' is given to *Ignorance, Doubt* and *Misconception* (and not to mere *negation of validity*); as has been declared by the revered Kumarila Bhaṭṭa—'Invalidity is three-fold, as consisting in misconception, ignorance and doubt;'—here what is meant by the term 'ignorance,' is the cognition of something other than the real thing; as the same author speaks of it (in another place) as the cognition of another thing. Now certainly all these three cannot be mere *negations*. Even though cognitions are possessed of intrinsic validity, yet there can be nothing incongruous in their becoming *invalid* by reason of defects (in their cause); just as even though fire is intrinsically *hot*, yet it is found to be *cool* when its *heat* is suppressed by means of incantations. If you ever entertain a doubt as to the *invalidity* of cognitions being *intrinsic*, how could you explain the activity that results from even invalid cognitions, until the recognition of the presence of defects in their origin [when alone the said activity ceases]?

"It is in view of all this that the theory is accepted (by the Veḍānṭin) that it is *validity* that is *intrinsic* in cognitions. Such being the case, if the Veḍānṭin now asserts that 'Brahman Knowledge' stands in need of Deliberation, why should it not be regarded as involving the 'abandoning of tenets' on his part?"

L

[Deliberation is not incompatible with the Self-validity of cognitions. It operates effectively towards the accomplishment of the Knowledge of Brahman.]

[*Page 103*] To the above arguments of the Opponent we make the following reply: The arguments put forward do not affect our position. Because all that Deliberation does is to remove the obstacle in the way (of True Knowledge). Though in reality Brahman is self-luminous, and Word (in the form of scriptures) is perfectly capable of bringing about the direct cognition of Brahman,—yet it is quite possible that there may be obstacles (in the way of the requisite Knowledge of Brahman), in the shape of (*a*) past sins, (*b*) contrary functioning of the Mind, (*c*) total inapprehension of the subject, and (*d*) misapprehension of It as consisting in the Body, the Sense-organs and such other things (as are not Brahman); and on account of these obstacles an unshaken direct cognition (of Brahman) fails to appear. Now of the obstacles, (*a*) past sins are wiped out by the due fulfilment of the duties pertaining to the life-conditions of the man; (*b*) the contrary functionings of the Mind are checked by the practice of calmness, self-control, &c.; (*c*) the total inapprehension of the subject of the Unity of *Jiva* and *Brahman* is set aside by Deliberation, which consists of cogitation and pondering; and (*d*) Meditation brings about that one-pointedness of the Mind which removes all misapprehension and renders the Mind capable of apprehending the subtlest of subjects; then finally becomes accomplished that unruffled direct cognition (of Brahman) which is brought about by means of the Word (of the scriptures). That the word of the *Upaniṣaḍs* is the means of bringing about the direct cognition of Brahman is indicated by the nominal affix in the word '*aupaniṣaḍam*' (*described in the Upaniṣaḍs*') which appears as the epithet of Brahman in the passage—'I am asking about that person *described in the Upaniṣaḍs*';—where what the nominal affix means is that *it is only by means of the Upaniṣaḍs that the said person can be rightly known*. Then again, the cognition of Brahman, which (being self-luminous) is directly (immediately) cognisable, cannot be indirect or mediate; hence the conclusion is that at the very outset the cognition (of Brahman) arising from Word is *direct*; and this same cognition becomes fixed and steady on the removal of obstacles. Or, just as the direct contact of the sense-organ brings about Perception, and then again, with the aid of impressions left by the previous cognition of that thing, it brings about the *recognition* of that same thing,— exactly in the same manner it may be that Word, at the very outset brings about the *indirect* cognition of Brahman, and subsequently, being helped by the removal of the above-described obstacles, it brings about the second cognition, which is *direct*. Nor need the *indirect* cognition of the self-luminous Brahman be necessarily a misconception; for (in ordinary experience) we find that even though a certain person's cognition is itself self-luminous, yet the cognition that other persons have of that cognition is only inferential, which is *indirect*. In this manner even though at the very outset Word does bring about the cognition—direct or indirect*—of Brahman, it remains as good as *not brought about*, by reason of its not having acquired the position of an unruffled direct cognition; and when contemplation and meditation are duly practised, as a result of these the knowledge of Brahman becomes duly steady, and thence comes to be spoken of as having been *acquired*.

---

* The presence of वा indicates the correct reading to be परोक्षापरोक्षं, which also appears to be required by the context.

[Against this process, the Opponent raises the following objection]—"If such be the case, then, inasmuch as the final result appears after meditation, this meditation should be regarded as the principal factor, and hearing and contemplation should, in that case, be only auxiliaries to meditation, and should, as such, have to be regarded as subordinate factors."

It is not so, we reply; for the simple reason that as a matter of fact, meditation can never be the means by which cognition is actually brought about. There is no such means of cognition as 'Meditation;' hence Meditation, by itself, could never be a cause in the bringing about of any cognition. *Hearing*, on the other hand, consists in the ascertaining of the import of the potency of words; and as such being a special feature of Word, which is a Means of Cognition, the said Hearing itself may be looked upon as the 'means;' so that it is the *hearing* that should be regarded as the predominant factor. Contemplation and Meditation, on the other hand serve only to remove powerful obstacles, and serve to bring about certain effects on the Mind, which help in the accomplishment of the result; so that these (Contemplation and Meditation) should be regarded as subordinate auxiliaries to the final result. Contemplation sets aside the inapprehension of the subject and thereby removes all doubts from the Mind; and Meditation sets aside all misconception and brings about the one-pointedness of the Mind. *Steadiness* (Self-control), &c., as also Sacrificial Performances, serve as indirect auxiliaries; and as such come in useful as constituting the entire process (whereby Brahman-Knowledge is obtained). Among these latter again, Steadiness, &c., are the more intimate auxiliaries; as it is there that serve to remove such visible defects as the contrary functionings of the Mind and Sense-organs, which obstruct the capacity for right *Hearing*; while Sacrificial Performances are only remote auxiliaries, inasmuch as these serve to remove only the Unseen (supernatural) defects. From all this we conclude that in the bringing about of the unruffled direct cognition (of Brahman), the principal cause is *hearing*, as aided by the aforesaid auxiliaries, which help in the process (of that cognition being obtained). That Hearing however, which, prior to the operation of the auxiliaries, brings about either only *indirect* cognition, or an *unsteady* direct cognition, may be regarded as subordinate to *Meditation*; and this would not militate against our tenets; as the *Hearing* that we insist upon regarding as the predominant factor, is only that which brings about such *direct* Brahman-Knowledge as serves to put an end to all metempsychic troubles.

LI

[The purpose of Brahman-Knowledge consists in the removal of evil.]

[*Page 104*] Says the Opponent—"The Knowledge of Brahman cannot be regarded as putting an end to metempsychic or worldly troubles; because as a matter of fact we find that worldly troubles continue even when the said knowledge has been attained."

This is not right; because it is a fact fully established by the scriptures that whenever there is direct cognition of truth, there is cessation of all *Aḍhyāsa* or Illusion from its very root, and where there is no such cognition, there is no cessation of Illusion. "But the cognition of truth, even though contrary to *Aḍhyāsa*, may not entirely remove it; just as the mere cognition of the Self as distinct from the Body &c., even though opposed to *Aḍhyāsa*, does not entirely destroy it." This can not be; as the two cases are not analogous; the cognition of truth is contrary to the Root-Ignorance (the Ignorance that lies at the root of all Illusion); which is not the case with the cognition of the Self merely as different from the Body &c. "In that case the Root-Ignorance having been destroyed by the Cognition of Truth, the Body should fall away forthwith." Not so; as it is possible for the Body &c., to continue for a while, by the force of the impressions or momentum set up Ignorance and its effects. "But such impressions are known to exist only in the case of Cognition and in that of the revolution of wheels; and not anywhere else." It is not so; for we do find impressions in the case of Smell and such other things also. "As a matter of fact, on the removal of the Flower, what still produces the notion of smell is, not any *Impression*, but, the subtle flower-particles, such as subsist in every flower." Even so, it will have to be admitted that at the time of Universal Dissolution, there remain the *impressions* left by all the effects that had appeared during the closing cycle. Those persons who will not admit these should be meet by the following inference—'the final destruction of the effects must be due to impressions,—because while being something other than the destruction of impressions, it is a destruction, like the destruction of Cognitions (which is brought about by impressions).' "But this inference would be annulled by the well- known fact that impressions are possible only for actions and Cognitions!" Well, if that be so, then, inasmuch as Nescience and its effects are also only mistaken *cognitions*, they could, as *cognitions*, give rise to Impressions. "It may be that, even though the witnessing Consciousness, pertaining to Nescience &c., is eternal, yet the *vṛiṭṭi* relating to the wrong cognition qualifying that Consciousness is transient, and hence the said Impression may be possible; but even so, how can the *direct cognition* of Duality arise from *Impressions,* which are productive of *Remembrance* only?" What we say in reply to this is that Impressions are a defect attaching to that Consciousness which is the cause of the direct cognition of worldly phenomena; just for instance, as Dimness affecting the eyes, which are the means of direct perception, becomes the cause of direct cognition in the form of misconceptions. It will not be right to argue that "pure Consciousness cannot be the substratum of Impressions;"—because Consciousness can be the substratum of Impressions in the same manner as it is the substratum of Nescience. Then again, even though Impressions are effects, they do not require a constituent cause, being, in this respect, like Destruction; specially as it is only positive products—with the sole exception of Nescience and Impression—that require constituent causes. So that, even though in other cases Impression must subsist in its own constituent cause, yet, in the case in question, it is quite possible for it to subsist in Consciousness, which is not its constituent cause.

[*Page 105*] The postulating of Impressions does not necessarily imply the denial of '*Viḍēhamukṭi,*' 'Deliverance during Life;' for the said Deliverance is accomplished at the exhaustion of such Karmic forces as have been set going, when Impressions cease by reason of the recollecting of True Knowledge. "But Nescience having ceased, and there being no constituent cause for Impressions, how could the Body &c. continue without a constituent substratum?" Well, in that case, 'Deliverance during Life' may be explained as arising on the acquiring of True Knowledge—the taint of Nescience (and the consequent connection with the Body &c.) continuing till the exhaustion of the active Karmic forces; and when the obstruction of these Karmic forces has been removed, even the slight taint of Nescience ceases entirely, by the force of True Knowledge.

From all this it follows that the purpose of the Vēḍānṭa texts consists in the acquiring of that Knowledge of the Unity of Brahman which puts an end to all metempsychic troubles. Though there are certain Vēḍānṭa texts which lay down the worshipping of Brahman with attributes, yet these should be taken merely as a side-issue, a bye-activity,—like the laying down of the milking vessel (which is laid down as a sub-subsidiary, helping in the main action of the Sacrifice); and hence these also should be taken as pointing out that same *absolute* Attributeless Brahman which is spoken of (in these texts) as the object of worship. And as regards the qualities that are laid down as objects of worship, they serve the useful purpose of helping in the comprehending of the true nature of Absolute Brahman,—by the method of assuming a character (for It, hypothetically) and then rejecting it (as unsuitable; and thus by the process of elimination, getting at the *Absolute*, free from all attributes). And before the said attributes have been actually rejected, the Brahman qualified by them may be taken as one whose worship is laid down for the accomplishing of certain ordinary results (and not of the highest result of Deliverance).

"If the injunction of worship, based upon the wrong imposition of qualities on Brahman, is only for the purpose of bringing about (by the process of elimination) the due comprehension of the nature of Brahman, by the person seeking Final Release,—then in that case (these injunctions being for the purpose of the seeking after Final Release), persons entitled to worship would be just these persons who are entitled to Final Release; just as in connection with the *Ḍarsha-Pūrṇamāsa* sacrifices, we have the text 'the fetching of the water should be done with the milking vessel;' and the person entitled to the use of this 'milking vessel' is the same who is performing the *Ḍarsha-Pūrṇamāsa.*"

This does not affect our position. In the example cited, it being a fact that the fetching of water is possible only for one who is entitled to the performance of the *Ḍarsha-Pūrṇamāsa,*—it follows that the injunction of the 'milking vessel' to the used if cattle is desired is also meant for those who are performing the *Ḍarsha-Pūrṇamāsa.* In the case in question however, the injunction (of worship) may be taken as referring to persons not necessarily seeking Final Release; as it is possible for these persons also to comprehend, by means of the texts concerned, what is imposed upon Brahman; so that in this case it does not necessarily follow that the persons entitled to the worship are the same as those entitled to Final Release.

"It may be that those Vēḍānṭa texts that lay down the worshipping of the qualified Brahman help in the bringing about of the comprehension of the true nature of Brahman; but the same cannot be said of those texts that lay down the worshipping of the Prāṇas and such other things."

Not so; as these latter also ultimately lead to the same end, through the purification of the internal organ (accomplished by means of the worship of the Prāṇas &c.).

Thus then, we conclude that Brahman forms the *subject-matter* of all Vēḍānṭa texts;—their *purpose* consists in the removal of evil by means of the attaining of Knowledge of Brahman; so that of the Science of Vēḍānṭa also, those same are the Subject-matter and Purpose.

LII

[That the subject-matter and purpose of the Vēḍānṭa are as described is implied by the first Vēḍānṭa-Sūṭra; as the Potential affix always denotes the means of accomplishing a desired end.]

Says the Opponent— "All that the first Sūṭra lays down is the fact that an enquiry (into the nature of Brahman) should be held; how is it then that you are now putting forward in connection with the Inquiry into Vēḍānṭa, a subject-matter and a purpose that are not even mentioned in the Sūṭra?"

Our answer to this is as follows: The said purpose and subject-matter are actually implied in the Sūṭra (even though they are not mentioned in so many words). We shall show later on that all injunctive affixes—the Injunctive, the Imperative and the Potential—denote the means of accomplishing a desired end. So that when the first Sūṭra stands in the form—'for the purpose of knowing Brahman, the Vedanta texts *should be pondered over*'—what the potential affix (in the term 'should be pondered over') denotes is the fact that what is expressed by the Verbal root (to 'ponder'),—*i.e.* the *pondering* or *reflection*—is the means of accomplishing some sort of a desirable end, in general;—and when the question arises as to what particular desirable end it is that is accomplished by means of the said *reflection,* it is Final Release that comes to be regarded as that end; for the simple reason that it is the desire for Final Release that distinguishes the person undertaking the said Reflection or Inquiry; just as (in the case of sacrificial performances) Heaven &c. come to be regarded as the end to be accomplished [by reason of the fact that it is desire for these that distinguishes the man undertaking the performances]. And as for the 'Knowledge of Brahman,'—it being the direct result of the *Reflection* expressed by the verbal root,—and also the direct means of bringing about Final Release,—it comes in as an intervening agency; just as *Apūrva* (being the result of Sacrifices and the cause of Heaven) does in the case of sacrificial performances.

The Opponent (Prābhākara) raises an objection—"The Injunctive affix signifies, not the *means of accomplishing as desired end,* but only *injunction* or *command;* as it is only this latter that cannot be cognised by any other means of cognition; so that the injunctive affix urges the person addressed to the undertaking of what is denoted by the verbal root; and it goes on to imply that what is denoted by the verbal root is the means of accomplishing the desired end."

There is nothing in this view; as there is no possible incongruity (for the avoiding of which such an implication or presumption would be necessary). That is to say, in the absence of the fact that what is denoted by the verbal root is the means whereby the desired end is accomplished, (*a*) would the form of the Injunction itself be impossible? or (*b*) would its urging power be impossible? (*a*) It could not be the former; as in the case of the obligatory and occasional duties, we have the injunction in its complete form, even though there are no results. (*b*) In the second case, when the Injunction urges the agent, does it do so through the desire for results, or by itself? If the former, then the urging might be done by the *desire* itself; and what would be the use of the Injunction? Specially as in the case of perceptible things, we find the *desire* doing the *urging*, independently by itself. If it be the latter, then the Injunction would, like the force of the stream, forcibly urge forward a person who may not have any desire at all for the result (accomplished by the action to which he is urged); and such *urging* (of persons without desire) would be possible even in a case where what is denoted by the verbal root is not the means of accomplishing any desired result at all! Otherwise it may be possible that the force of the stream also would be urging (the drowning man) towards an action leading to a desirable result!

"Even though the Injunction alone may not presuppose the connection between the result and the action signified by the Verbal root,—yet, when the Injunction becomes recognised by a person desiring the result, it does certainly come to establish that connection."

[*Page 107*] Not so; as even so there would be no incongruity, even in the absence of such a connection. For instance, even though the desired result were not one to be accomplished by the action expressed by the verbal root, there would be nothing in the way of the desire for the said result being the qualification of the person entitled to undertake the act; because in the case of such offerings (the *Agnihōtra* f.i.) as are laid down to be made 'as long as one lives,' the qualification of the performer consists in *being alive*, which certainly is not something accomplished by the act of *offering*. "But even though this may be so when the qualification concerned is one that is not capable of being accomplished; yet in cases where the qualification—in the shape of the result—is such as is capable of being accomplished, the result cannot be a qualification unless it be capable of being accomplished by means of the act denoted by the verbal root." This is not right; for when you speak of 'capable of being accomplished,' does it mean 'capable of being accomplished *by what is signified by the verbal root*?' Or merely 'capable of being accomplished' in general? If it is the former, then what is presupposed and what presupposes being the same, it involves the absurdity of a thing resting in itself. If it is the latter; then is the fact of Heaven being capable of being accomplished known directly from words? Or is it only implied? It cannot be the former; as there is no word expressing the idea. Nor can it be the latter; as there is nothing that could imply it; inasmuch as we do not see anything that would be inexplicable except on the basis of Heaven being regarded as something to be accomplished. "Well, if Heaven were not something capable of being accomplished, it could not have any connection with persons desirous of it." Even so, Heaven could not be a qualification of the person entitled to the performance of the act,—on the strength of which we could assume the fact of its being capable of being accomplished by what is expressed by the verbal root. Then again, when one says 'Ḍēvaḍaṭṭa has a dry stick,' the *stick* is the qualification of Ḍēvaḍaṭṭa, and *dryness* is the qualification of the stick,—so when it is said 'one desiring Heaven is entitled to the performance of actions,' the *desire* is the qualification of the person entitled, and *Heaven* is the qualification of the Desire. "But even Heaven may, through the Desire, be regarded as the qualification of the person." Even so, it does not follow that Heaven is accomplished by means of the act denoted by the verbal root. For example, in the case of the sentence 'one desirous of study should live on alms,' even though the *study* is something *to be accomplished,* and it enters into the qualification of the person entitled to perform the act referred to, yet it is not recognised as something capable of being accomplished by *living on alms*, which is the act denoted by the verbal root '(*charēṭ*'). "But we also find the contrary to be the case in such sentences as 'desiring riches one should serve the king'." Well, in that case (what we would urge is that), it is extremely difficult to determine how *Heaven* and *desire for it* can serve the purpose of qualifying the Agent; for in the first place the term 'desiring heaven' does not preclude the non-connection of the Agent with the Injunction of the *Ḍarsha-Pūrṇamāsa;* as the preclusion of this non-connection is already accomplished by the force of the obligatory Injunctive word itself;—nor can the term be taken as precluding the connection of other things (than the *Ḍarsha-Pūrṇamāsa*);for if persons not desiring heaven were to be precluded from the *Ḍarsha-Pūrṇamāsa* Sacrifices, this preclusion would be incompatible with the obligatory character of the Injunctive word; specially as the Obligatory Injunction is something entirely different from the Optional Injunction. "But these objections cease to apply if we take the preclusion to be of both, the connection of others and the non-connection of the *Ḍarsha-Pūrṇamāsa.*" It is not so; for though it is true that the obligatory injunction is expressed by the passage laying down the *lifelong* sacrifice, while the optional injunction is expressed by the passage speaking of 'desiring Heaven,'—yet in reality there is no difference between the two injunctions,—as it is easily recognised that it is the same *Ḍarsha-Pūrṇamāsa* along with its subsidiaries that figures in both Injunctions. Then, as for this distinction between 'obligatory' and 'optional,' that may be explained as bearing upon the difference in the character of the person entitled to the performance. Nor will it be right to argue that—"if the *desire for heaven* is not a qualification for the Agent, the term 'desiring heaven' would be absolutely futile." For, just as in the case of the passage 'holding the stick the priest recites the *Praiṣa* manṭras,' we find that the priest reciting the *Praiṣa* manṭras having already been spoken of elsewhere, all that this passage does is to speak of the *stick* as the qualification of the Priest, the sense being—'when the Priest recites the *Praiṣa* manṭras he should hold a stick,'—in the same manner, the term 'desiring Heaven' may be taken as pointing to the Heaven as the qualification; as has been declared by Pārṭhasāraṭhi—'as the result to be accomplished is what is desired, the term *desire* must be taken as referring to that; how a mere qualification can be the predominant factor in a sentence has been shown in the case of the term *holding the stick.*' Even if the term 'desiring heaven' is taken merely as pointing to the *result* (and not as qualifying the Agent), the real character of the Agent would be recognised by implication. For instance, the fact of the Sacrifice being the means of accomplishing Heaven having been made known by the Injunctive and other affixes, the Agent, by himself, realises that the action mentioned is the means of accomplishing something that he desires, and thus comes to recognise himself as entitled to the performance of that action. Thus in this manner the term 'desiring heaven,' pointing to the result, becomes capable of being construed along with the sentence speaking of the means of accomplishing that result. And this is possible only if the Injunctive, the Potential and other affixes denote the fact of a certain act being the means of accomplishing something desirable, and not when they denote mere *Injunction*. Hence *Injunction* cannot be accepted as forming the denotation of the Injunctive and other affixes.

Other writers hold that what is brought about by the Injunctive and other affixes is the cognition of the relation of cause and effect between Heaven and the action denoted by the verbal root. Their position may be summed up as follows:

[*Page 108*] What is expressed by the injunctive sentence is the Injunction as along with (qualified by) the subject-matter and the Agent. The subject-matter is the *sacrifice*, the person desirous of heaven is the *Agent*; and with a view to render the Injunction effective, we presume the mutual relation of Action and Doer to subsist between these (the Agent and the subject- matter),—without which relation, as the subject-matter would not be put into action by the Agent, the Injunction would not be effective. Thus then, just as in the case of the man *holding the stick*, it is found that that which is connected with the *man holding the stick* is also connected with the *stick*,—in the same manner when the *Sacrifice* would be related to the *urged Agent who is desirous of heaven*, it would become related also to the Heaven, which is a qualification (of the Agent). This *relation* cannot be any other that that of the 'Primary and Secondary' (the Principal and Subordinate). So that *Heaven* being the predominant factor, the *Sacrifice* becomes related to it as the subordinate factor, and it follows that there subsists between these two the relation of cause and effect (the *Sacrifice* being the cause and *Heaven* the effect)."

There is nothing in this theory. For in the manner described, there might be a connection of the *Sacrifice* with even such qualifications of the Agent as *living, burning of the house* and so forth.' "Let there be this connection—what is the harm?" Well, if there were such connection, the question would arise—does this *being alive* become connected as the subordinate factor in regard to what is denoted by the Verbal root? Or as the predominant factor? If the former, then, it would come to this that the *being alive*, which is a qualification of the Agent entitled to the obligatory *Ḍarsha-Pūrṇamāsa*, being subsidiary to this sacrifice, would have to be connected also with the *Saurya* and other ectypes of it. That the *Saurya* sacrifice, laid down in the sentence 'one desirous of Brahmic glory should offer the rice to Sūrya,' is an ectype of the *Ḍarsha-Pūrṇamāsa* is made clear by the force of the injunction of the 'offering;'—this being so, in view of the 'law of transferences' that 'the Ectype is to be performed like the Archetype,' the subsidiary details of the *Ḍarsha-Pūrṇamāsa* become applicable to the *Saurya*;—and inasmuch as *being alive* is as much a detail as any other, this also becomes connected with the *Saurya*; and thus the meaning of the injunction of the *Saurya* would be that 'one should offer the rice to Sūrya *throughout his life*.' "But inasmuch as the *Saurya* has been laid down for the person having a particular desire (that for Brahmic glory), this precludes the possibility of the connection of such details as pertain to an *obligatory* act; so that the said incongruity cannot arise?" This is not right; because the conditions of the obligatory and optional acts should all be as applicable to the Ectype as to the Archetype (in view of the general law of Transference).

If, on the other hand, the *being alive* becomes connected (with the denotation of the Verbal root) as the predominant factor,—then, in that case, being the predominant factor, the *being alive* should be looked upon as *something to be accomplished*, just like *Heaven*. From all this it follows that the term 'desiring Heaven,' which speaks of a particular result, becomes connected with the injunctive word, in virtue of the fact that every injunctive word in general signifies the means of accomplishing something desirable.

Another objection is raised—"If the Injunctive affix signifies the means of accomplishing a desirable end, then there should be no instrumental ending in the sentence '*Jyotiṣṭomēna yajēṭa;*' as the instrumental is laid down as to be used only for the signification of such *instrumentality* as is not already signified by conjugational or nominal or verbal affixes [and in the case in question the desired instrumentality is *ex-hypothesis* already signified by the conjugational injunctive affix in '*Yajēṭa.*']

This objection does not affect our position. Even though the injunctive affix (in *Yajēṭa*) expresses the instrumentality of 'sacrifice' in general,—which is what is denoted by the verbal root '*Yaj*' (in '*Yajēṭa*')— yet, it does not signify the instrumentality of the *particular* sacrifice *Jyotiṣṭoma* (for the signifying of which we require the instrumental ending in '*Jyotiṣṭomēna*']. Thus there need be nothing incongruous in the fact that the means of accomplishing a desirable end is denoted by the injunctive affix.

Now, when the *Sūṭra* stands in the form—'one who desires Final Release should reflect upon the Vēḍānṭa texts'—what it signifies is the fact that *Reflection* is the means of accomplishing a desirable end *in general*; but it follows from this that *Final Release*, which is a particular kind of *desirable end*, is the final purpose of that Science of Reflection. And the term '*Brahmajijñāsa*', serves to point out also the subject-matter of that science. Though in reality the *subject-matter* of the Science is dealt with in a later chapter (called the *Samanvāyāḍhyāya*), and the *Purpose* in the Fourth Chapter,—yet it becomes necessary to indicate these in the opening Sūṭra also; as a due understanding of these is necessary before one undertakes the inquiry embodied in the Science.

Thus then the purport of this section is that, inasmuch as this Science has a subject-matter and a definite purpose, people should undertake its study.

Index